TANSU

TANSU

TRADITIONAL JAPANESE CABINETRY

by Ty & Kiyoko Heineken

New York • WEATHERHILL • *Tokyo*

The endpapers are reproductions of two pages from the *Musashi Abumi* (1661), which show the townspeople escaping from the Meireki fire of 1657, taking their possessions with them in wheeled trunks.

First edition, 1981
Fourth printing, 1988

Published by John Weatherhill, Inc., of New York and Tokyo, with editorial offices at 7–6–13 Roppongi, Minato-ku, Tokyo 106, Japan. Printed and first published in Japan.

Library of Congress Cataloging in Publication Data: Heineken, Ty. / Tansu: traditional Japanese cabinetry. / Bibliography: p. Includes index. 1. Chests—Japan. 2. Cabinet-work—Japan. I. Heineken, Kiyoko. II. Title. / NK2725.H44 745.593 / 81–3032 AACR2 / ISBN 0–8348–0162–0

To the men and women
of the Craftsmen's Guild—
hands and hearts keeping tradition

CONTENTS

Maps and a chronology appear on pages 6–7

FOREWORD

Unlike the artistic tradition of China, which is an aristocratic one and appeals primarily to a cultured elite, that of Japan has a much broader base with aesthetic taste and sensibility existing in all classes of Japanese society. In keeping with this phenomenon it is not surprising that much of the best art produced by the Japanese people is not of the so-called fine arts, made by highly trained professional artists for the refined few, but folk art made by ordinary people for their own use and enjoyment. This type of art, which is today referred to as *mingei,* has rightly enjoyed a special place of honor in contemporary Japan. As Sōetsu Yanagi, the leading spokesman of the folk-art movement and the founder of the Mingeikan, or Folk Art Museum, in Tokyo, said: "*Mingei* is a people's art, a term which is to be understood as inclusive of all artisans' works made for the general public. Its products are those of the unelaborate arts of the craftsman, and not the works of art by geniuses. The consumers of these products are also the general public."* Although originally made for purely utilitarian reasons and sold at the local markets of Edo-period Japan without any thought to their being artistic masterpieces, these humble products are today eagerly collected and highly valued both in their native country and abroad for an intrinsic beauty and simple, unpretentious appeal. Mirroring an older traditional Japan, these common objects used by the peasants and artisans of the eighteenth and nineteenth centuries fill us today with nostalgia for a world that has vanished.

When modern Japan, like other technologically advanced countries, is inundated with cheap, mass-produced goods, these pre-industrial folk articles are greatly valued for their diversity of style and technique. During the Edo period there were many local art centers all over the Japanese isles, each developing and preserving its own artistic tradition

* Sōetsu Yanagi, *Folk Crafts in Japan* (Tokyo: Kokusai Bunka Shinkōkai, 1949), p. 7.

and nurturing its own types of crafts. Although Japan was a far poorer country then, and the people in the rural areas were very isolated, there was nevertheless an abundance of folk art being produced. This state of affairs unfortunately began to change after the Meiji Restoration of 1868, when Western ideas and methods of industrial production transformed the country. However the process was a gradual one, for well-made handicrafts were still being produced in the more backward, rural regions of Japan right up to the Second World War.

During the postwar era, true folk art practically ceased to be produced as modern industry undermined the very existence of this type of art. At the same time, however, due to the enthusiasm of the lovers of *mingei* and the sponsorship of the folk-art movement, there was a maintenance of folk crafts and even a revival of interest with new centers of artistic production being established. If this modern *mingei,* made for the urban crafts shops rather than the rural populace, should be considered genuine folk art is debatable. But that this new *mingei,* often following traditional models and made by rural craftsmen, has a beauty all its own and satisfies a real need cannot be disputed. Even if we call them *mingei*-style modern crafts, these contemporary products are aesthetically pleasing in their own way.

In the United States, the first to appreciate and collect Japanese folk crafts was Langdon Warner, the late curator of the Fogg Museum, Harvard University, who was a close personal friend of Dr. Yanagi and other leading figures of the Japanese Folk Art Society. It was through his advocacy and influence that good examples of this type of art entered American collections and museums and became popular with the American public. Numerous younger scholars and collectors, among them the late Professor James Plummer of the University of Michigan and this author, became interested in Japanese folk art. Several exhibitions were held in the U.S., notably the 1965 *mingei* show at Asia House in New York and the 1978–79 exhibition "Folk Traditions in Japanese Art," which was organized and circulated throughout the United States by the International Exhibitions Foundation.

Now that this field of connoisseurship and collecting has become popular, it remains to explore the various particular aspects of this art in more specialized studies and exhibitions. It is in this context that a book on tansu, the traditional cabinetry of Japan, by Mr. and Mrs.

Heineken is to be welcomed. Having studied and collected *mingei* for many years, this couple, with roots both in the West and Japan, are ideally suited to undertake such a work, and it can only be hoped that this will be merely the first of many such specialized studies of the various aspects of *mingei*.

Hugo Munsterberg

PREFACE

In 1964 we purchased our first tansu with little consideration of age, provenance, or authenticity. Our home in Tokyo was small, and the modularity of a chest-on-chest suited our needs for storage in two separate rooms during the summer and in one room for the cold, winter months. Our tansu was far from the level of sophistication one might expect from furniture with fine veneering and dovetail joinery. It was, in truth, a purely functional box with interesting hardware reminiscent of British "campaign" chests. Perhaps it was the subtle but persistent jesting of Japanese friends at our use of a tansu as a piece of furniture that led to an association of these chests with the steamer trunks of "Grand Tour" Europe. Indeed, it was a practical and mobile box but not intended to function as furniture. Proceeding from this point of view, an awareness of tansu as a unique form of cabinetry, ignored or at best misunderstood in ethnological history, began to unfold.

A decision ten years later to coalesce the fragmented, often inconsistent information available, present materials and structure from a conservationist point of view, and place the development of tansu within a simple outline of socioeconomic history, may be attributed to two sources of knowledge and encouragement. In Japan, members of the Craftsmen's Guild, especially in the snow country of Tōhoku, gave of their time to teach us not only what their hands were trained to do but why there should be pride in the creation. In the United States, we shall always be grateful for early moral support and professional advice from our friends in the Oriental Arts Department of the Brooklyn Museum, one of the very few museums to have recognized the significance of Japanese *mingei,* or folk art.

In the preparation of this book, one person stands out as both a contributor with immense sympathy for our task and a connoisseur of tansu without exception. Mr. John Gruber of Washington, D.C., and Nikkō,

Japan, has been a valued friend and a source of inspiration. As a group of successful ladies and gentlemen committed to the accurate documentation and study of tansu, the members of the Tonami Wa-dansu Kenkyūkai of Toyama Prefecture were unwavering in their cooperation. The collection held by this group represents the most outstanding cross section of tansu yet documented. We are also indebted to Mr. Yasuharu Takeuchi, custodian of the Tokyo Furniture Museum, for his insight and cooperation in making the museum's exceptional inventory available.

The photography is principally the creation of Mr. Toshiji Sekine, a close friend of many years with an aesthetic eye profoundly sensitive to bonsai in particular and art in general. His urbane control of difficult situations was very often a deciding factor in the success of each day's work. From New York City, we were fortunate to be able to entice Mr. John Kennard, a young photographer of exceptional ability, to Princeton for the shooting of pieces from our family collection. Mr. Kiyoshi Sonobe of Tokyo is well recognized as a don in ethnological photography. To him, as both a photographer and an outstanding artist, we are most grateful.

Line drawings were rendered by Ms. Sanae Sasaki of Musashino Bijutsu University based upon amateur sketches, which her patience and special abilities were able to overcome. From Mr. Ryūshin Makino of Kaga, author of a definitive presentation of ship *ema* painting, we were able to borrow his only print of an extraordinary ship *ema,* a kind of votive offering.

Although the research for our book was very largely the result of our own wanderings and probings, several people were most effective in certain specialized areas with which we were unfamiliar. Dr. Hans Wagener, our oldest Dutch friend, took time from his international responsibilities to transliterate the Zacharias Waganaer diary into twentieth century language. Messrs. Roessingh and van Opstall of the Algemeen Rijksarchief of the Netherlands provided a readable rendering of the Waganaer diary on which to base our research. Cooperation in the deciphering of obscure names, titles, and subjects by the library staffs of the International House, Tokyo, and the Tokyo Toritsu Chūō Toshokan Bunkō-shitsu, are especially appreciated. As well, we are obliged to Dr. Heinrich Taut for his research on our behalf regarding quotations from his illustrious father.

In order to put the manuscript into a cohesive format, the professional guidance and suggestions of several people were sought. Our respected friend Prof. Marius B. Jansen of Princeton led us to a deeper insight into Japanese history. Prof. Madoka Kanai of Tokyo University was a guide to us in the unanticipated complexities of classic Dutch. Dr. P.H. Pott, director of the Rijksmuseum voor Volkenkunde in Leiden directed us to the Dutch national archives, and Messrs. Yuki, Ishizuka, Nakajima, and Ōtake with their respective families allowed us to temporarily discombobulate their lives.

In appreciation of a special relationship and for protecting our isolation, we must thank Mr. and Mrs. Ernie Salomon of Tokyo.

We accept responsibility for any omissions, inconsistencies, and mistakes; however, for virtuous bursts of professionalism that may be apparent, please blame our patient editor at Weatherhill, Meg Taylor.

We did not intend this book to be simply an introduction to tansu nor a definitive study of the subject. This is the first book on tansu separate and distinct from a classification as furniture, in either Japanese or English. We hope that it will invite both controversy and a stimulating reappraisal of Japanese functional forms in cabinetry.

January 1981
Point House, Moro Iso

Illustration Credits

Mr. T. S. Heineken, 50
Mr. Scott Hyde, photographer, 36
Mr. John Kennard, photographer, 23, 27, 29, 120, 126, 145, 161
Kōgei Shuppan, 39, 43, 159
Mr. Shizuhiko Kōsetsu, 13
Mr. Dana Levy, photographer, 69–73, 91–97, 130–32, 135, 163
Mr. Ryūshin Makino, 76–77
National Diet Library, 33, 51–53
Mr. K. Onuki, 162
Mr. John G. Roberts, 127
Mr. Mamoru Sakamoto, photographer, 37, 68, 78, 84, 103, 128–29, 136–37, 160, 199
Ms. Sanae Sasaki, line drawings on pages 13, 19, 188–89
Mr. Toshiji Sekine, photographer, 8, 24, 26, 28, 30, 32, 34–35, 40–42, 46, 57–59, 62, 64–67, 74–75, 79–83, 85–90, 98–102, 104–19, 121–25, 133–34, 139–44, 146–50, 152–53, 156, 158, 164–98, 200–206, 208–24, 226–97
Dr. Franz Philipp von Siebold, 225
Shibundō, 7
Shōgakukan, 154–55
Shōkokusha, 6
Shunjūsha, line drawings on pages 63–64, 97–98, 176, 190–91, 193
Mr. Kiyoshi Sonobe, 31, 38, 47–48, 60, 207
Tankōsha, 22, 151
Mr. John B. Taylor, photographer, 63
Tokyo Toritsu Chūō Toshokan, 2, 14–18, 25, 44, 49, 54–56, 61

INTRODUCTION: A REVERENCE FOR SPACE

"*That which functions well, looks well.*"—Bruno Taut

Japan is probably the only civilization to have developed without a tradition of stationary household furniture. Until barely one hundred years ago, the well-decorated home was comparatively bare. This phenomenon, rather than being merely a peculiarity of an isolated nation, was the result of a complex blend of physical factors that came together to form the character of an exceptionally pragmatic people.

The Japanese archipelago stretches along the same latitudes as eastern North America from Montreal to Florida and encompasses a broad range of landscapes and climates, including heavy snowfalls along the Japan Sea coast and frequent volcanic activity. From earliest times the Japanese people have sought to understand their unpredictable environment through a belief in spirits residing within nature. The very rocks and trees became animate to them. Based on this belief, they developed Shinto, an indigenous religion involving purification rituals to attain harmony in nature.

Both the belief in an inherent spirit in each object and the Shinto emphasis on purity contributed toward a unique aesthetic that utilizes space and materials most effectively. This aesthetic is evident in every facet of Japanese culture, and it is especially prominent in traditional architecture.

The teahouse style of architecture exemplifies the Japanese reverence for space and respect for materials. This style, called *sukiya,* developed from the farmhouse-inspired simplicity of tea-ceremony rooms and buildings in the early part of the Edo period (1603–1868). Rustic elements were borrowed and adapted for residential structures, while retaining the Zen austerity of the tea ceremony. The designs are efficient and flexible, involving modular units and standardized materials, and relying on the simplicity of the arrangement and the natural beauty of the materials.

Upon visiting Katsura Detached Palace, a classic example of *sukiya* architecture in Kyoto, Bruno Taut, the eminent German architect, observed in 1933: "The entire arrangement, from whichever side one might care to look at it, followed always elastically in all its divisions the purpose which each one of the parts as well as the whole had to accomplish, the aim being that of common and normal utility, or the necessity of dignified representation, or that of lofty, philosophical spirituality. And the great mystery was that all three purposes had been united into a whole and that their boundaries had been effaced." Professor Taut found in Katsura support for his functionalist theory, yet he perhaps felt instinctively that there was much more to be learned from this seventeenth-century creation.

Above all, space is respected at Katsura. There is a flow between the garden and the structures, wedding interior and exterior spaces; through this, living space and the surrounding environment are united. In every indigenous design, from farmhouses to aristocratic villas, Japanese architecture is oriented toward the efficient use of space and respect for building materials.

In a similar quest for purity, the Bauhaus in the 1920s postulated the design precept "less is more," approximately one thousand years after Japan had developed a similar aesthetic. Perhaps even more closely analogous to the Japanese experience than the Bauhaus are the Shaker communal experiments of the nineteenth century. Although the strict religious tenets of the Shakers may not be relevant, their glorification of God through the effective utilization of time and resources developed into a Western aesthetic based upon purity in some ways strikingly similar to that of the Japanese.

A comparison of cabinetry reveals that, for both the Japanese craftsmen and the Shakers, form was primarily determined by function. Simplicity, balance, utility, and durability are common characteristics. In their specific approaches to materials and techniques, both cultures relied upon local woods, avoided decorative joinery, and shunned veneers in favor of the honesty of solid woods. In terms of utilization, the Shaker tendency to build case pieces into the room structure, use structural ''dead space'' for storage, and leave floor space open is paralleled in the nineteenth century only in Japan.

Outside influences eventually left a foreign mark on Japanese house design. Although a room for performing the tea ceremony and a garden symbolically representing the universe appear to have been easily assimilated into the Shinto aesthetic of purity in spite of Chinese origin, Western taste has often been expressed in Japan by decorative excess in the twentieth century. Furniture occupying fifty percent of the floor space, fluorescent lighting, multiple man-made textures on a single surface, and hermetically sealed windows are not uncommon.

On the other hand, the traditional Japanese house with its sparse contents invites an appreciation of space. The use of tansu was entirely consistent with this will to eliminate anything extraneous from the flow of balanced forms, both nature's and man's.

Comparisons cannot easily be made with the great decorative furniture traditions of Europe and China. Japanese chests are not stationary furniture. Rather, they can accurately be described as mobile cabinetry, used by the individual to keep personal possessions and clothing outside of the season for which they were intended, by the merchant to store important records and valuables, and by the family for ready access to objects of daily use. Tansu were kept in storehouses adjacent to homes and businesses, in storage rooms, on the raised area of a shop, and on some coastal ships for the owner or captain. With only a few exceptions, they were not visible in the house except at certain times and in specific situations. It is perhaps due to the fact that tansu have been judged according to the same criteria as conventional furniture that they have not until recently begun to gain international recognition.

PART ONE

HISTORY

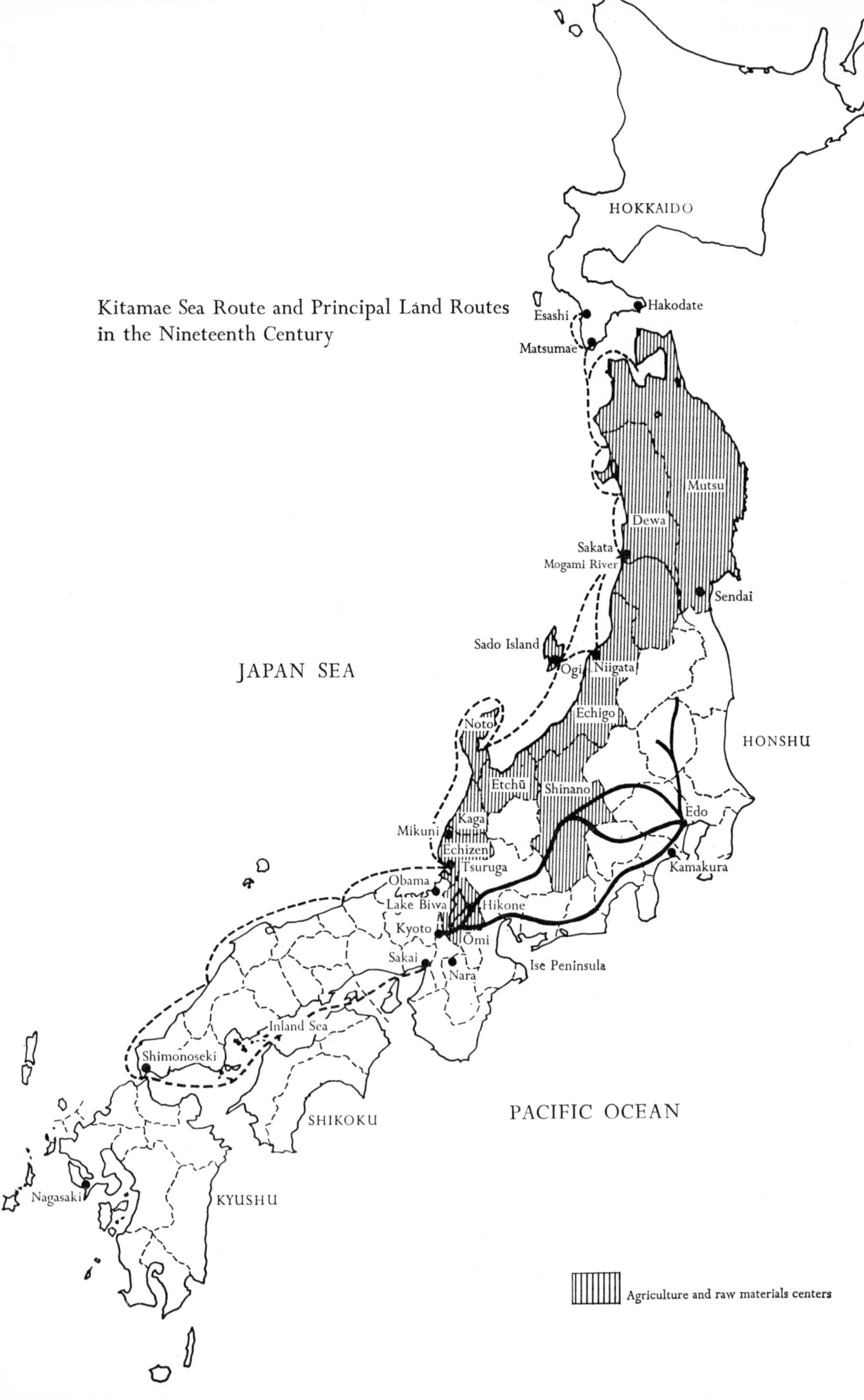

Kitamae Sea Route and Principal Land Routes in the Nineteenth Century

Chronology

Nara period	646–794
Heian period	794–1185
Kamakura period	1185–1336
Muromachi period	1336–1568
Momoyama period	1568–1603
Edo period	1603–1868
Modern period	1868–present
Meiji era	1868–1912
Taishō era	1912–26
Shōwa era	1926–present

Meiji-era Regional Tansu Centers

CHAPTER ONE

ORIGINS AND EARLY DEVELOPMENT

We have chosen to define tansu as Japanese mobile storage chests in order to accommodate cabinetry within changing life patterns from the early Edo period through the Meiji era in a single definition. Tansu are primarily a product of Edo and Meiji times. The word tansu was first recorded in the Genroku era of the Edo period (1688–1703). The two components, *tan* 簞 and *su* 笥, appear to have initially represented objects with separate functions: the storage of food and the carrying of firewood. Since the bamboo radical appears in each of these characters, it may be conjectured that wood was not as yet used.

In 1713, the *Wakan Sansai Zu-e,* a popular encyclopedia, decried the use of the term tansu as a substitute for *tate-bitsu,* a category of storage containers popular at that time in the ruling military class. The broader term tansu perhaps gained acceptance in time over *tate-bitsu* because of its roots in colloquial speech. It is interesting to note that the second character for *tate-bitsu* 堅櫃 contains the radical for wood; therefore, it is in truth a more precise nomenclature than tansu.

In contemporary Japanese language, there is no uniformly accepted definition for tansu separate from the term *wa kagu,* literally Japanese furniture. This is indeed unfortunate, since the collector might be inclined to consider Japanese cabinetry with an eye prejudiced by Western decorative furniture traditions.

We have sought to find points in history at which the tansu was produced as a craft, beginning with the boxmaker and the joiner and ending with a transition to mass production. As a chronological guide, the following dates may be used. Pre-tansu: 646 (in the Nara period) to 1657 (Meireki fire); tansu: 1657–1923 (early Edo period through the Meiji and Taishō eras to the Great Kanto Earthquake); post-tansu: 1923 to the present.

The development of the tansu as a utilitarian possession for the common people can best be understood with an appreciation of the changing socioeconomic face of Japan from early times to the present. The sophisticated culture of T'ang-dynasty China had an especially profound influence on seventh and eighth century Japan. Although a flow of Buddhist mysticism and images from the continent had been in progress for several centuries, the Taika Reform of 646 forced the ruling court to emulate a Chinese model of political institutions based upon Confucian legal codes. Until this time, government was based upon tribal kinship and the Shinto religion. Evolution to a more centralized state with a supporting bureaucracy brought about the establishment of Japan's first permanent capital of Nara in 710. The symmetrical plan of this city was entirely Chinese in character.

In cabinetry, Japan is most fortunate to still have several examples of early craftsmanship preserved in the Shōsō-in, an imperial storehouse within the grounds of Tōdai-ji, a temple in Nara. Four pieces stored in the eighth century are particularly important: a cabinet of lacquered wood, a cypress bed, a coffer, and free-standing shelves. These will be examined in some detail.

The cabinet, called a *zushi,* is constructed of zelkova wood burl and lacquered. At the time this piece was stored in the Shōsō-in, it had already been used by several successive rulers beginning with Emperor Temmu in A.D. 673. It is described in the *Kemmotsu-chō,* an inventory, as being constructed of *bunkanboku,* an archaic term for zelkova burl. The floriate paneled base, much admired by Chinese furniture scholars for its pure T'ang form, was unsuccessfully restored in the 1890s. It is unfortunate that the aesthetic sense evident in this famous cabinet has been consistently credited to a non-Japanese origin. Upon examination of the materials and construction technique, there is little support for this long-standing assumption except for the base, the removable mullion, and general proportions.

Unlike Chinese and Korean furniture, the construction of this cabinet did not rely upon panels floating between mortise-and-tenoned frame members. Case construction uses simple lap joints secured by iron nails with large heads covered by silver leaf. The shelves are housed in the sides and secured by nails. The doors are each of one board, and these are cut into three sections in the classic *hashikui*-style tenoned and mitered clamp joint to prevent warping, a technique that has continued into the twentieth century. All the wood has been book-matched in nearly perfect symmetry.

Hardware on this cabinet is almost completely original, yet it seems to be a curious mixture. Consistent with the silver-headed nails, the staple receivers for the removable mullion that covers the two doors are solid silver. The padlock and hinges, however, are green gold.

There is a faint red tone to the wood resulting from application of boiled tannin from sapanwood, a red dyewood from the East Indies. This was a popular practice, the sapanwood acting as both a stain and an astringent. Over this stain, a clear lacquer was applied.

The Chinese-style bed is constructed of cypress and dates from the reign of Emperor Shōmu (724–49). Originally finished with a white chalk wash, the *onshō,* a platform bed, was used in a pair before the introduction of the *chōdai,* a tatami-covered platform, and later it was used on the *chōdai* in the private living quarters of an aristocratic residence. Silk-bound straw mats, silk cushions, and coverlets filled with cotton wadding were placed on the bed. With the evolution to tatami-covered platforms, the structured bed became symbolic, used only for ceremonial occasions.

The horizontal frame members, 7 cm square, are joined by rebate mitered dovetails. The eight inner slats are tenoned into the outer frame, supported by two transverse braces tenoned into the legs, and further secured by 11.6 cm iron nails at each of the sixteen crossing points. The entire leg, brace, and outer frame configuration is enforced by right-angle iron plates considered to be the originals dating from the early eighth century.

Although most probably of Japanese origin, the coffer exhibits a strong design influence from the continent, possibly coming from the Paekche kingdom of Korea with the dissemination of Buddhism. The scholar Sekine has observed that unrevised inventory records of the Shōsō-in designate such coffers with the character *kan,* which was originally associated with the Korean peninsula, even though it was pronounced *kara,* literally T'ang China, from the mid-eleventh century.

Four short legs of zelkova wood are connected to a cryptomeria body by iron nails and further secured by transverse braces between the legs to support the case floor. The braces are tenoned into the legs. The cover and all four sides are each one board, interconnected by *rokumai-gumi* (a six-part-tenon, open-mortise box joint) secured with iron pins. The indentations in the legs were for ropes used in a carrying sling. That this *kara-bitsu,* or "T'ang coffer," has lacquer covering only its joints, to seal the case against moisture, indicates that it was intended for storage of personal papers, not religious documents.

The multi-level shelves are built of natural cryptomeria. Each level is constructed from a board 3.5 cm thick. For passage of the vertical frame members, there are holes cut in the shelves. Transverse wood braces, grooved and flared at each end, support the shelving. All surface wood has been convexly carved to inhibit warping. The base is of cross-lap construction.

This piece was originally intended for keeping perishables in the imperial kitchen, but in later generations it inspired shelves of similar design used in aristocratic residences for display and personal effects.

In the middle of the Heian period, the mid-tenth century, the ruling Fujiwara family encouraged the introduction of a new residential style for the aristocracy, the *shinden* style, modifying Chinese design to Japanese convenience and a growing native aesthetic sense. With the development of the *shinden* style, Japanese concern for a balance of components, rather than perfect but separate statements in decoration, began to assert itself. The Kyoto Imperial Palace is an example of this style.

Other than a departure from strict symmetry, the principal change in room-interior configuration was the elimination of chairs and beds for daily use. *Shinden* style allowed for one large room without fixed walls or windows, a series of sliding panels being used instead, and incorporated raised platforms of wood covered in part with tatami mats. In the arrangement of the living quarters, as opposed to a formal reception hall, four additions were required:

CHŌDAI: a platform of two tatami mats in the middle of the room, for sleeping, with a rigid shoji canopy from which curtains could be hung for privacy.

TATAMI: mats of woven straw, each approximately 242 cm long and 106 cm wide, with a thickness of 6 cm. Three were placed to the left and one to the right of the *chōdai*.

TANA: free-standing open-framework shelves, usually in a pair,

Japanese-style splayed leg (soriashi) *of the Muromachi period.*

The Heian-style nikai-dana *base superimposed on the Chinese-style interconnected-frame base of the Nara-period cabinet from the Shōsō-in.*

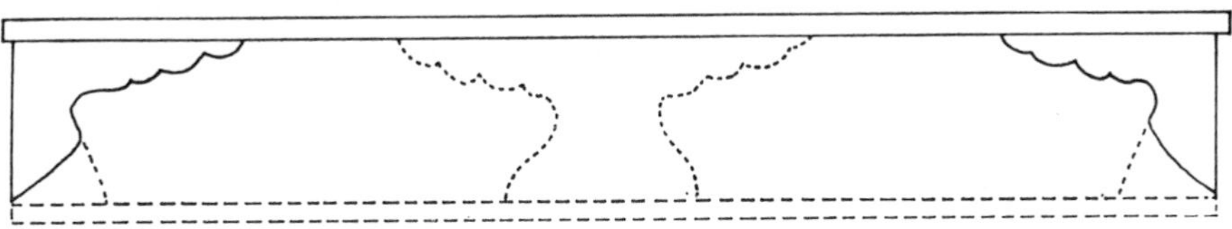

placed on the floor directly behind the three tatami mats to the left of the *chōdai*.

BYŌBU: a pair of folding screens set on either side of the *chōdai* behind the *tana* to the left, and behind the single tatami mat to the right.

In their domination of the imperial court through intermarriage, the Fujiwara clan was eventually able to reign as well as rule by their monopoly of the government bureaucracy and control of private tax-free estates. In order to perpetuate this power, the Confucian tenet that position should be determined by individual merit was abandoned in favor of inherited rank and status.

The fertilization of Japan by Chinese civilization, followed by its isolation from any external threat, was responsible for the evolution of a sophisticated indigenous culture. By the late Heian period, parallel with the development of the *shinden* style, storage cabinetry for the aristocracy began to acquire a more distinctly Japanese character.

Cabinets in the T'ang-dynasty style (Fig. 1) came to be combined with free-standing open-frame shelving (Fig. 3), resulting in two new types of furniture:

NIKAI-ZUSHI: an asymmetrical unit often finished with decorative etched lacquer. The interconnected frame base has been superceded by four splayed legs in the pure Japanese style with double front-opening doors on full-face hinges under an open shelf.

NIKAI-DANA: a partially enclosed framing of two shelves over four splayed legs. This shows a clear modification of the T'ang interconnected frame base.

Through attrition of family members, rivalries, and a decentralization of enforceable power, the Fujiwara family lost control of the country in the mid-twelfth century. For the next 170 years, first the Heike, then the Genji, and finally the Hōjō families were able to maintain a semblance of control through a patronage system using conquered lands in reward for loyalty. Unfortunately, lack of charismatic leadership, decentralized power, and a breakdown of loyalties brought a chaotic end to the Kamakura period and the beginning of feudalism under less than absolute control by the Ashikaga family.

In the fourteenth century, a new architectural style, the *shoin* style, emerged from the needs of the samurai class. Since the Kamakura period, when tatami began to be more widely used as inset floor covering, the *shinden* style had been gradually changing. The rambling pavilion configuration of loosely connected modules was broken into smaller separate buildings for specific functions such as general living, entertaining, storage, staff housing, and religious activities. The *chōdai* in the *shinden* residence was incorporated into the structural plan with sliding panels, known today as shoji and *fusuma,* replacing the impermanent canopy and curtains of the Heian period. The influence of the growing popularity of tea ceremony as a social function, requiring increased space for the entertainment of guests, was considerable in the evolution to the *shoin* style. In the course of this development, an alcove specifically for objects to be enjoyed aesthetically, recessed shelves both open and covered, and a naturally lighted nook for reading came to be part of the integral structure. The *ninomaru shoin* of Nijō castle in Kyoto may be considered a mature example of *shoin* style.

During these years of regional factionalism and constant war, the *hitsu,* a coffer with or without legs, was the mainstay of storage cabinetry among all people of means, regardless of class. While *hitsu* were adequate for personal possessions, they were not principally designed for mobility, requiring a complicated rope sling to secure the coffer to a carrying pole.

This style of storage trunk was not known as a *wa-bitsu,* literally a Japanese coffer, until the 1050 recodification of the Shōsō-in inventory.

Prior to this time, all *hitsu,* with or without legs, were known as *karabitsu,* "foreign" *hitsu,* later considered to be of T'ang-dynasty influence. Although this piece has been considered by some scholars to be non-Japanese in origin, the use of indigenous cryptomeria wood makes provenance beyond Japan difficult to accept. Further, a design without legs implies that the piece was intended for storage on a wood floor, not on the fine stone flooring of Chinese homes at this time. Each face is one solid board, the body interconnected by *gomai-gumi* (a five-part-tenon, open-mortise box joint) secured with iron nails and sealed with black lacquer. Two horizontal bars are of zelkova wood with two inner recesses on each bar for the passage of sling ropes to facilitate carrying.

Although Ashikaga family rule during the Muromachi period gave little respite to the common people from war and political strife, it provided a positive climate for the dissemination of Zen Buddhism throughout Japan under the shoguns' protection. Introduced from China in the twelfth century, Zen Buddhism, with its emphasis on self-discipline, scholarship, and austere habits, was not only appropriate to the warrior spirit of the samurai, but also a necessary balance against the power of numerous Buddhist sects with overt political ambitions. Zen helped keep intellectual interests alive during very uncertain years. The refinement of borrowed Chinese culture and the continuing influence of Chinese principles can largely be attributed to the Zen scholars.

Important to our interest in design, the Zen aesthetic was compatible with Shinto reverence for the spiritual nature of all things. The natural characteristics of materials came to be accepted and resulted in various interesting cults of appreciation for the inexactitudes of nature. The unpretentious, the spontaneous, the directly stated, found favor with the Japanese aristocracy. This new aesthetic stood in marked contrast to both Chinese and European artistic traditions. Because of this shift in the direction of taste, craftsmen, over the following centuries, tended to progressively eliminate the extraneous in a quest for intuitive awareness of reality as expressed in the creative process. Form from function in cabinetry is but one manifestation of this mentality.

The last half of the Muromachi period saw an enormous expansion of regional rivalries. Factionalism tore the fabric of the central government to threads. Tightly self-contained feudal states relied upon their productive capacity to finance political ambition through warfare. The lord of each state, or daimyo, actively supported commerce in order to generate revenue for the purchase of means to greater power. Agriculture, forestry, mining, weaving, sakè brewing, and numerous other primary as well as secondary occupations were encouraged.

Of special relevance to this discussion of cabinetry, new techniques emerged that expanded the efficient use of materials and manpower. A two-man saw, used vertically for ripping large timber, facilitated the construction of superstructures for castles and large residences. A plane with an adjustable blade that could be easily resharpened supplemented the traditional inshave and adze, thereby permitting very thin wood to be cut accurately.

These innovations became available to the common boxmaker and joiner sometime during the Sengoku period of civil wars (1482–1558) from whence there emerged two significant storage containers:

NAGAMOCHI: a wooden trunk of cryptomeria, paulownia, or cypress with a hinged lid, the size and proportions being most similar to the *hitsu* without legs. Large U-shaped iron handles on each of the two short sides allowed the trunk to be carried easily and efficiently on a wooden pole borne between two servants. Within the samurai class, *nagamochi* were usually lacquered and often covered with a light-blue silk bearing the crest of the owner when carried in a procession. The *nagamochi* of wealthy townsmen, on the other hand, almost always had a natural finish prior to the Meiji era.

TSUZURA: a woven rectangular box originally made of wisteria vine with a removable cover, three-quarter to full, of an identical material. For strength, the corners were often reinforced with leather before iron hardware was used for the same purpose on wood tansu in the next century. Although most *tsuzura* were certainly intended for relatively stationary use, woodblock prints from the sixteenth century indicate that they were used to carry personal possessions in wedding processions and were carried by peddlers on their backs. The *Shin Sarugaku-ki,* published before the Edo period, mentions one Makito Hachirō as a leader of peddlers with trading activities from northern Honshu to southern Kyushu island, involving at times over one hundred pack horses.

With the seizure of Kyoto in 1568, the subjugation of separatist Buddhist sects outside the city, and the consolidation of power into a central government in 1573, the general Oda Nobunaga began the process of bringing peace again after one hundred years of civil wars. This stability stimulated expansion of established commerce beyond the primary and secondary sectors. The local merchant began to prosper as well. His customers for fans, silks, writing brushes, hair ornaments, and many other small items were not only samurai families, but also the families of other merchants. As the samurai rivaled each other for status through power and influence, the merchants did likewise for profit.

With this new prosperity, novel ways were sought to conveniently classify merchandise in storage. Multilevel free-standing shelves, an adaptation from those of the upper classes, evolved into a direct predecessor of the tansu, *shōhin hikidashi,* literally merchandise drawers, built into shop walls. It is not possible to conjecture a date for this development, but we do know from a book of woodblock illustrations, *Kōshoku Ichidai Otoko* by Ihara Saikaku, published in 1682, that such cabinetry was not uncommon among urban merchants. It seems reasonable to assume that this development came about sometime between the last decade of the sixteenth century and the first half of the seventeenth century, in the Azuchi-Momoyama or the early Edo period. At this time, two new types of conveniently sized personal storage containers also appeared:

KŌRI: very much like *tsuzura* but proportionately smaller, of leather originally and later of woven bamboo or willow vine, for storing small objects of daily use.

HASAMI-BAKO: literally "scissors box," a conveniently mobile, small trunk constructed of leather, cryptomeria, cypress, or *washi* (handmade paper) treated with persimmon tannin. The interesting name owes its origin to the earlier use by samurai of bamboo poles to hold bundled possessions. These poles were split along a middle length and pressed open, whereupon bundles were inserted. The pole then held the bundles in a scissors-like vise. In addition, the side handles on the trunk each resemble a pair of open shears when in a raised position for carrying the unit on a bar by one man. Prior to the Edo period, *hasami-bako* were used only by samurai.

Especially within the higher levels surrounding the shogun, samurai became increasingly inclined to display status through material possessions. Following this trend, four styles of free-standing shelving for samurai residences and castles came into use in cabinetry, inspired by the *nikai-zushi* and *nikai-dana* of the late Heian-period aristocracy discussed previously:

ZUSHI-DANA: three-tiered shelves finished with decorative etched lacquer, for writing utensils and incense preparation materials. With an increase in height over the Heian *nikai-zushi*, the full-face hinged double doors were positioned in the middle level. The "brush-stop" rolled edge on the top and Chinese-style splayed legs recall the earlier influence of Chinese designs.

KURO-DANA: three-tiered shelving in essentially the same configuration as the *zushi-dana*, for utensils used in personal care. Here we can see the evolution of the indigenous splayed leg of the Heian period into a straight leg flared only on the outer side.

SHO-DANA: three-tiered asymmetrical shelving for books and related objects, with sliding doors on the lower level and a base without legs.

TEA-CEREMONY TANA: shelving in a variety of configurations and sizes. These *tana* were either finished to complement textured materials used in the structure or opaque lacquered. As the popularity of the tea ceremony and the culture associated with it grew, shelved cabinets for tea-ceremony accoutrements developed in a pure Japanese style.

Nobunaga's success in subduing civil strife set Japan in a position of acquiescence to policies dictated by his successor Hideyoshi. These policies proved to be profoundly important to the stability of the country over the next 260 years. Especially important to our considerations are the following points: first, all rice fields were recodified as the principal source of tax revenue for the government; second, the peasant class was forbidden to possess arms; third, samurai were pressed into exclusive service to the state and were not permitted to live as farmers or engage in entrepreneurship; fourth, the government seized control over and severely restricted all foreign trade.

With the death of Hideyoshi at the end of the sixteenth century, the Edo period began and Tokugawa Ieyasu took the position of shogun. Although the Tokugawa homeland was Nagoya, approximately one hundred kilometers from Kyoto, Ieyasu wisely chose to build his gov-

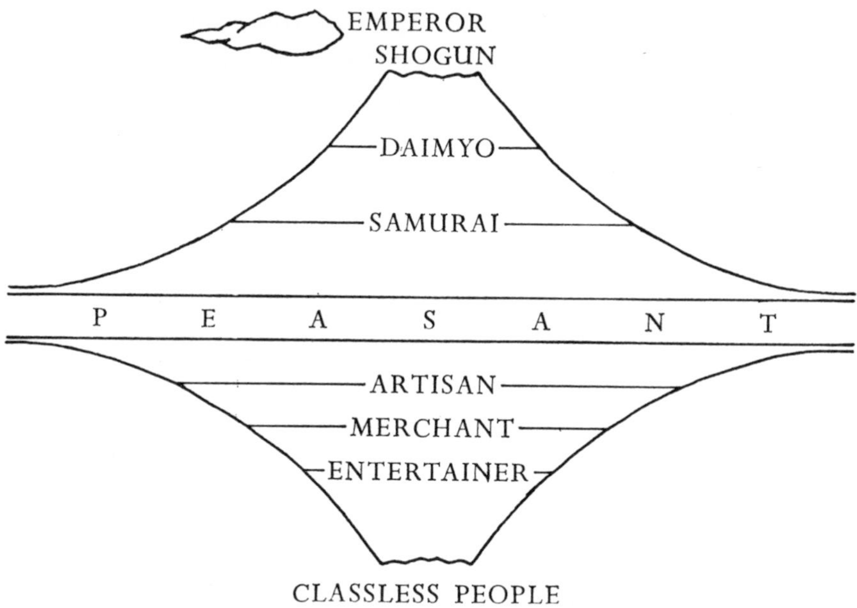

Based on a sketch of the Edo-period social order from Houses and People of Japan *by Bruno Taut.*

ernment on the extensive eastern lands of the Kanto Plain, which had been granted to him by Hideyoshi in gratitude for his loyalty. Kanto is the plain where present-day Tokyo is located, then a fishing village called Edo. With great patience, Ieyasu built a centralized feudal bureaucracy with society divided into the four classes of warrior, peasant, craftsman, and merchant.

Since the Imperial Court and its supporting aristocracy residing in Kyoto had almost no political power and little direct cultural influence, the warrior class of samurai families stood at the apex of the hierarchy. They not only ruled the country but also bore responsibility for the peace, collecting taxes and tending to administrative duties assigned by the shogunate. Each daimyo of the approximately 250 fiefdoms had an obligation to spend alternating years in residence in Edo, the capital, with an appropriate retinue to show his support of the shogun. When the lord was in his home domain, his family was required to maintain residence in Edo. On guard against conspiracy, the shogunate closely regulated the travel routes of lords and their families.

The peasants who farmed the lands were indirectly the principal source of revenue through taxation in rice for both the Tokugawa bureaucracy and the local daimyo with his liege samurai. Perhaps due to the situation in earlier times when the managers of lands, those who actually farmed the land, and the protectors of those lands had often been the same people, the peasant class was treated with considerable respect by the shogunate. Villages were not infrequently left to run their own affairs under the leadership of a family with samurai origin.

There was no differentiation between craftsmen and artisans within the *shokunin* class. This division cannot be applied to the Japanese situation, though there did exist differences in status among the craftsmen. For example, a carver of combs did not have the status of a swordsmith, but they both were of the same designated class. More appropriate to Japan is an understanding of the urban and countryside differences. In the towns, there were two groupings: the *chōnin,* or townspeople, and the samurai. In the countryside, farmers engaged in cottage industry to generate supplementary income. Products in which a province excelled either through technique or the availability of raw materials were encouraged by local governments. The handmade paper of Shirakawa, iron casting from Takaoka, silk woven at Yonezawa, and Wajima lacquerware are but a few examples of regionally specialized production within the craftsman class encouraged by the Tokugawa rulers.

At the bottom of the class structure, merchants were regarded as unproductive and consequently looked down upon. Agriculture was the tax base and source for the fixed incomes of samurai. Trade as a generator of tax revenue was curiously not exploited by the Tokugawa government. Consequently, as techniques developed for the transportation and distribution of materials, with a reliable monetary system in support, the modestly taxed merchant class began to reap rewards from the nation's economic integration.

The shogunate, concerned with the consolidation and security of its power, insulated itself with a matrix of regulations that were interpreted in varying ways and only enforced at the convenience of the government. In spite of considerable restriction and enforced isolation under a firm policy of seclusion from foreign countries from 1638 until 1853, Japan at peace quietly prospered.

History offers a documented point in time when it can be said that tansu as mobile storage cabinetry were a common possession. On March 2, 1657, in the third year of the Meireki era of the Edo period, a fire broke out at the Honmyō-ji temple in the Hongō district of Edo after many rainless months. Swept on by high winds, flames took three days to consume most of the capital, killing 107,000 people.

At the time of the conflagration, a trade mission from the Dutch East India Company on Dejima island in Nagasaki harbor had just concluded an agreement with the shogunate and were in Edo at an inn in what is now the Nihonbashi area of Tokyo, awaiting permission to return to Dejima. Zacharias Waganaer, head of the mission, recorded in careful detail his observation of the panic ensuing from the fire. The Waganaer diary records the experience of a foreigner on the fringe of survival in the core of a holocaust. It is not objective, and was perhaps penned not for the private historical reference of the writer at some later date, but from the habit of a disciplined diarist. Several passages from the Dutch are offered here, corroborated by several woodblock prints concerning the fire from the seventeenth century *Musashi Abumi,* a historical commentary published in 1661.

Zacharias Wagenaer Diary

In the midst of extended praise for Dutch medical science, our host was interrupted by a young man who, it seemed, warned him that something was seriously amiss. Shortly thereafter he excused himself, presumably to give the situation his personal scrutiny. Thus now alone, we ventured our own investigation by stepping out on to the verandah of the villa. Judging from a rising column of black smoke to the north and a wind of exceptional force, we immediately ascertained that a fire of considerable magnitude had begun to rage. The young man who had brought the first news returned to us and advised that his master was obliged by the situation to remain absent, nevertheless he continued to extend the hospitality of his household. We acknowledged this honor but desisted from acceptance, fearing for the security of our lodging. Thus having taken leave properly, we mounted our horses and rushed back, although it had been determined that the fire was still more than one and a half miles away from our quarters and therefore not yet a danger.

Upon arriving at slightly past four o'clock, I found that my assistant

Cornelis Mulock, with the help of a Japanese servant, had packed my papers and personal belongings in crates and placed them in our fireproof storehouse [*kura*]. In fear of the fire's erratic path, people were hastily crating provisions, gifts, and silver for like storage. Although lookouts from our roof advised that a change in the wind was now taking the fire away from us, we felt torn between hope and despair when seeing people carrying away their belongings. Our Japanese government intermediaries and interpreters agreed with the landlord that nowhere would our valuables be safer than in the aforementioned storehouse, which had withstood such a fire only one year before. This I agreed to but I felt that the company vault holding our cash should best be sent on by guarded palanquin to the Edo villa of Joffiesamma [European reading of the name of the second governor of Nagasaki] for safekeeping. As we pondered our course of action, we saw more than one thousand citizens pass by, burdened miserably with old people and children. Our traveling companion, a Dutch medical surgeon, then appeared from the rooftop and prevailed upon me to view the conflagration from an elevation in order to realize our peril. With fear and trepidation, I realized that our lodging would soon be lost to lightning flames no less voracious than those at Troy or any great conflagration in history. The entire sun, which otherwise would have been shining brightly, was completely obscured by black smoke as though it would never be seen again! Although the fire was still about a quarter mile away, we could feel its strength and heat through the winter cold, driven on by a north wind. The rolling sea of flame was a mile wide running from east to west and it pressed forward with fire sparks falling like a strong rain so that the east side was always ignited before the west side.

We all now realized that escape was our only choice. Servants and retainers hurried this way and that. By the time our senior Japanese staff had sealed the storehouse and organized our flight, I saw that the flames were but a pistol shot away from our door. With our realization of the gravity of the situation at about half past four, our senior Japanese bodyguard, with a long staff in hand, led us into the street with instructions to stay together at all costs. This was indeed almost impossible because of the crowds of panic-stricken refugees, many trying to carry away their belongings in big chests on four wheels [*nagamochi kuruma*].

Since nobody wished to be last, they had so congested the gateways and crossings that often hundreds of thus burdened citizens were waiting just to pass through, with the number growing with each passing moment. Those who were empty-handed climbed over the chests and packs, finding safe escape. We did likewise, as well as climbing over roofs, in our race to outrun the insatiable flames that caught those wretched people who could not pass with their possessions. God save their souls! By this time our Japanese staff had become more concerned for our safety than for their own survival, and had found a sufficient number of escape passages to allow us to now consider how to face the cold night without shelter.

The streets of Edo were very narrow and planned with numerous gates and right angles in order to inhibit insurrection. In addition, most of the townspeople's residences had thatch roofs that tended to smoulder and smoke profusely. The chests on wheels observed by Waganaer, pulled and pushed by the citizenry and severely clogging the streets, were the earliest type of massive mobile storage cabinetry, the *nagamochi kuruma,* intended to carry all of the owner's personal, and often also mercantile, possessions in one unit. Although there is no conclusive official verification of Waganaer's observations of the Meireki fire, suffice it to say that the Tokugawa shogunate in the following years restricted the use of thatch and tile, regulated building design, and in 1683 prohibited the construction and use of *nagamochi kuruma* in Edo, Kyoto, and Osaka.

As the Edo period progressed, tansu developed rather strictly in accordance with class and function. The samurai rulers utilized cabinetry to both reflect the privileged position of the owner and to provide convenience within the stylized life into which they had been born. Examples of samurai tansu include:

SHO-DANSU: a chest for storing books of poetry, music, religion, and epic fiction for personal use. Usually *sho-dansu* were built with an enclosed frame of cryptomeria or cypress, and multiple shelves covered by one or two full-height, drop-fit doors, known as *kendon-buta*.

KATANA-DANSU: a chest for the safekeeping of sword blades 30 to over 62 cm in length, as well as accompanying sword fittings. When not carried on a day-to-day basis, swords could be easily disassembled into components. Sword tansu are usually of a uniform size in unfinished paulownia wood. A vertical locking bar generally reflects greater age than individually locking drawers.

CHA-DANSU: a portable cabinet for the storage of tea-ceremony bowls and utensils. In that formal tea was properly offered out-of-doors as well as inside, *cha-dansu* were as necessary as *chanoyu-dana*. Construction material and finishing varied with the season and inclination of the owner; however, quite often a drop-fit *kendon-buta* door was part of the total elegant configuration.

GOYŌ NAGAMOCHI: a trunk for clothing and official documents, usually of cypress lacquered black and bearing the family crest of the owner in a deep vermilion or maroon. These pieces were little different in size and style from the *nagamochi* used by wealthy townspeople, as in the woodblock print of the Meireki fire where they appear abandoned on the bridge (Fig. 25). A principal difference, though not entirely reliable, lies in the use of cypress for samurai pieces and cryptomeria for those of the townspeople. *Goyō nagamochi* of cypress without a finish were also used, in which case the unit was fitted with a blue silk cover bearing a crest in white when carried by retainers.

KOSODE-DANSU: a chest for storage of short-sleeved silk kimonos. When not needed in the house, these small tansu could be carried from the living quarters to the family storehouse, or *kura*. The piece illustrated in the *Wakan Sansai Zu-e* is an accurate representation of how *kosode-dansu* were often used when in the home: the vertical locking bar removed, allowing easy access to the drawers. In that an opaque black lacquered finish was preferred by samurai families for most convenience cabinetry that might be seen by non-family members, *kosode-dansu* usually had cypress for the body and drawer faces, and paulownia for the drawer interior wood.

TEMOTO-DANSU: a small chest for the samurai woman's use in the privacy of her rooms. Because *temoto* were small, for personal use, and only rarely moved about, they tend to reflect a sophisticated feminine character. Fine wood finished to complement the grain, elegant hardware, and paneled sliding doors painted by artists of the highest repute were desired features. Preferred woods included zelkova, black persimmon, mulberry, and boxwood.

ISHŌ-DANSU: a clothing chest with multiple drawers. For the samurai man who was of necessity preoccupied with the give and take of obligations, a chest to store his official clothing was essential. Different seasons and situations necessitated a multitude of costumes, so a samurai storehouse could be quite full of such units. It was not uncommon for these tansu to be brought in and out of the main living area on numerous occasions by the male retainers in the course of a year.

Ishō may be considered a general term for personal clothing in the context of cabinetry, common to both townsmen and samurai. Certain characteristics are to be found in samurai *ishō-dansu:* the use of black opaque lacquer; a preference for chased bronze or copper hardware; and a depth of over 50 cm for men's tansu to accommodate the "winged" shoulders of their formal *kamishimo* overgarments.

For *ishō-dansu* used by samurai women, a clear distinction from those used by the townspeople is more difficult since they relied primarily on woven *tsuzura* baskets set into the built-in closets covered with sliding doors that are still such an important feature of Japanese rooms today. However, since lacquer was a samurai preference, the *ishō-dansu* depicted in Edo-period woodblocks (Fig. 33) and known historically as Edo *ishō ryōbiraki kasane,* literally Edo-style double-door chest-on-chest, might best be considered as tansu of the merchant class or those used by women of the leisure world, unless the artist intentionally darkened the chest in his print.

The farmer of the Edo period, unless he was the master of his own land, was too poor to have anything in need of storage in a tansu. For those very few people who either controlled land or performed some function for the government through the local bureaucracy, two tansu types might be expected:

NAGAMOCHI KURUMA: a general storage trunk on wooden wheels with a hinged, removable lid, generally kept in the *kura,* or storehouse, of a wealthy family or in a storeroom of the main house on an earthen floor. Although these chests had been banned from Edo, Kyoto, and Osaka as an indirect result of the Meireki fire, they persisted in many rural towns, especially in the mountainous Tōhoku area of northern Honshu. They were usually constructed of zelkova or chestnut, both hardwoods, and occasionally these two woods were used in combination. If finished, a thin layer of oil and lacquer was applied. Unfortunately, few of these very early tansu have survived, mainly because their high-quality wood was readily recyclable.

MIZUYA: an enclosed framework of shelves covered by sliding doors, with outer drawers and other compartments depending upon the wealth of the owner. This multi-function chest was constructed usually in two sections and was kept adjacent to the kitchen primarily for the storage of eating utensils and food. By late Edo and early Meiji, the design had become sophisticated in visual balance with the addition of more compartments and air circulation panels not unlike the pioneer American bread safe in principle. Pine was often the dominant frame member, with cryptomeria for the panels and interiors.

In a rather special category, an official documents chest was used by village headmen. Unlike the formidable *goyō* chests of the samurai, the farmer's *goyō,* called *nōmin goyō,* was rather like a small *hitsu* without legs. Hardware used functionally over a natural zelkova, chestnut, or cryptomeria body was common, as was a small, lockable drawer for seals. The most important characteristic in these very rare pieces in the unobtrusive, almost hidden presence of the crest of the local daimyo to whom the headman was, in fact, liegeman.

As the economy developed to a point where local products could be marketed by urban merchants, the craftsmen began to rise as a class above mere subsistence. Especially in the cities and the castle towns, the swordsmith, the ironmonger, the tinsmith, the barber, and the oculist were very active. Even the boxmaker and joiner, as predecessors of the tansu maker, had expanding business as the people began to have enough possessions to require storage containers.

The *Shomin Shokunin Futokoro Nikki* of 1713 observed that tansu makers in Edo were so busy, they had customers waiting. Other than small multi-drawer wooden boxes or built-in drawers for the storage of products, the Edo craftsman with his own workshop relied upon simple woven *tsuzura* for safekeeping of the tools and materials required in his occupation. An interesting exception is found in those itinerant craftsmen who plied their trade from door to door. The chests they carried were often ingeniously designed. There fortunately still exist some excellent examples of the itinerant craftsman's toolbox as well as the peddler's box, which will be discussed in more detail below.

At the bottom of the class structure enforced by the Edo shogunate, merchants and peddlers made considerable use of tansu especially after the Genroku era (1688–1703). In the eighteenth century, those people who could openly display the material accoutrements of status or affluence were either born into, married into, or functioning on behalf of the Edo government, directly or through the domain of a subordinate daimyo. The merchant class, officially considered unproductive and motivated solely by selfish considerations, gradually came to direct the prosperity of the country through their control of distribution, local commerce, and moneylending. A wide gulf developed between merchant wealth and samurai power, aggravated by monetary indebtedness of the samurai to the merchant.

Initially, the impact of the merchants on the evolution of tansu was an urban phenomenon limited primarily to Edo, Kyoto, and Osaka and falling within the three categories of storage, administration, and personal use:

SHŌHIN HIKIDASHI: built-in drawer units for the storage of merchandise, used in shops from early Edo. Their convenience stimulated the creation of numerous types of chests for use in the front shop area, with multiple drawers for specific functions.

Prominent among these designs were the *kusuri-dansu,* or medicine chest for keeping medicinal herbs, and the *kaidan-dansu,* a staircase chest. Whereas *kusuri-dansu* were always of paulownia wood for lightness since they were carried on the backs of salesmen if necessary, *kaidan-dansu* were intended to be stationary, their foremost purpose being an efficient utilization of available structural space. A majority of Edo *kaidan-dansu* for shops seen by the authors indicate a preference by the cabinetmaker for framework and steps of pine, drawer and door face members of zelkova, and vertical paneling and drawer interiors of cryptomeria.

The *gyōshō-bako,* or peddler's merchandise box, can be considered a mobile storage container. Whereas the craftsman carried his trade box in order to perform a service, the peddler went from place to place in order to sell merchandise and services, usually because he could not afford to have his own shop.

As in Europe in the Middle Ages and eighteenth century America, the peddler even in the pre-Edo years was not only a primary distributor of urban merchandise but also a distributor of the popular culture and news of the time. At a neighborhood level, the majority of peddlers were merely hawkers of fresh daily produce and staples, moving about with a shoulder balancing bar from which inventory containers were suspended at either or both ends. On a larger scale, peddlers concentrated on purchasing luxurious items in developed areas such as Kyoto and carrying them to the countryside. Originally, these backpacks of merchandise were known as *senda-bitsu,* literally a coffer carried on the back, but as designs proliferated the term *gyōshō-bako* became popular.

Following the prohibition against wheeled *nagamochi* trunks, urban merchants came to rely upon recessed or free-standing enclosed shelves for the storage of inventory, and even other cabinetry of a more specific function such as account and money boxes. If these *todana-dansu* were not meant to be seen by the public, there would have been little or no hardware with the framing wood of cryptomeria natural or protected by a single coating of oil and lacquer.

Cabinetry used in conjunction with shop administration has come through time to be collectively called *chō-dansu,* literally account chests. Usually in the public view, it was expedient for the merchant to have these pieces constructed of fine woods in combination with substantial iron hardware in order to convey an impression of prosperity and reliability. The *chōba,* a tatami-covered elevated area where business was conducted, contained a variety of objects of ethnological interest to a collector (Figs. 58–59):

CHŌBA-GŌSHI: a two- or three-sided semi-open screen, usually of cypress, designed to imply desired privacy around the accounts desk. As in numerous other cultures, the physical handling of money was most proper when private. Each right-angled section of the *chōba-gōshi* was connected by hinges enabling the piece to be folded up completely for storage.

CHŌBA-ZUKUE: low desk with a solid top, often zelkova or chestnut, and foliate legs of one piece of cryptomeria running the full depth of the top. The addition of a single drawer between the legs is a Meiji-era modification of the simple Edo design.

KAKESUZURI: writing box with a hinged cover usually carried whenever the master left his shop on business, containing *sumi* ink with an ink stone, writing brushes, paperweights, and rolled writing paper. The best of these pieces at the end of Edo and into Meiji were of zelkova, many more were of paulownia or chestnut. Very early pieces such as our example from the Gruber Collection were considerably larger with a full front-opening door on half-faced individual hinges, usually four in number. Four inner drawers fulfilled the same function as the later hinged cover pieces and allowed space for more seals, scales, and money. A *kakesuzuri* somewhat identical to Mr. Gruber's, in a Sado Island museum, is dated 1628. Though these pieces were conceived for land use, there is no question that they sparked the first recognizable design in ship's cabinetry, about which more will be said later.

IN-BAKO: a late Edo addition enabling the merchant to keep the shop seals of less than official importance in one box so that any residue ink could be blotted by replaceable paper. *In-bako* are rarely lockable and are usually of paulownia wood. As well as pieces with only a hinged cover, there are some of slightly larger size with a single drawer opening at the face for writing brushes, paper, etc. These larger boxes appear to be a Meiji development, combining in part the *in-bako* and *kakesuzuri* function, both types having a *mochiokuri*-style handle in the cover center for carrying.

MASUTSUKI ZENI-BAKO: money box with the coin slot shaped like a traditional Japanese volume measure, called a *masu*. For a larger shop where the master may not have wished to become involved in small purchases, the *zeni-bako* was convenient for use by the sales employees. The *masu*-shaped coin slot is now used extensively on auto expressways and at self-service toll stations in many countries, but curiously not yet in Japan. *Zeni-bako,* with and without the *masu,* were used in temples, shrines, public baths, and shops. They were, with few exceptions, constructed of very thick chestnut or zelkova. Access is by removal of the slotted half-lid cover after the hasp on the face edge has either been unlocked or had its padlock unbolted.

CHŌ-DANSU: usually a single-section tansu with numerous sliding doors and drawers for keeping most anything related to shop administration, including tea service paraphernalia for serving the customer in some examples. It was not uncommon for the lower quadrant sliding door area to conceal a small secret compartment structured into the molding. In the Edo period, ledger account books were not yet in use. Notes of obligation were written on long papers bound together as books, called *daifuku-chō*. The craftsman who made these up for sale would use bold characters on the front cover: 大福帳. Filled books were kept in the *chō-dansu,* while one in daily use might be either laid on the shop desk or hung from the *chōba-gōshi* screen.

To complete our picture, at least one abacus and often several in varying lengths were essential. In that the principle of an abacus is based upon a decimal progression of tens raised by one power for each new vertical line of beads counting from right to left, calculation using multiplication could require a unit of considerable size for a successful business. Abacuses of over 60 cm in length are not uncommon.

With increasing affluence, merchants naturally wished to enjoy more conveniences in life. They eagerly sought services, entertainment, and material objects but were progressively frustrated by the Edo government. An appropriate example applicable to an interest in the development of tansu may be found in a series of reforms, in fact sumptuary laws, implemented under the shogun's regent Matsudaira Sadanobu, in 1789, and collectively known as the Kansei Reform. At the time Sadanobu attained his position, the government treasury was sorely depleted. The rural population, still dependent upon a rice-harvest barter economy, was starving after year upon year of harvest failure; the citizens of Edo and Osaka were rioting against price increases of rice to six and seven times the normal level. Only the merchants seemed to prosper. The pleasure quarters of Edo were thriving and tansu craftsmen were in demand by the merchants not only for storage and administrative cabinetry, but also for personal chests in which to keep their possessions. The production of chests in the category of *ishō-dansu,* or clothing chests, had been expanding rapidly into an assortment of styles and configurations ever since the Hōreki era (1751–63).

The regent's intentions were not rooted in a desire to persecute merchants but motivated by what he perceived as a need to instill a sense of social austerity in order to reverse the indebtedness of the government and the supporting samurai class. His solution, in part, was to lower the overt profile of the merchant class through legislation.

The key point in the Kansei Reform applicable to our interest concerns a strict control of clothing-chest design produced by tansu makers. Sadanobu chose to limit tansu makers to a style which had begun to be popular in the mid-eighteenth century: Tokyo-style, double-door, chest-on-chest of paulownia wood. This limitation pressed urban tansu makers into a lower level of creativity persisting into the nineteenth century. In addition to regulation of clothing chest design, the Kansei Reform imposed numerous other controls applicable to the merchant class:

1 Barbers and hairdressers were prohibited from practicing their profession.

2 House repairs were forbidden unless a residence was in a state of collapse.

3 Anyone who wore garments unsuitable to his or her position was punished according to law.

4 Betting or gambling in any form was now illegal.

5 Non-samurai women were prohibited from embroidering garments.

6 The size of children's dolls was restricted to not more than 20 cm.

7 Separate accommodations for men and women at public baths became strictly controlled.

These restrictions, especially the first, fourth, and the seventh, impinged upon joys of the common people. Most certainly the position of Sadanobu was not enhanced by suppression of this sort. However the will of the shogunate was all-powerful; not to comply with such edicts invited harsh punishment. By the end of the Edo period, there was the appearance, if not the reality, of economic chaos in the traditional class hierarchy. Those of privilege were of little means and those of means were denied privilege. While there was an awkwardly balanced prosperity, there was also a substantial latent demand for self-expression through materialism.

The restoration of imperial authority in 1868 ended a system of enforced adherence to what had become an imposed class structure. The primary concern of the new Meiji government was to bring Japan into the modern industrial world. To this end, emphasis was placed upon capital goods, primary infrastructure, a modern military, and national education. The craftsman class was essentially left untouched by this modernization except that the craftsmen could now anticipate a wider range of customers.

A traditional system of apprenticeship had become irrefutably entrenched during the Edo period, and the necessary philosophy to maintain it voluntarily. With its ethic of mastery through practice and refinement without innovation, it enabled the craftsmen of Japan to enter the Meiji era with a discipline, training, and dedication associated only with artisans in other cultures. Left alone to prosper in a new materialism, the temptation to affluence through a rationalization of techniques in favor of a broad commercial base did not touch the craftsmen until the early twentieth century. With the Meiji restoration, the occupational specialization of the tansu maker eventually became discernible from those of the boxmaker and the joiner.

It is rather difficult to generalize about tansu types and styles in the Meiji era because of disintegration of the rigid class structure and the development of distinctive regional characteristics. In order to enjoy the exciting diversity of designs that flowered especially at centers of production on the main island of Honshu, tansu as storage cabinetry for the people should be appreciated by locality. Chapter three examines the Meiji tansu region by region.

1. *Lacquered zelkova-burl cabinet of the Nara period. Shōsō-in.*

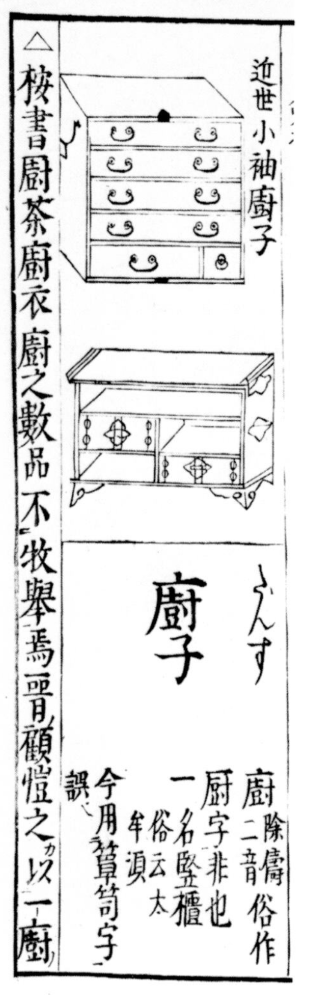

近世小袖廚子
廚子
ずんす
廚 除儔 俗作
厨字非也
一名竪櫃
俗云太牟須
今用簞笥字
誤
按書廚茶廚衣廚之數品不牧舉焉晋顧愷之以一廚

2. Tate-bitsu, *ancestor of the tansu. From* Wakan Sansai Zu-e *by Terajima Ryōan, 1715.*

3. *Free-standing shelves of the Nara period. Shōsō-in.*

4. *Chinese-style bed of the Nara period. Shōsō-in.*

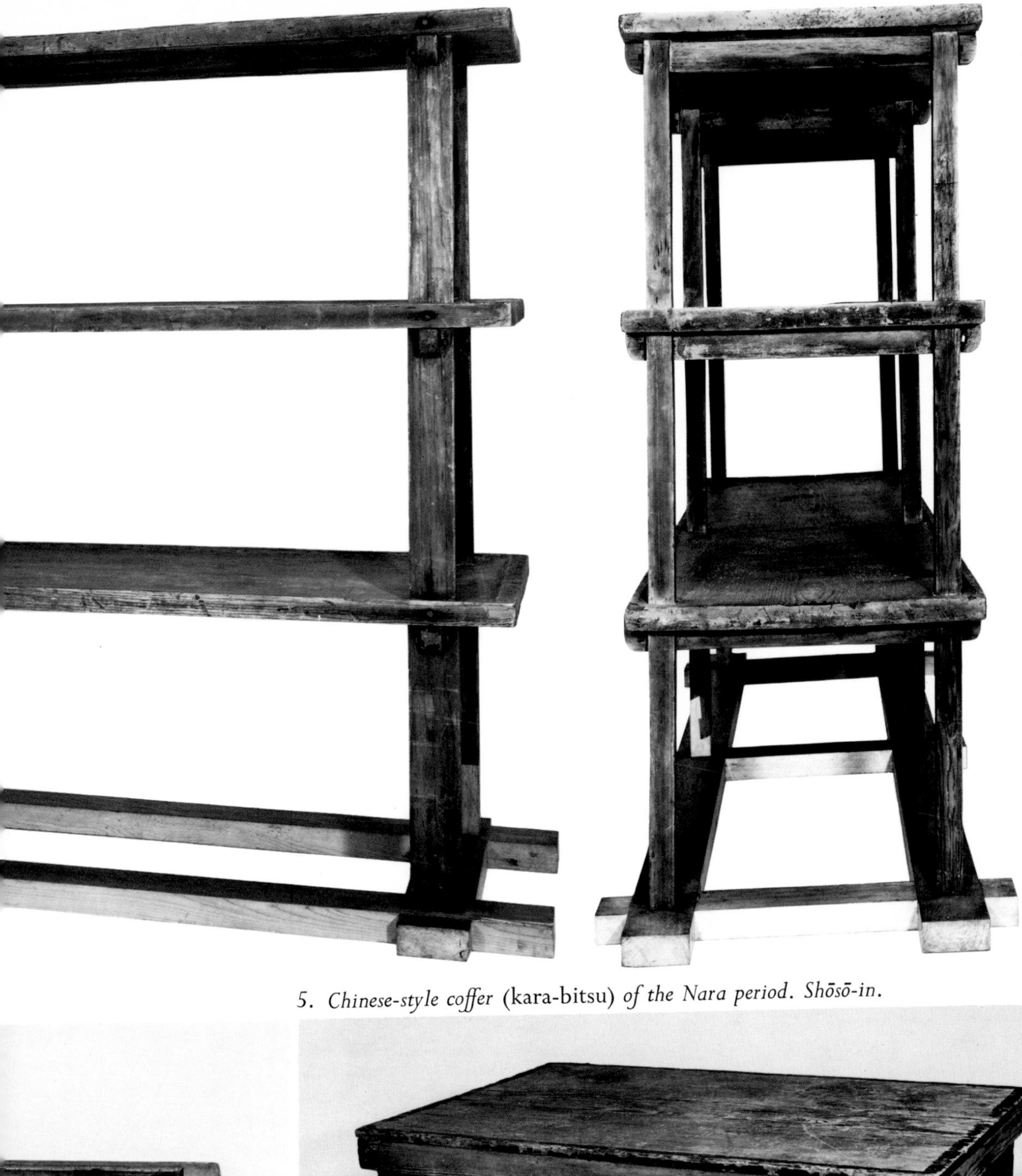

5. *Chinese-style coffer* (kara-bitsu) *of the Nara period. Shōsō-in.*

6. *Drawing of the* shinden *style of architecture originating in the Heian period.*

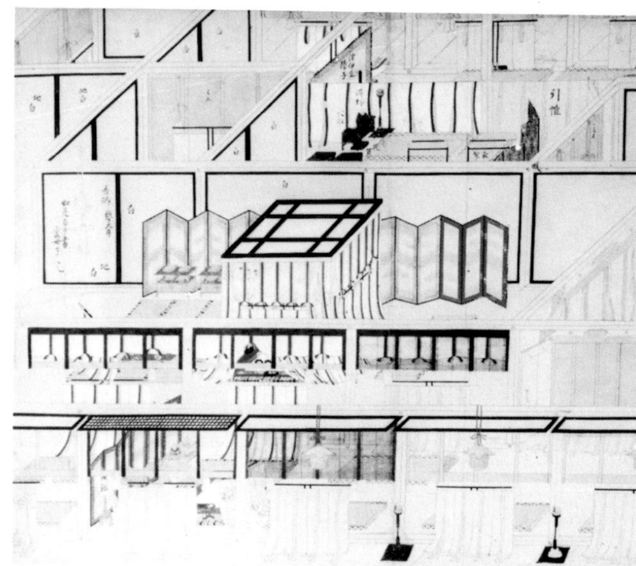

7. Shinden-*style* interior. *From an Edo-period copy of* Ruiju Zōyōshō.

8. *Classic* shoin-*style interior with recessed shelving, a tokonoma, and a reading alcove in the Kanda family teahouse of Tonami, Toyama Prefecture.*

9. Nikai-dana, *a two-level framed shelf, made for the Kyoto Imperial Palace. Heian-period style. H. 79* x *w. 76* x *d. 40 cm. Tokyo National Museum.*

10. Nikai-zushi, *a partially enclosed cabinet, made for the Kyoto Imperial Palace. Heian-period style. H. 61* x *w. 87.5* x *d. 42 cm. Tokyo National Museum.*

11. *Japanese-style coffer* (wa-bitsu) *of the Nara period. Shōsō-in.*

12. *Coffer carried in a rope sling. From* Kokawa-dera Engi Emaki. *Twelfth century. Collection of Kokawa-dera.*

13. *Two-man saw* (oga). *From* Sanjūniban Shokunin Uta-awase Emaki, *late fifteenth century.*

14. *Trunk* (nagamochi) *carried by samurai. Illustration by Kitao Masanobu from* Untsuku Tarozaemon banashi, *1781.*

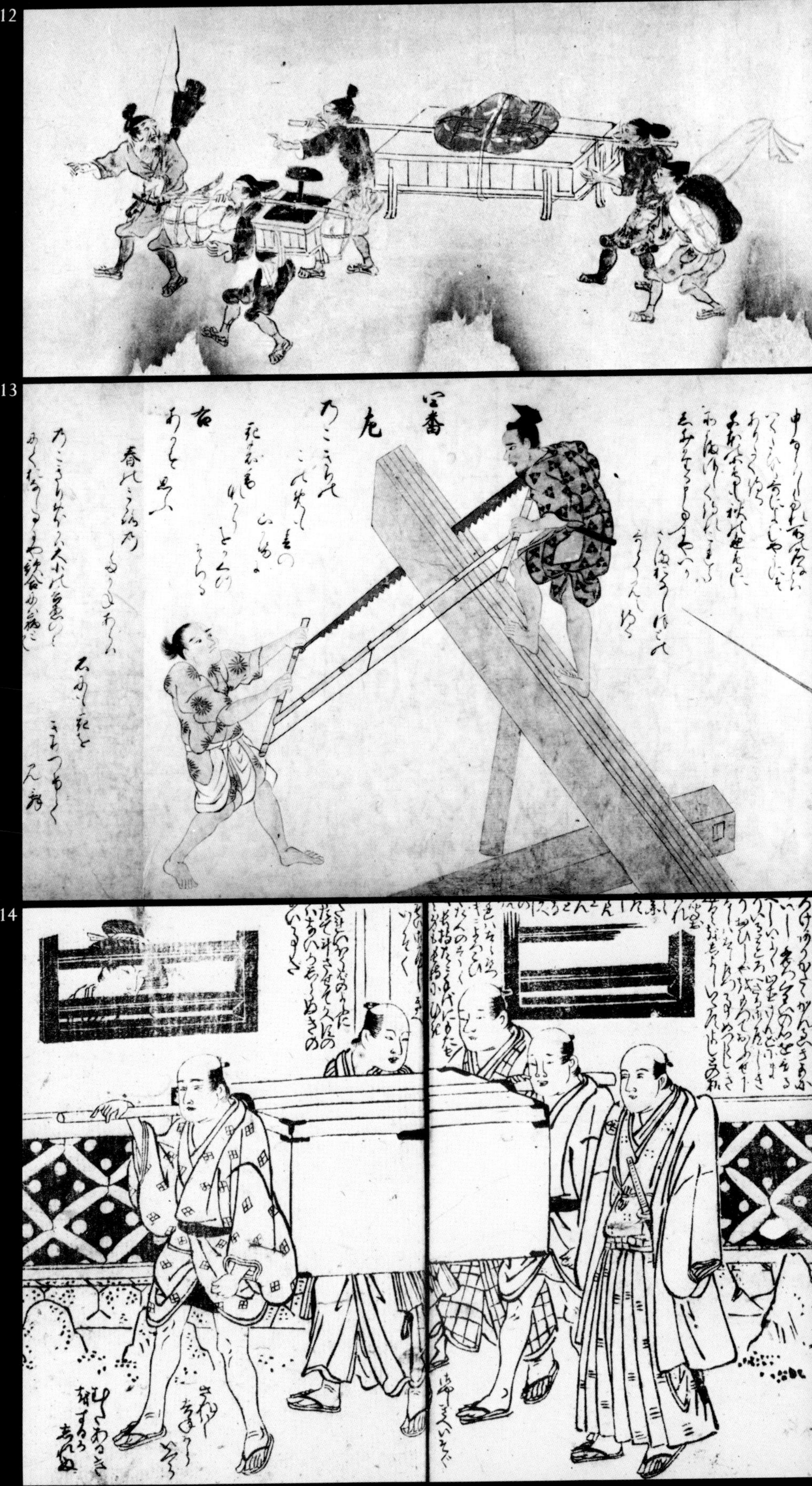
12
13
14

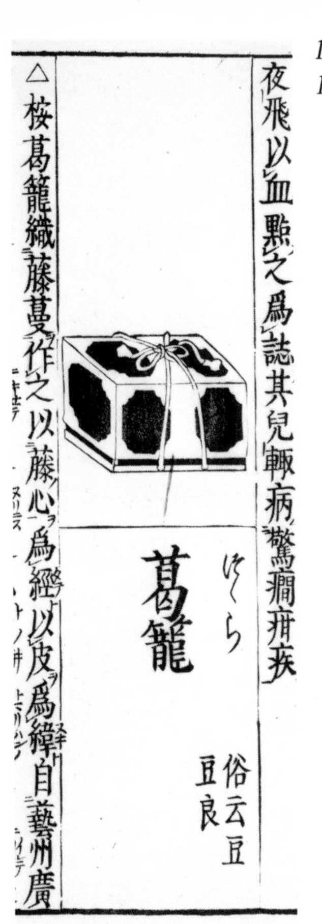

15. *Woven box* (tsuzura) *from* Wakan Sansai Zu-e *by Terajima Ryōan, 1715.*

16. *Fan shop with merchandise drawers. Illustration from* Kōshoku Ichidai Otoko *(The Life of an Amorous Man) by Ihara Saikaku, 1683.*

17. *"Scissors box"* (hasami-bako). *From* Wakan Sansai Zu-e *by Terajima Ryōan, 1715.* ▶

18. *"Scissors box"* (hasami-bako) *carried by samurai. From* Nihon Fūzoku Zu-e, *vol. 5.*

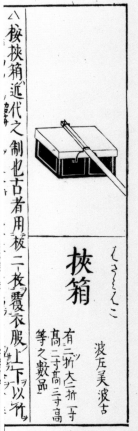

19 20

21 22

19. The zushi-dana *from a set of wedding cabinetry bearing the Tokugawa crest. H. 76* x *w. 152* x *d. 40 cm. Edo period. Okayama Museum.*

20. The kuro-dana *from a set of wedding cabinetry. H. 68 x w. 78 x d. 38 cm. Edo period. Okayama Museum.*

21. The sho-dana *from a set of wedding cabinetry. H. 100 x w. 96 x d. 44 cm. Edo period. Okayama Museum.*

22. Tea-ceremony taṇa *in a traditional winter style.*

23. *Book chest* (sho-dansu). *Drop-f doors with open shelves behind. De signed to be carried on the back Zelkova and cryptomeria. H. 61* x *w 43* x *d. 30 cm. Edo period. Heineke Collection.*

24. *Wheeled trunk* (nagamochi kuruma) *of chestnut. H. 85* x *w. 124* x *d. 62 cm. Edo period. Heineken Collection.*

25. *Edo townspeople escaping from the Meireki fire with their possessions in wheeled trunks,* Musashi Abumi, *1661.*

26. Sword chest of paulownia. H. 44 x w. 111 x d. 32 cm. Late Edo period. Tokyo Furniture Museum.

27. Sword chest of paulownia with a small-door compartment and sao-tōshi *handles. Oil and lacquer wiped finish. H. 50 x w. 116 x d. 42 cm. Edo period. Heineken Collection.*

28. Sword chest of cryptomeria and zelkova. H. 37 x w. 106 x d. 34 cm. Edo period. Tonami Wa-dansu Kenkyūkai.

9. Bamboo tea-ceremony chest with hinged double doors and drop-fit doors. Viped lacquer finish. H. 73 x w. 51 x d. 30 cm. Edo period. Collection of Kiyoko Heineken.

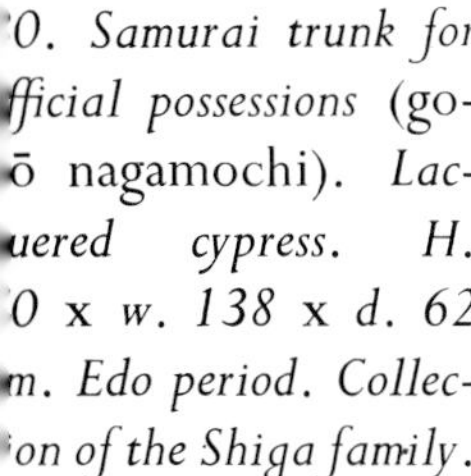

0. Samurai trunk for fficial possessions (go-ō nagamochi). *Lacuered cypress. H. 0 x w. 138 x d. 62 m. Edo period. Collecon of the Shiga family.*

31. Chest for short-sleeved kimono (koso-de) *with locking bar, brass hardware, and* tame-nuri *lacquer. H. 96 x w. 98 x d. 42 cm. Edo period. Tokyo Furniture Museum.*

32. *Small personal chest for a woman (te-*moto-dansu). *Zelkova with* kijiro *finish and lacquered copper hardware. Five opaque-lacquered drawers behind the double doors. H. 96 x w. 98 x d. 42 cm. Edo period. Tokyo Furniture Museum.*

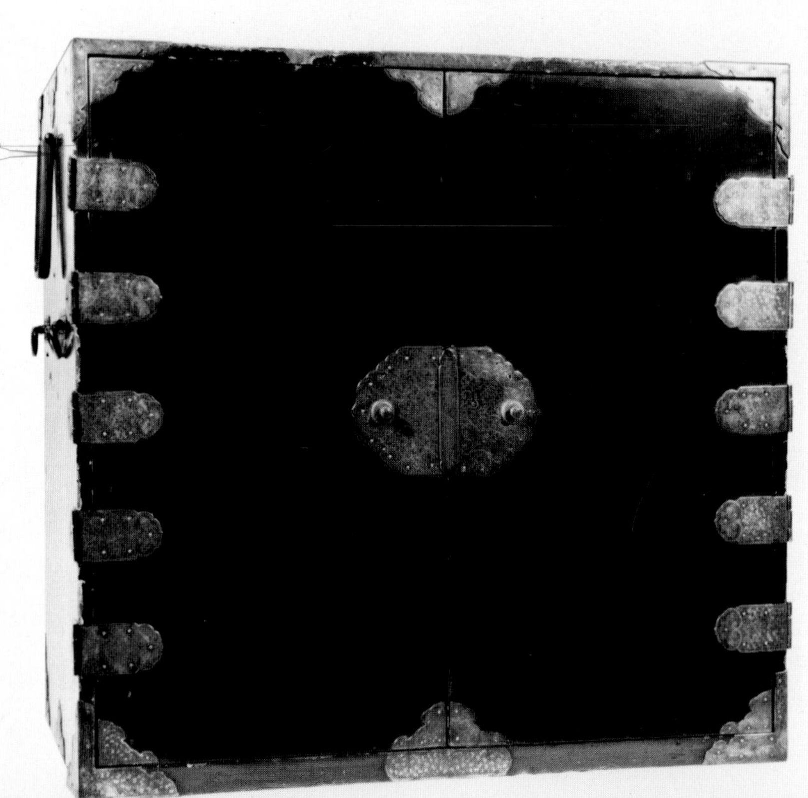

33. *Double-door chest-on-chest* (ryōbiraki kasane-dansu). *Illustration by Torii Kiyonaga from* Sono Kazukazu Sake no Kuse, *1779.*

34–35. *Views of large, double-door clothing chest. Opaque* tame-nuri *lacquer over cypress with brass hardware. Inner drawers are close-grained paulownia. H. 107 x w.110 x d.73 cm. Edo period. Tokyo Furniture Museum.*

36. *Wheeled farmer's trunk* (nōmin nagamochi kuruma) *of zelkova with cryptomeria drawer-interior wood. H. 78* x *w. 95* x *d. 44 cm. Mid-Edo period. Collection of Mrs. P. A. Aron.*

37. Farmer's chest for official documents (nōmin goyō). *The Maeda family crest suggests that this piece was used by a village head who acted on behalf of the daimyo. Cryptomeria. H. 58* x *w. 80* x *d. 55.5 cm. Edo period. Collection of Mr. John Gruber.*

38. Farmer's kitchen chest (nōmin mizuya). *Zelkova frame with cryptomeria panels. H. 176* x *w. 121* x *d. 44 cm. Late Edo period. Tokyo Furniture Museum.*

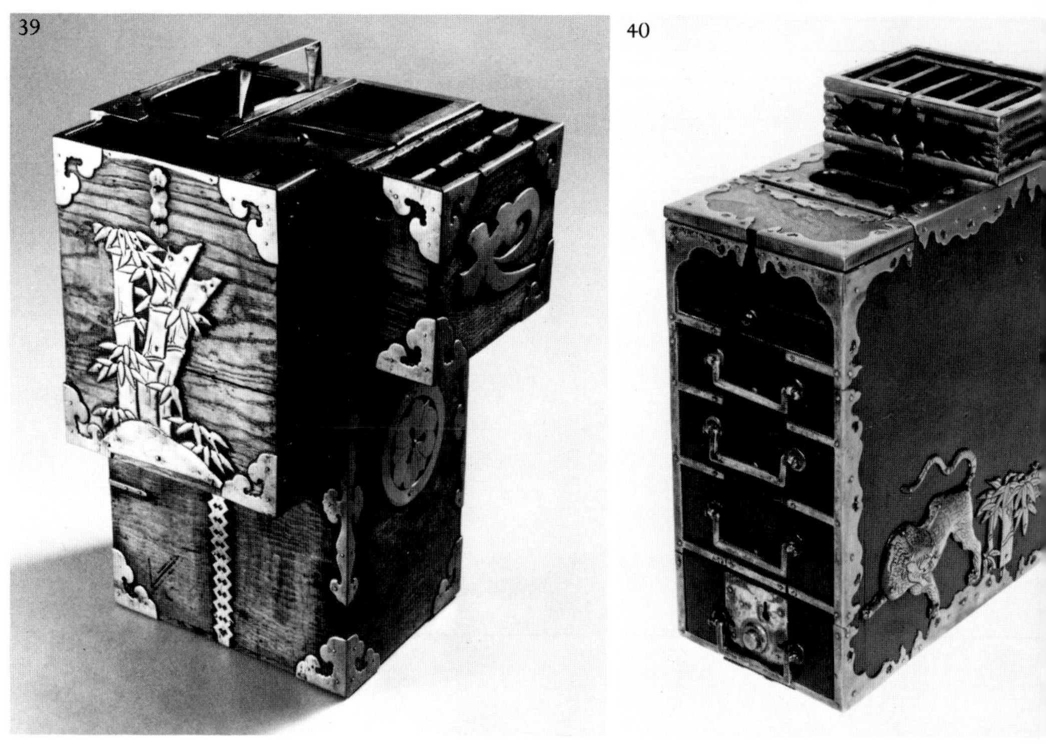

44. *Armorer. Illustration by Katsushika Hokusai from* Ehon Azuma Asobi, *1799.*

45. *Ironsmith. From* Shokunin Zukushi-e *by Kan Yoshinobu. Momoyama period. Collection of Kita-in*

9. *Itinerant barber's box* (bindarai) *in Osaka style. Zelkova with copper hardware. H. 42* x *w. 22* x *d. 25* *n. Edo period. Mombushō Shiryōkan.*

0. *Itinerant barber's box* (bindarai) *in Tokyo style. Lacquered, with copper hardware. H. 35* x *w. 15* x *d. 27* *n. Edo period. Tokyo Furniture Museum.*

41. *Wig peddler's box* (katsura gyōshō-bako). *Cryptomeria with copper hardware; oil and lacquer wiped finish. H. 51* x *w. 30* x *d. 15 cm. Edo period. Heineken Collection.*

42. *Pipe peddler's box* (rauya gyōshō-bako). *Paulownia with iron hardware. H. 88* x *w. 27* x *d. 36.5 cm. Edo period. Heineken Collection.*

43. *Medicine peddler's box* (kusuri gyōshō-bako) *of* jōsai *type. Zelkova; vertical locking bar. H. 75* x *w. 51* x *d. 32 cm. Edo period. Tokyo Furniture Museum.*

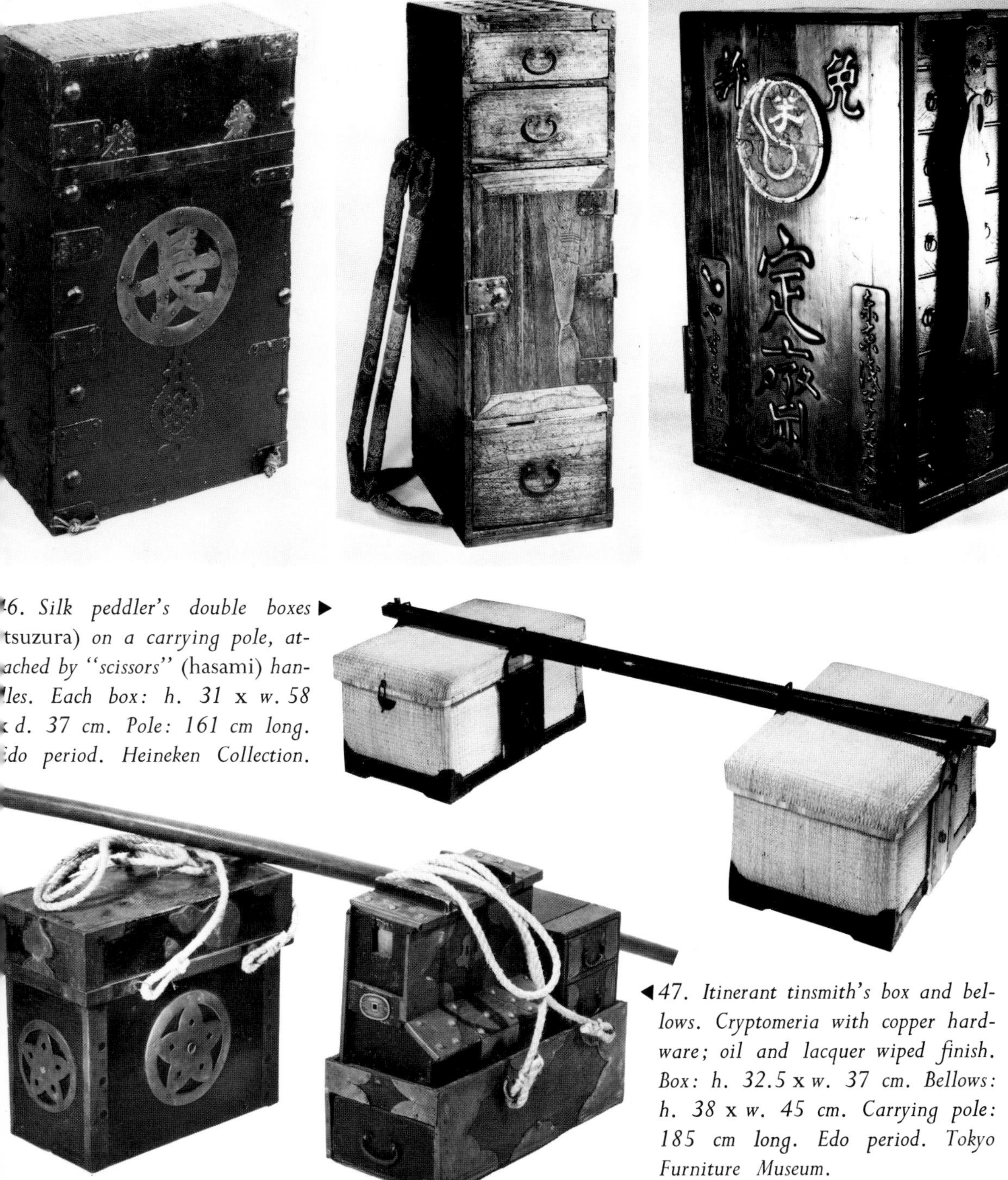

41 42 43

6. *Silk peddler's double boxes* ▶ (tsuzura) *on a carrying pole, attached by "scissors"* (hasami) *handles. Each box: h. 31* x *w. 58* x *d. 37 cm. Pole: 161 cm long. Edo period. Heineken Collection.*

◀47. *Itinerant tinsmith's box and bellows. Cryptomeria with copper hardware; oil and lacquer wiped finish. Box: h. 32.5* x *w. 37 cm. Bellows: h. 38* x *w. 45 cm. Carrying pole: 185 cm long. Edo period. Tokyo Furniture Museum.*

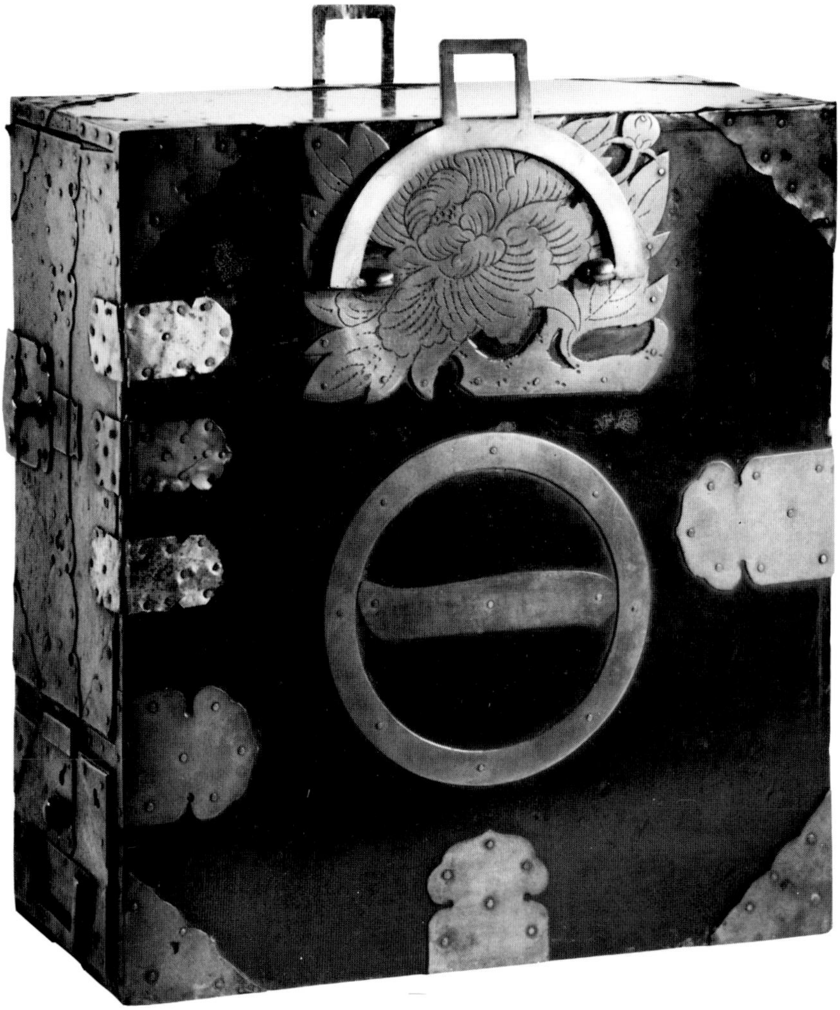

48. Medicine peddler's bo of magotarōmushi *type Cryptomeria with coppe hardware. "Scissors"* (ha sami) *handles for carryin pole. H. 36.5* x *w. 34 d. 16 cm. Edo period. Mom bushō Shiryōkan.*

49. Medicine peddler. From Nihon Fū-zoku Zu-e, *vol. 7, 1730.*

50. *Barber at work. From* Toba-e Akubi-dome, *1793.*

51. *Tobacco salesman. Illustration by Utagawa Kunisada from* Irohabiki-dera Irisetsuyō, *1828.*

52. *Pipe peddler and hardware peddler. Illustration by Kitagawa Morisada from* Morisada Mankō.

53. *Itinerant tinsmith. Illustration by Kitagawa Morisada from* Morisada Mankō.

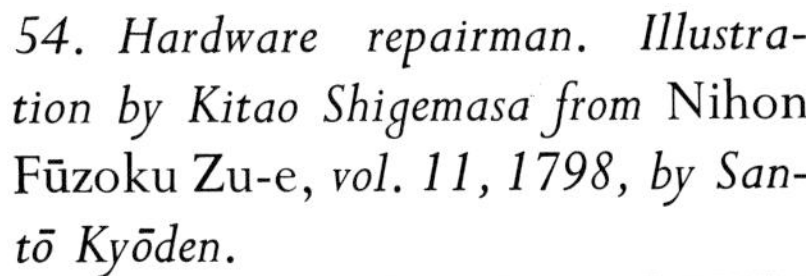

54. *Hardware repairman. Illustration by Kitao Shigemasa from* Nihon Fūzoku Zu-e, *vol. 11, 1798, by Santō Kyōden.*

55. *Seaweed shop in Asakusa showing merchandise drawers* (shōhin hikidashi). *Illustration by Katsushika Hokusai from* Ehon Azuma Asobi, *1799.*

56. *Shelves with sliding doors* (to-dana) *and a tansu inside. Illustration by Torii Kiyonaga from* Oyaji Nunoko o Tombi ga Saratta, *1780.*

57. *Merchant account box and safe.* (chō-bako). *H. 44* x *w. 35* x *d. 46 cm. Similar to the* chō-bako *and* kakesuzuri *used on ships. Zelkova. Late Edo period.*

58–59. The chōba, *a tatami-covered elevated area in a shop where business was conducted. a) Screen* (chōba-gōshi), *h. 45 x w. 206 cm. b) Desk* (chōba-zukue), *h. 26 x w. 105 x d. 33 cm. c) Writing box* (kakesuzuri), *h. 30 x w. 24 x d. 34 cm. d) Seal box* (in-bako), *h. 15 x w. 12 x d. 20 cm. e) Money box* (masutsuki zeni-bako), *h. 42 x w. 30 x d. 51 cm. f) Ledger chest* (chō-dansu), *h. 97 x w. 99 x d. 45 cm.*

60. Medicine chest (kusuri-dansu) *for shop use, hinged for use as a peddler's box. Paulownia. Closed size: h. 77 x w. 92 x d. 18 cm. Tokyo Furniture Museum.*

61. *Chest-on-chest with double doors* (ryōbiraki kasane-dansu) *carried on a pole. Illustration by Utagawa Toyokuni from* Katakiuchi-domori no Watakushi, *1807.*

62. *Chest-on-chest with double doors* (ryōbiraki kasane-dansu) *of paulownia. H. 103* x *w. 95* x *d. 42 cm. Edo period. Tokyo Furniture Museum.*

CHAPTER TWO

SEA CHESTS

From the Edo period into the Meiji era, there was one prominent category of mobile cabinetry that maintained absolute continuity in design. The pieces in this category are known as *funa-dansu,* literally ship chests, but known as sea chests in translation. These chests were used on merchant vessels plying the Sea of Japan and the Inland Sea between Osaka and Hokkaido. This route, known historically as the Kitamae, was active from March through November.

With political stability enforced by the Tokugawa shogunate, merchants were increasingly inclined to risk investment, especially in the supply of raw materials and food to the expanding city of Edo. In that it served the interests of the government to control the merchant guilds, free trade was encouraged and eventually supported by a law in 1623 ordering open trade between the provinces and forbidding the establishment of private groups to control business. This significant incentive was in part restrained by the poor state of the national land transportation system. With few exceptions, land routes were extremely difficult, and their use further complicated by checkpoints, permits, and obstreperous samurai. Enterprising merchants saw that water routes offered great potential. Although not entirely free from bureaucratic hindrances, river, canal, and lake transport of high-volume cargoes was a growing business in the early seventeenth century. An expanded interest in sea-route transportation soon followed. As early as 1619, cargo vessels were being sent from Osaka to Edo with oil, sakè, and cloth, and from Sendai on the north Pacific coast to Edo with taxation rice from government lands.

A continuing fear of foreign interference by proselytizing religions and international trade caused the shogunate in 1636 to prohibit the construction of ships having a keel, more than two masts, or a cargo capacity of more than 500 *koku* (89,760 liters or 2,550 U.S. bushels). Although the decree was intended to prevent Japanese from navigating in foreign waters and trading in foreign countries, it was also interpreted as a specific prohibition against the construction of fighting ships by individual daimyo. Because shipping merchants could not effectively trade using ships within the legal cargo capacity, they quietly built vessels capable of carrying as much as 1,100 *koku*. And perhaps because the government needed taxation rice in the capital from outlying regions, the 1636 decree was never strictly interpreted.

As the need for trade grew with the population of Edo and numerous catastrophies there, the shogunate was soon hard pressed to both expand and stabilize sea-route transportation. In 1670, the responsibility for reorganization was given to a dynamic merchant who had made a considerable fortune by cornering the lumber market after the Meireki fire of 1657. Kawamura Zuiken's task was considerable. Because ships were not permitted to have a keel, they were forced to run with the wind, never facing the open seas. Along the northeast Pacific coast, the problems of wind and ship were further complicated by purloining of the cargo by the crew. Kawamura overcame much of the problem through seeking the advice of the most experienced sailors in the area. By riding the outer currents past Edo and then doubling back along the coast, transit time was reduced and transshipments eliminated, even though the total distance of the voyage increased. Honesty was subsidized by large wage increases and enforced by allowing traders more power in their contractual agreements with shipping companies.

On the Japan Sea, the traditional route for rice from the northwest coast to Edo required as much as one year with an incredible loss factor through accidents and theft occurring during transshipments. Starting at Sakata, a town in northwest Honshu, ships brought cargo down the coast to the towns of Obama or Tsuruga, then the goods were taken by pack horse and oxen 300 km across the mountains to Lake Biwa, the length of the lake by boats, by pack animals again to the Ise Peninsula, and finally on to Edo by cargo ship. Even though the Maeda family, lords of the Kaga fief, had been relying upon a sea route for the transportation of their taxation rice for sale in Kyushu, the southernmost main island, and on the Pacific coast of Honshu for many years, the influence of powerful merchant cliques controlling various stages of the traditional route seems to have inhibited earlier progress to a more efficient course. Kawamura proposed that a single vessel could sail from Sakata with stops at specified ports along the entire Japan Sea coast, round Honshu at the port of Shimonoseki, follow the Inland Sea to Osaka, and even proceed on to Edo without transshipment, a total distance of about 800 km requiring three months in transit. In concert with his master plan, watchtowers were erected along the coasts to monitor dangers to the ships, and the profession of piloting was introduced to reduce the chance of mishap in treacherous waters.

The success of Kawamura Zuiken in reorganizing marine transportation was most evident in a subsequent leveling out of regional commodity prices throughout the country in the late seventeenth century. It was during this period that the sea chest originated.

The vessels used on the Kitamae route were properly called Kitamae ships but popularly known by their theoretical capacity in rice cargo, one thousand *koku*—the equivalent of 150 tons. Even though many of the ships used on the Japan Sea route were smaller than their implied capacity, the name "thousand-*koku* ship" was in time applied to all ships in the trade.

Whereas shipping and trading progressed as separate occupations for the Osaka-Edo sea route, with the shipowner functioning as a professional transporter, the Kitamae route was quite different in nature. The owner as captain was very common, but there were also many examples of hired captains who were permitted to trade with their own merchandise as well as representing the cargo of the shipowner.

The course of trade most representative of a typical merchant ship on this route followed a profitable sequence. Purchase of daily necessity items such as sakè, noodles, oil, cotton, tobacco, and clothing were negotiated in March so the vessel could sail from Osaka by mid-April. Along the Inland Sea, salt, paper, sugar, and bamboo came aboard; iron from Tottori on the Japan Sea coast; straw products from the towns of Obama, Tsuruga, and Ogi; rice and sakè from Sakata in the Dewa fief. By mid-July, the ships were at their destinations: the towns of Matsumae, Hakodate, or Esashi on Hokkaido, where there was a market for their cargo. The salt was immediately used for herrings, which were pickled for food or processed for fertilizer. Daily necessities brought from Osaka were in high demand by the townspeople, as was the used clothing for barter with the Ainu aborigines. Most ships tried to be under sail on their return voyage by mid-August with a cargo of sea products. Taxation rice from government storehouses established by Kawamura Zuiken was taken on at Sakata and Niigata. Generally, captains ran for the protection of Inland Sea shelters as soon as possible in order to avoid the worst days of the typhoon season in September. Herring processed into fertilizer was very salable among the Inland Sea islands, where a considerable portion of the cargo from Hokkaido was sold.

Not only were the men on the Kitamae route performing a service to the shogunate as transporters of harvest surplus to areas in need, but they were able as well to amass considerable wealth without surrendering their independence. Status as "privileged merchants" was not unknown in the Edo period among townsmen serving the samurai, but for shipowners and captains reflecting a broad rural background, their special position was exceptional.

Although various forms of functional cabinetry had most probably been in shipboard use for a considerable time, evidence indicates the Kyōhō era (1716–35) as the beginning of specific designs in use on the Kitamae route.

The term sea chest represents a cabinetry grouping and was first used as such by the twentieth century scholar Sōetsu Yanagi. However, distinct names for three popular chest styles built primarily at Ogi on Sado Island, Sakata at the Mogami River, and Mikuni in the Echizen area appear to have been in colloquial use in the eighteenth century.

There is little dispute that sea chests represent the highest achievement of joinery and hardware in consort during the Edo period and through the Meiji era. The reasons for this excellence are rooted in functional demands that forced the sea-chest maker to surpass in technique most all tansu constructed for land use.

Most of the ships in the Kitamae-route Japan Sea trade were smaller than the "thousand-*koku*" size, in part because of the fear of government regulation but more certainly because of the cost of construction. Being flat-bottomed, without a keel, and rarely over twenty-seven meters in length, the ships were not well designed for bad weather. The Japan Sea is an uncertain friend to those who sail, and therefore the ships, the men, and their accoutrements had to be rigorous. In the chests, density and strength were essential. For this reason, zelkova was always the primary wood for the face, top, sides, bottom, and structural members. All external joints were covered and reinforced by iron plating of 1.2 up to 3 mm in thickness.

Among the crew of up to eleven men, only the captain and shipowner possessed chests. Because these two men, or often one in a combined role, functioned as commercial agents buying and selling for their own account, appearance of status was important. The sea chests, ceremoniously unloaded and carried to a place of business negotiation, were then carefully positioned to most effectively impress a local merchant.

There is a third functional consideration that is still hypothetical. In the early and middle development periods, there are indications that chest builders intended their pieces to be watertight and easily identifiable in case of storm, shipwreck, or pirates. In support of this assumption are the following points:

1 Chests were occasionally lined with paulownia wood at the lips of the drawers and in most examples use this highly flexible wood for all inner compartments within compartments. The use of *sammai-gumi* (a three-part-tenon, open-mortise box joint) for the drawer corner joinery permits paulownia considerable flexibility given the wood's unique ability to swell in humidity. If a craftsman intended his creation to be secure against the dangers of the sea, the pegged tenon would be a better choice for drawers than the simple pegged and glued lap joint most often found in land-use tansu cabinetry. Indeed, there is a fable that suggests that the well-designed chest could float just under the surface of the water beyond the sight of an attacking pirate, yet still attached to the ship by a rope of silk. In fact, because most pirates were Japanese, they rarely bothered the Kitamae-route ships, obliged by design to hug the coast.

2 It was most usual for sea chests to bear either a family crest or a merchant's trademark, usually in an abstract form or a language character. Some sea chests bore both on the front face, often of brass for high visibility. For land-use chests prior to the Meiji era, concern for conspicuous identity was common only on official cabinetry or ceremonial *nagamochi,* a kind of trunk.

3 For coastal vessels sailing to the inner side of the deep water currents of the Japan Sea, the tide would draw in a floating object and wash it to the shore.

4 It is not unusual to find false hinges for doors that actually slide and lift out instead of swing, or drop-fit doors with false keyholes and obscure latches intended to hinder curiosity.

5 Whether or not sea-chest craftsmen truly intended their chests to float, there can be no doubt that they had the technique to accomplish such an exacting task.

The oldest of the three representative sea-chest designs is the *kakesuzuri*. Originally quite small and intended for land use, the *kakesuzuri* chest had a single swinging door on half-face hinges, multiple drawers, and one carrying handle on the top center in the *warabite* style. Quite probably, land-use pieces such as the seventeenth-century-style chest in the Gruber Collection were introduced to shipboard function for all-purpose personal use. The evolving ship's *kakesuzuri* had an average size of h. 44 x w. 39 x d. 48 cm and became structurally more substantial in time through the use of thicker wood and additional hardware. The development of the very early, door-center, vertical iron brace into a detailed frame for a crest and trademark took approximately 150 years. The inside configuration varied but usually included two full-width and two or three half-width drawers of paulownia wood. Land-use pieces continued to be made well into the twentieth century as small writing boxes with a side-hinged top lid instead of the full-face door. Even with the size reduced to an average h. 21 x w. 18 x d. 29 cm, the name *kakesuzuri* persisted, modified in some regions to *suzuri-bako*.

The *hangai*, a second style of sea chest, evolved from a storage container with a detached lid. Even though the *hangai* is the largest in size of the three most representative types of sea chest, it is considerably smaller than the land-bound *hitsu* (coffer) from which it derived. Used exclusively for clothing storage, the name means literally half-*hitsu*, but it was in most early instances a chest-on-chest with each of the two units having a full-face removable door panel of zelkova wood. By using the ancient technique of *hashikui*, the Japanese mitered clamp joint, observed initially in cabinets at the Shōsō-in in Nara, the doors remained stable under atmospheric change. In the usual inner configuration, the top unit had two drawers of equal size and the lower unit, one large drawer entirely of thick paulownia wood. The standard size for each unit

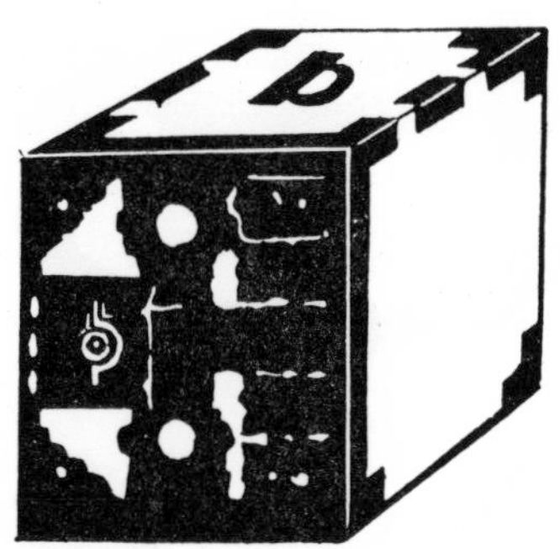

The three most representative kinds of sea chest: *kakesuzuri*, *hangai*, and *chō-bako*.

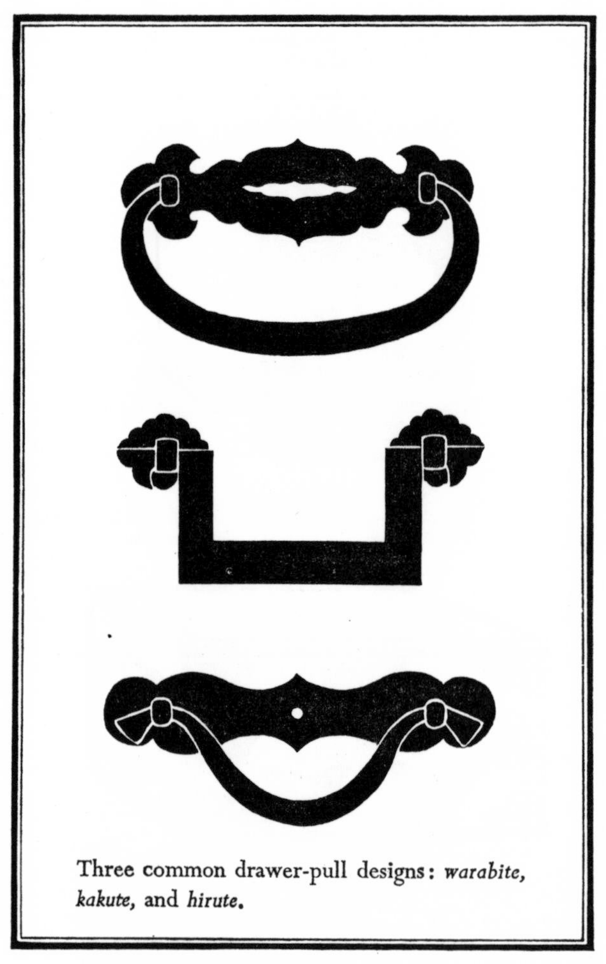

Three common drawer-pull designs: *warabite, kakute,* and *hirute.*

was h. 45 x w. 76 x d. 42 cm. However, there was considerable variation in height and width with a tendency to size reduction in the Meiji era. Chest-on-chest *hangai* frequently have a lockable latch at each of the two shortest sides, not unlike a contemporary suitcase hasp, to secure the stacked units to each other. These locks are unique to *hangai,* but are not a reliable indicator as to whether the unit was originally single or a stacking pair. Door-panel hardware on *hangai* is not only impressive but also entirely functional. While the door is secured by only one lock at top center, the false lock latches at mid-level and the two iron face braces tenoned into the case frame hold the panel rigid. Use of a family crest and a trademark at the center of the

63. Kakesuzuri *sea chest. Zelkova with iron openwork in intertwined Japanese and Chinese ivy pattern. Brass family crest. Five paulownia inner drawers and a drop-fit door with removable money box and secret compartment for seals. H. 44.5 x w. 39 x d. 47.5 cm. Late Edo period. Heineken Collection.*

64. Kakesuzuri *sea chest. Ze-kova with iron sash hardware o bias. Door face plating in gour and-ivy pattern. H. 49 x w 45 x d. 52 cm. Edo perio Tonami Wa-dansu Kenkyūkai.*

65. Kakesuzuri *sea chest. Zelkova with iron crest and brass trademark. H. 44.5 x w. 40 x d. 50 cm. Edo period. Tonami Wa-dansu Kenkyūkai.*

66. Hangai *chest-on-chest for a captain's or shipowner's clothing. Zelkova. Upper chest: h. 41 x w. 83 x d. 45 cm. Lower chest: h. 36 x w. 83 x d. 45 cm. Late Edo period; probably from Ogi. Tonami Wa-dansu Kenkyūkai.*

67. *Outstanding example of iron sash hardware on doors of chest-on-chest.*

72. Chō-bako *sea chest of zelkova. H. 48 x w. 63 x d. 40.5 cm. Late Edo or early Meiji; Ogi. Collection of Mr. John Gruber.*

73. Chō-bako *sea chest with built-in desk. Zelkova case, paulownia drawer interiors. H. 44 x w. 55 x d. 39 cm. Meiji era. Collection of Mr. John Gruber.*

74. Chō-bako *sea chest. Zelkova-burl front backed by close-grained paulownia. Other faces are open-grain zelkova.* Kijiro *finish. H. 57 x w. 58.5 x d. 45 cm. Meiji era. Tonami Wa-dansu Kenkyūkai.*

75. Ship's safe. Probably used on the Kitamae route. Zelkova with iron plating and sash hardware. Lock plate on double doors pictures the god Hotei. H. 52 x w. 64.5 x d. 46.5 cm. Edo period; Echigo area. Tonami Wa-dansu Kenkyūkai.

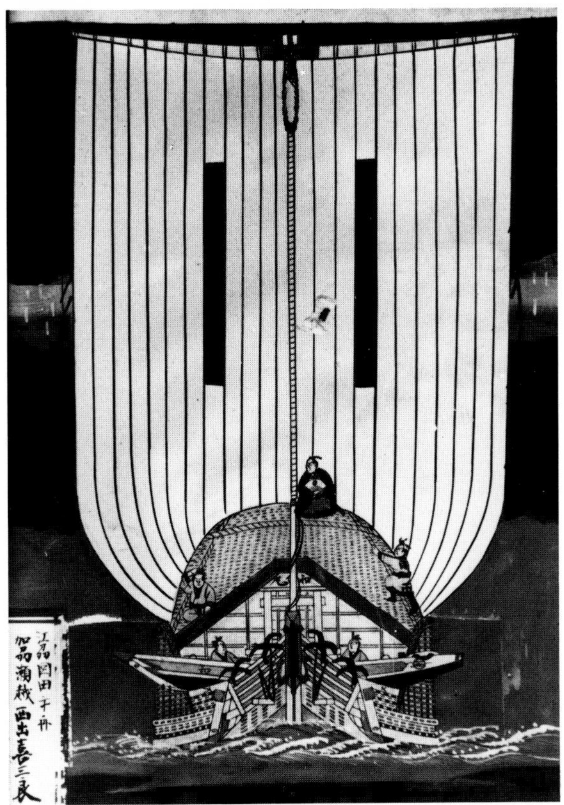

76. *Ship's* ema, *donated to the Hakusan Shrine, Segoe, Kaga. Early Meiji era.*

77. *Votive painting* (ema) *of a "thousand-*koku *ship," made for a shipowner and presented to a Shinto shrine for good fortune. Early Meiji era.*

78. Kakesuzuri *chest, transitional from land to shipboard use. Zelkova with paulownia drawers. H. 40 x w. 32 x d. 42 cm. Edo period. Collection of Mr. John Gruber.*

80. *Slat construction on bottom of chest for stability, indicating shipboard* ▶ *use. Inscription reads: "1840, ordered in June from Mambako Shiirejo, in Sado, Namo-gun, Ogi, [supplied or delivered by] Wataya Tōichiryō."*

79. Kakesuzuri *sea chest.* See *Figure 64.*

81. *Three intricately crafted iron keys.*

82. *Paulownia drawers and* kendon-buta *doors. Inside face of zelkova body partially backed with paulownia for protection against moisture.*

83. *Zelkova money box with* kijiro *finish, matching tansu body, behind* kendon-buta *door. Two staples on latch prevent hasp from being pried open.*

84. Hangai *sea chest. Zelkova body with single paulownia drawer. H. 39 x w. 78.5 x d. 43 cm. Late Edo period. Collection of Mr. John Gruber.*

86. *Side-locking latch unique to* hangai *chest-on-chest.*▶

85. Hangai *chest-on-chest for captain's or shipowner's clothing.* See *Figure* 66.

87. *Three paulownia drawers. Zelkova faces backed with paulownia.*

88. Ship's hangai *chest-on-chest. Individually lockable paulownia drawers with floating dust covers.* Shunkei *finish over* bengara *stain. Crane-and-tortoise lock motif. Each chest: h. 41 x w. 79 x d. 43 cm. Late Edo or early Meiji; inscribed with "Sado Island, Ogi." Tonami Wa-dansu Kenkyūkai.*

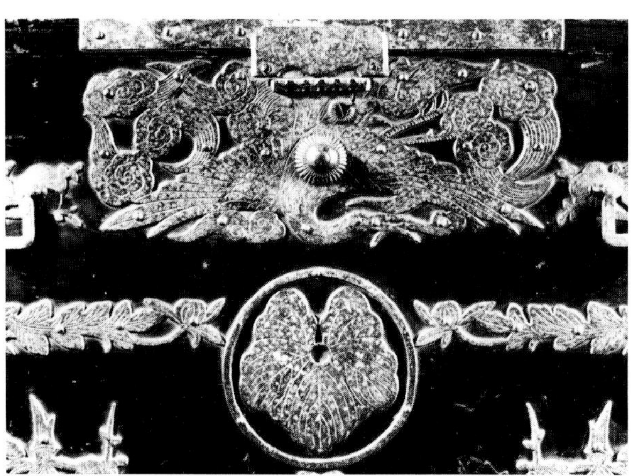

89. Iron family crest in shape of Japanese ivy.

90. Iron trademark.

91. Chō-bako *sea chest of zelkova. H. 48 x w. 63 x d. 40.5 cm. Late Edo or early Meiji; Ogi. Collection of Mr. John Gruber.*

◀ *92. Each compartment in lower level covered by* kendon-buta *door.*

93. Lower left compartment holds zelkova money box and paulownia case with kendon-buta *door, behind which is an inner case with sliding lid for documents. Lower center compartment has large, removable money box. Lower right compartment has small drawer with ring pull for inkstone, often lacquered black inside.*

94. Four half-lapped braces, on bottom, characteristic of the best chō-bako *serve as a frame for inscription identifying purchase at Ogi, Sado Island.*

95. Chō-bako *sea chest with built-in desk*. See *Figure*

96. *With double doors open and sliding door remove zelkova desk can be taken from its narrow housin*

97. *Three compartments with removable boxes under three drawers. Left and right boxes probably for papers. Center box, behind drop-fit door, for money.*

98. Chō-bako *sea chest. See Figure 74.*

99. With large drop-fit door removed, two inner drop-fit doors are exposed, behind each of which is a zelkova money box.

00. Since this tansu was very heavy hen full, hemp loops attached to arrying handles helped distribute the ad.

101. Chō-bako *sea chest. Zelkova with* shunkei *finish. H. 47.5 x w. 53 x d. 44 cm. Early nineteenth century; Ogi or Mikuni. Tonami Wa-dansu Kenkyūkai.*

102. With hinged door open and sliding door removed, five paulownia drawers are exposed. Atypically, the vertical jamb is covered with iron plating.

03. Chō-bako *sea chest. Zelkova with paulownia interior. Rare single compartmentalization. H. 35* x *w. 48* x *d. 36.5 cm. Early Meiji era; probably from Sakata. Collection of Mr. John Gruber.*

04. *Case of* chō-bako *sea chest. Zelkova with drop-fit door joined with mitered clamping. Crest of prominent* ▶ *ukui Prefecture family on door. Case: h. 48.5* x *w. 61* x *d. 44.5 cm. Meiji era. Tonami Wa-dansu Kenkyūkai.*

05. *The chest inside. Zelkova-burl drawer faces, double doors, and drop-fit sliding door are backed with close-grained zelkova. Both case and chest have* totte *side carrying handles. Usually, if a case was used, the* chō-bako *did not have side handles. Chest: h. 43* x *w.* 55 x *d. 39 cm.*

104

106–7. Lower section. Above: three paulownia-lined drawers. Below, from left to right: full-depth drawer, removable document box, and removable writing-utensils box.

108. Zelkova box in center behind kendon-buta *door conceals paulownia box. When zelkova writing box on right is removed and panel behind is slid aside, zelkova seal box is revealed.*

109. Chō-bako *sea chest of zelkova. Oil-and-lacquer finish. H. 50 x w. 58 x d. 45 cm. First half of nineteenth century; Sado Island. Tonami Wa-dansu Kenkyūkai.*

110 111

10. Inside of hinged doors shows mitered clamp construction. Hirute *drawer pulls indicate considerable age. aulownia drawer interiors.*

11. Removable money box behind drop-fit door. Corner tenons and open mortises are dovetailed.

112. Chō-bako *sea chest of zelkova. Burl drawer and door faces backed with paulownia. Tarnished brass fami crest on doors. H. 51.5 x w. 58 x d. 45.5 cm. Mid-Meiji era; possibly from Sakata. Tonami Wa-dansu Kenkyūka*

13. Sliding doors with sophisticated lock system. Upper button is head of long pin, pulled out when single-action ɔck is unlocked. Visible drawer faces and doors are zelkova.

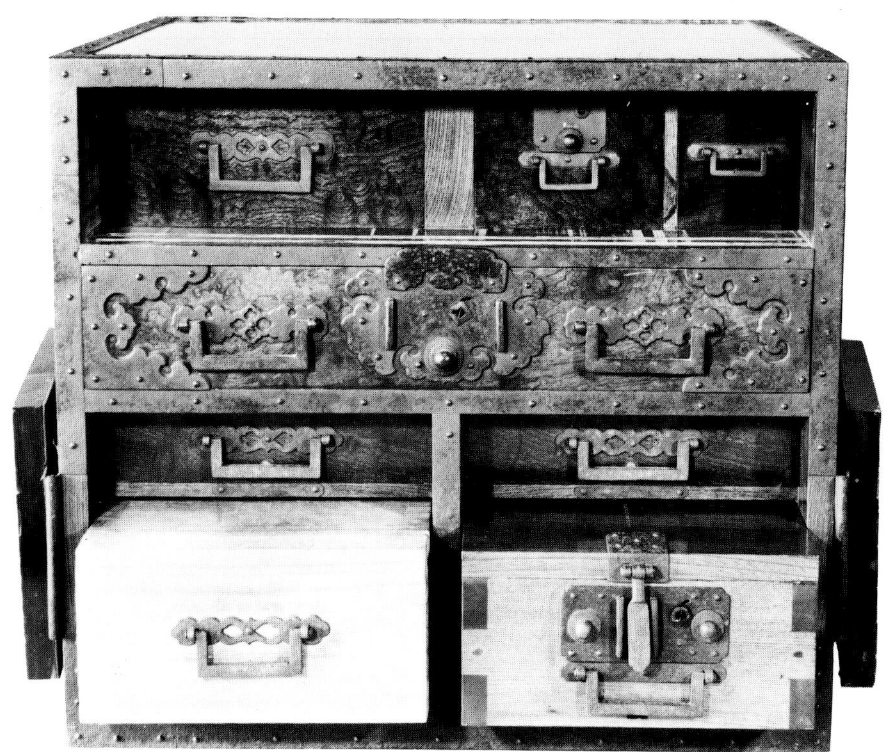

114. *With* kendon-buta *doors removed, two boxes revealed. Paulownia box for documents on left. Zelkova money box uses characteristic pegged-tenon open-mortise joints.*

115. *Paulownia box is actually a case with vertically sliding door to secure drawer with sliding cover.*

116. Chō-bako *sea chest. Zelkova-burl face backed with paulownia. Absence of side handles indicates the was once a case. Hexagonal cut in lower center plate originally for crest or trademark, but replaced by rosett H. 50 x w. 52.5 x d. 43 cm. Meiji era; probably from Sado. Tonami Wa-dansu Kenkyūkai.*

117. With outer door removed, unusual symmetrical configuration revealed. Since not sealed with paulownia, this chest probably not intended for shipboard use.

118. Center interior door with removable zelkova money box. Drawer pulls in form of pins with large heads are unusual except on very small tansu.

119. Detail of drop-fit door with fals keyhole next to slide-latch button.

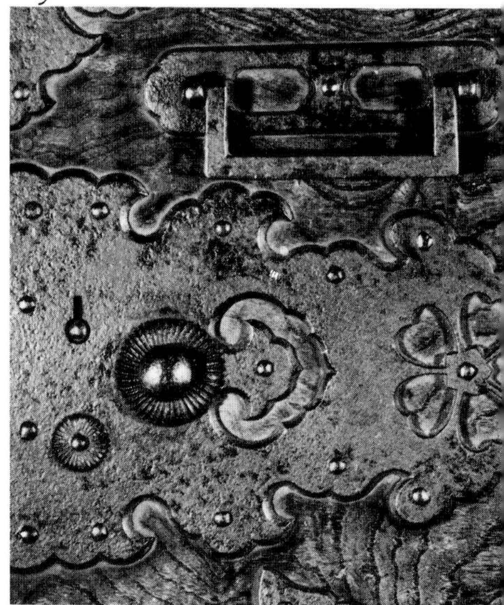

120. Chō-bako *sea chest of zelkova.* Kijiro *finish on door; other exposed zelkova has oil-and-lacquer finish. Embossed* shishi *(lion-dog) on* kendon-buta *door indicates late production. Interior is drawers only. H. 35.5* x *w. 50* x *d. 38 cm. Meiji era. Heineken Collection.*

121. *Ship's safe.* See *Figure 75.*

123

122. *Individually lockable inner drawers with silver locking buttons* (kikuza tegakejō). *Lock plate of upper drawer cut in shape of the god Daikoku and delicately engraved using the* sembori *technique.*

123. *Back center plate inscribed with the date, 1814, and the Japan Sea coast location of Echigo Murakami.*

24. *Ship's desk of zelkova with* kijiro *finish. Burled face wood backed with paulownia. Recesses cut into sides for rrying. Dovetailed mortise-and-tenon joinery, similar to that used on many hibachi of the period. H. 28 x 59.5 x d. 44 cm. Meiji era. Tonami Wa-dansu Kenkyūkai.*

125. *Inner configuration: open compartment to left for account book, lockable drawer to right for seals, and two small drawers to far right for inkstone and brushes. Paulownia drawer interiors.*

126. Ship's desk box for charts and maps. Lockable box with single drawer that opens from either end. Zelkova top carved with name of ship: Hokushin-maru. Blind tenons join sides to top; corners below drawer use through-dovetail joints. Flower-diamond motif indicates probable origin in Ogi or Sakata. H. 18.5 x *w. 29* x *d. 41 cm. Heineken Collection.*

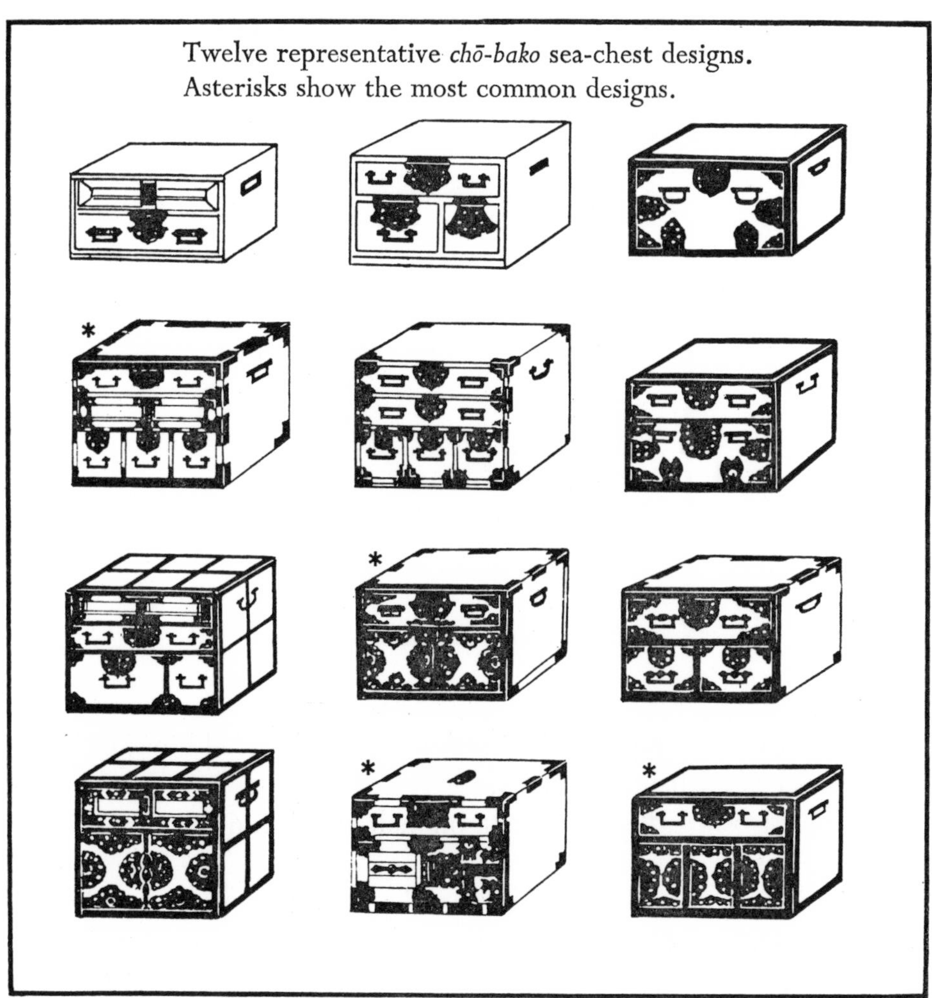

Twelve representative *chō-bako* sea-chest designs. Asterisks show the most common designs.

door of the top unit and the bottom unit respectively was popular throughout the production history of *hangai*.

The final sea-chest style to emerge, *chō-bako,* literally account box, had the broadest range of exterior configurations. Although it developed from the land-use *chō-dansu,* it in turn strongly influenced, as well as was influenced by, *chō-dansu* design. In all its variations, especially in the Meiji era, there are six characteristics of which at least two in combination were common to any *chō-bako* sea chest:

KENDON-BUTA: drop-fit door either cut into the case or inside the case as a cover for the removable money box.

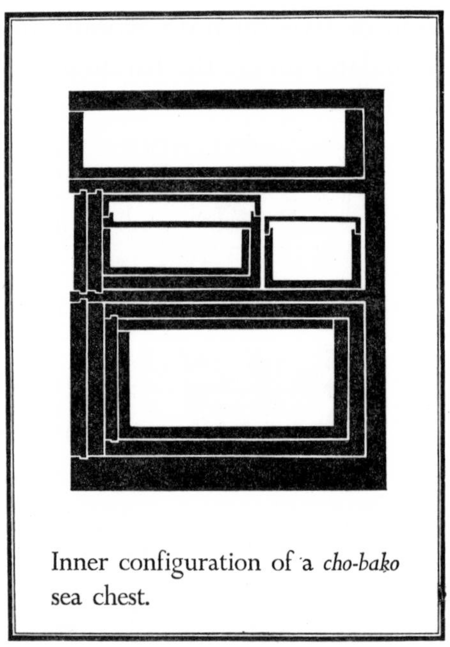

Inner configuration of a *cho-bako* sea chest.

KOBIRAKI-DO: a small swinging door on a half-faced hinge or hinges in the lower right-hand quadrant.

RYŌBIRAKI-DO: double doors on half-faced hinges in the lower half of the case.

DEZURA HIKIDASHI: one or two drawers that pull out directly from the exterior face.

HIKI-DO: removable double sliding doors running full width in either the upper or middle third of the case.

ZURI-DO: removable single sliding door in the lower half, left-hand quadrant, most typically used in conjunction with the *kobiraki-do.*

Within the multiplicity of emerging styles in the Meiji era, four types are particularly representative with an average size of h. 48 x w. 55 x d. 42 cm. All pieces used zelkova for the case, inner separations, and face woods. Only rarely was zelkova burl wood used for the chest face prior to the Meiji Restoration. Usually, we find 2.4 cm open-grain wood for the sides of Edo-period *chō-bako* sea chests, with a careful book-match of two separate boards for a single side on very early pieces. The original purpose of the iron banding on exposed sides was to secure and protect the connection of two separate woods, in that gluing at that time was not reliable. In later pieces the banding was still used primarily to discourage potential thieves. The inner wood for drawers and removable compartments is paulownia with zelkova used for the face wood of inner compartments in late pieces. However, the money box found behind a lockable drop-fit door panel is always totally of zelkova in Edo-period and Meiji-era examples. As with *kakesuzuri* and *hangai* chests, there was often planned space in the center of a door or as a hardware inset for the owner's family crest or business trademark. Because burl is inherently unstable as well as costly, zelkova burl as a face wood in many Meiji *chō-bako* was often backed with a closer-grained zelkova for strength. Use of paulownia as a backing wood to the zelkova burl was a later advance toward greater stability made possible by improvements in bonding methods.

Although *chō-bako* literally means a box to keep account records, as sea chests they were in their early and middle development also for travel documents, the ship's manifest, charts, money, and seals of identity. With a decree in September 1853 by the Tokugawa government withdrawing the prohibition against construction of large ships, *chō-bako* sea chests grew in support of greater trade capacity with more specific functions of writing case, portable safe, desk, and accounts storage box. Particularly from the mid-nineteenth century, sea chests began to exert considerable influence upon many of the regional tansu produced throughout the country. This was facilitated by a tendency rooted in late Edo for sea-chest joiners and hardware makers to move from place to place primarily along the Japan Sea coast not unlike the journeymen of early North America. In the later development period, many pieces were never intended for shipboard, but were commissioned by people involved directly or indirectly in the coastal trade. There is no conclusive indication of an intentional modification in design from chests actually used aboard ship.

With a Meiji-government prohibition in 1885 against construction of traditional Japanese ships of more than 500-*koku* capacity, sea chests were no longer practical. A total prohibition against even the use of the wide beam, no-keel, "thousand-*koku* ships" promulgated in 1907 followed the introduction of safer and faster narrow-hull designs from the West, but indirectly dealt a mortal blow to traditional sea chests.

CHAPTER THREE

MEIJI ERA: THE REGIONAL TANSU

The development of distinctive regional tansu characteristics in the Meiji era was most conspicuous on Honshu. For this reason, we shall limit our introduction to the most active production areas on Japan's main island, including Sado Island, lying off the northwest coast of Honshu. This discussion will start in northern Honshu and move south through tansu centers along the Japan Sea coast. The major cities of Tokyo, Kyoto, and Osaka will also be included.

Sendai

Perhaps the most well-known design category of post-Edo tansu bears the name of Sendai, the largest city in northern Honshu. Documented and well researched by Japanese scholars, the rise and transition of the Sendai tansu is a representative microcosm of changes associated with the Meiji Restoration. Although numerous tansu styles were produced in Sendai, eventually encompassing every level of the social strata, the design that came to be considered the most representative was both personal and mercantile in function, most frequently in one section of large proportion and intended, most probably from its inception, for use in the *dei,* a tatami room for the entertainment of guests. Sendai pieces, though often large, were able to fit under the *oshiire,* a built-in closet 181.8 cm wide. An *andon,* a wooden or iron lantern, frequently stood beside the chest. In that all Meiji clothing chests from other areas were kept beyond view in the family storehouse or in the *nando,* a storage room, the placement of Sendai chests in a prominent position next to either the family altar or the tokonoma, an alcove in which a scroll may be hung, is an interesting exception.

Although the Meiji era brought greater liberty in self-expression, after more than two hundred years of repression under the Edo sumptuary laws, the change to a status-bearing purchase mentality was at first hesitant, but by 1887 had become firmly established. Because Sendai was both a castle town and a mercantile center of considerable power, there was with the Meiji Restoration a tendency toward luxury and sophistication in a desire to emulate the pre-Meiji life style of the now defunct military government. The development of the Sendai tansu from its inception in the last years of Edo through a peak at the turn of the twentieth century to a degeneration in favor of mass distribution can fortunately be documented through examples reflecting a broad spectrum of changes between 1850 and 1920.

The Sendai chest of pre-Meiji years was very simple in appearance. A vertical locking bar usually extended over two drawers. Individually locking drawers, if present, had flat single-action locks, usually without an engraved design motif. The cutting of a design into the hardware was limited to the locking-bar face plate, for which a pattern of connected ivy leaves was most popular. Both the body and face woods were soft cryptomeria and paulownia respectively, finished with either a persimmon stain or an oil-thinned lacquer over a *bengara,* or ferric oxide, stain. *Warabite*-style iron drawer pulls with plain horizontal back plates are common in the oldest pieces. This early type, though reflecting a time of low production and limited demand, persisted as late as 1880.

In early Meiji, a second type of Sendai chest emerged, intended to appeal visually to prospering merchants and land-owning farmers now liberated from their harvest obligation to the samurai class. Though the proportions did not change, the paulownia face wood without obvious grain was superceded by beautifully grained zelkova or chestnut. The hardware remained flat but with somewhat more cutting and carving, especially for the single-action lock plates of the upper drawer, which for the first time acquired the horizontal crane motif now frequently associated with tansu from the Sendai area.

While popularity of the second style continued to grow, especially with farmers, a new form was seen that for the first time eliminated the vertical locking bar in favor of individually locking drawers in addition to a door hinged on the right side. The forged-iron *warabite*-style drawer pulls formerly mounted with one-piece back plates were now cast in the *mokkō* style with two separate round escutcheons for each pull instead of a single plate. Though cryptomeria continued to be used for the body, as it was right up through the late Sendai tansu, zelkova for the face wood with a *kijiro* lacquer finish was increasingly preferred. An embossing technique, known as *uchidashi,* was employed for the first time on the cut, chased, and engraved lock plates. Because this third type incorporated a mixture of hardware styles and new techniques, we are inclined to consider it transitional rather than a step in development. Even though this tansu displayed considerable innovation, few were produced, indicating that it might have been intended for a limited number of sophisticated customers among the merchant families.

From Meiji 21, or 1889, a chest very definitely rooted in transitional pieces of ten years earlier came into extensive production. This chest is today considered representative of Sendai's finest tansu. Though massive, the balance of engraved and embossed hardware against zelkova face wood finished with *kijiro* lacquer over a deep reddish stain is impressive if not subtle. In this type there is complete reliance on the sand-cast *mokkō*-style handles influenced by the iron-kettle craftsmen of Iwate Prefecture. Elaborate ornamentation, skillfully executed, reached a peak for the upper drawer in Figure 145. For the first time traditional Chinese subjects such as leaves and mythical animals became dominant hardware motifs. Perhaps to emphasize symmetry, the structural face woods began to be finished in opaque black lacquer, obscuring any grain in the cryptomeria members when viewed full-face. This fourth type of tansu persisted into the twentieth century, remaining in production until the 1920s.

With the end of the Meiji era and the coming of the Taishō era (1912–26), the individualist position of tansu makers as neighborhood craftsmen with a limited clientele gave way to a broad distribution system for both raw materials and finished products, based upon the modern concept of "economies in scale and location." The introduction of systems for pre-cutting wood and mass-molding hardware was good for business but destroyed the local character of the Sendai tansu. The last example is degenerate only in style. Although it was the result of modern production techniques for a nationwide market, it is well built and carefully hand-finished. The hardware is inspired by production considerations and is rather contrived. The single-action lock is superceded by the modern double-action lock using a key for both locking and unlocking, thereby eliminating the need for the foliate button common to all Edo-period and most Meiji-era tansu. Representative Taishō- and Shōwa-era pieces are frequently built in two sections, but small single-section chests of no more than 90 cm width are also common. Early twentieth century examples tended to reduce the lock size to a 6 cm circular plate and eliminate the hinged door area. In production cabinetry from the 1920s onwards, large lock plates and an inner compartment area were once again emphasized.

Because the Meiji government concentrated its efforts for the modernization of feudal Japan upon the national infrastructure, regional tansu craftsmen did not experience pressure toward a system of efficient production and national distribution until the early twentieth century. In fact, evolution of the Sendai tansu mirrors changes in the national living style that the Restoration instigated. Although in origin a chest used by the merchant class, it was propelled by an expanding twentieth century prosperity into a category very close to decorative furniture.

Iwate

Tansu from Iwate Prefecture are frequently confused with Meiji-era Sendai chests owing to their use of elaborately embossed hardware. In fact, their origin and popularity among the farmer class indicate a rural character quite different from the tansu of neighboring Sendai.

By the Tenmei era of the Edo period (1781–88), the Iwate area called Iwayado had become prominent as a horse-trading center. Under the influence of a liberal commercial policy encouraged by the daimyo Iwaki Sonshō, secondary commerce with visiting horse-traders developed for numerous crafts encouraged by the local government such as umbrellas, lanterns, and tansu.

Whereas the chests of Sendai became synonymous in the Meiji era with the stationary personal tansu used in the house, now known generically as Sendai tansu, Iwayado tansu are accurately represented by a massive chest on wheels with multiple drawers for clothing storage or a single-section chest with a combination of drawers and a door-covered compartment for personal use. In both styles, vertical locking bars used singly or in a pair were a common characteristic into the twentieth century. The dominant face wood was zelkova with the case of either pine or cryptomeria. Drawer interiors are only rarely other than paulownia. Iwayado pieces have less intense *bengara* red stain in comparison with those of Sendai since the Iwayado tansu were intentionally muted with persimmon tannin. Although color can be an important indicator of provenance, structure and hardware should also be considered. *Kuruma,* or wheeled, chests often do not employ horizontal frame members tenoned into corner stiles as do the wheeled chests from other regions. Indeed, Iwayado *kuruma* rarely have a frame-and-panel structure, exhibiting instead the pegged-tenon, open-mortise, corner box joint of secured-case tansu.

In that there are no known surviving examples of chests built prior to the Meiji era, the embossed foliate drawer-pull back plates may be considered a reliable identification. Care should be taken not to be confused by early Meiji Sendai chests, which also used the vertical locking bar system. The finish and lock mechanism should then be considered in order to correctly establish origin and age. The tansu of Iwayado remained in demand throughout the Meiji era, with production gradually declining in favor of molded-hardware centers such as Tsubame and Sanjō in Niigata Prefecture during the Taishō era.

Yamagata

With an abundant supply of reliable woods and skilled ironsmiths experienced in the craftsmanship of sea chests, Yamagata Prefecture offered a favorable climate in the Meiji era for the production of land-use chests. The tansu produced at Sakata, a coastal city, reflect a profound influence from sea-chest hardware. The use of extremely thick iron of up to 3 mm, large staples through the lock plates, and square drawer pulls are common to Sakata as well as to most sea chests from the Japan Sea coast.

Because of its position at the Mogami River estuary, Sakata had been an important coastal trading port from the sixteenth century. The economic power of Sakata might seem small in comparison with the great Hanseatic League cities of Europe in the thirteenth and fourteenth centuries, but there are interesting similarities that articulated an independent spirit from the Azuchi-Momoyama period. Whereas city-states such as London, Hamburg, Lubeck, and Bremen extended regional political power through allied extra-national guilds, the *za,* and later *onaka,* of Sakata, Kyoto, and Sakai built power within their respective feudal states, securing the exclusive use of primary roads and monopolizing commercial privileges. Although the manifestation of self-government was less spectacular than European examples and eventually deteriorated under pressures from the central government, it was nonetheless unique in feudal Japan and set, especially for Sakata, an appearance of self-determination that influenced merchant-class attitudes through the Edo period.

In consideration of its favorable geographic location, the Edo government appreciated that a prosperous Sakata would bring prosperity to the entire Dewa Province area. Extensive leasing of privately owned storehouses from "privileged merchants" for taxation rice as part of the Kawamura Zuiken transportation reforms described in chapter two is an apt indication of Sakata's importance. Confidence and power were manifested in the bold execution of both merchant and personal tansu.

The design of lacquered chest-on-chest clothing storage pieces is quite consistent. Square drawer pulls set against back plates with a motif of four diamonds were used in conjunction with individual drawer locks affixed to the face wood by two identical vertical staples on either side of the locking button. Usually there is a small-door compartment in the lower right corner, hung on three or five half-face hinges. When zelkova was chosen for the face, a *kijiro* lacquer over a *bengara* stain was employed to accentuate the wood grain. The top, sides, and structural separations of cryptomeria were intentionally subdued by the use of lacquer diluted with oil. With rare exceptions, the interior for the drawers is paulownia. A chest for clothing, constructed entirely of natural paulownia and often in the double-door Tokyo style, is also occasionally seen, but does not exhibit a design consistency, though there is an inclination to favor the chrysanthemum-leaf pattern for lock plates among Meiji-era tansu from numerous Yamagata Prefecture towns.

Merchant chests for shop use reveal very little design continuity except for a uniform bold use of hardware in configurations consistent with the personal, lacquered chest-on-chest tansu. Zelkova was almost always used for the face wood and often for the case top and sides as well, with the exception of pieces where regular use had to be considered, such as a peddler's chest.

While Sakata was the coastal mercantile center, Tsuruoka, just eighteen kilometers away on the Shōnai plain, was the seat of political power as castle town of the ruling daimyo. Conservative and orthodox, the Edo traditions of Tsuruoka are evident in the Meiji-era tansu, which are detailed and decorative to an excess. As in a number of other areas, personal tansu were brought by a new bride to the home of her husband's family. In Tsuruoka these wedding chests bore certain distinctive characteristics that make them both visually striking and readily identifiable. Hardware was finished with a process used extensively at Tsuruoka until the twentieth century in which *bengara* stain was used as an undercoat for clear lacquer burned onto the iron. When applied to hot iron, pure lacquer will turn black. If applied to a calculated degree, the red tone of the *bengara* exudes an orange glow under the familiar matte black. In addition, on the wedding chests of Tsuruoka, the hardware motifs always incorporate the crane, the turtle, and the crest of the bride's family. Drawer pulls in the *warabite* style set against small round escutcheons with embossing on at least one of the locks or on the vertical locking bar are also common. Up to the end of the Meiji era there is usually a locking bar covering the three inset drawers of a wedding chest of either one or two sections. Although a black opaque lacquer over cypress was frequently used on the face of the majority of chests, there are numerous examples from the second half of Meiji with zelkova face wood finished with *kijiro* lacquer, using either cryptomeria or zelkova for the case wood. Many merchant chests were also produced in Tsuruoka, but because their specific provenance separate from other seacoast production areas is difficult to ascribe, they are not considered sufficiently representative.

At Yonezawa, located at the navigable beginning of the Mogami River, two separate factors influenced the development of one of the most prolific tansu centers of the late Meiji era. From Sakata, river trade exposed Yonezawa to bold designs and refined techniques. From the Mikuni area on the Japan Sea coast, family-altar makers had migrated to Yonezawa, bringing with them the highest skills of the joiner. Of the numerous designs in both merchant and personal tansu produced during the Meiji era, one particular chest-on-chest configuration is especially representative of the fine level of workmanship achieved toward the end of the nineteenth century. The Yonezawa *ishō kasane* was intended as a wedding chest to be kept in the family storehouse for the safekeeping of formal clothing outside of the season when it might be normally worn. The face wood is chestnut or zelkova, with paulownia chosen only rarely. The secured case and drawer interiors used cryptomeria with few exceptions. Very early examples position the small-door compartment in the lower right corner with two or three drawers to the left. The upper chest usually had two full-width drawers. By late Meiji, this early configuration had been reversed and the door compartment was located in the upper chest. Among late examples, there is a tendency for very wide pieces of over 120 cm to have the lower chest seem to be built slightly higher than the upper chest due to an attached, foliate frame on which the tansu stood, permitting air circulation. Tansu without the frame normally had sections of equal height when placed side by side.

Hardware is also distinctive. Specifically in chest-on-chest Yonezawa tansu, round lock plates were most prevalent. Dominant motifs include an engraved, five-petal cherry blossom within an arabesque of ivy and a butterfly with folded wings engraved and cut out of the plate, which was rimmed with a composite of copper and tin. Use of flat or two-facet *mokkō*-style sand-cast drawer pulls in combination with openwork and embossed drawer-pull back plates bearing an engraved pine-branch pattern is a very reliable indication of Yonezawa provenance. A tea-seedpod motif on drawer corner plates is usually considered a nearly foolproof indicator; however, this interesting pattern actually owes its origin to Sado Island in the Edo period. As well as in Yonezawa, it can be seen occasionally on tansu from Akita, Niigata, and Fukushima prefectures, thus implying the importance of water-route commerce in the dissemination of technique and design. For merchant tansu, including wheeled chests, the use of an iron pin with a "pine-nut" head at important overlapping hardware points or in the center of a prominent piece of face hardware is a very reliable clue for determining high-level craftsmanship in Meiji-era Yonezawa single-section cabinetry.

As for the finishing of Yonezawa chests, hardwoods used on the face such as chestnut or zelkova were coated with *kijiro* lacquer to accentuate the wood grain. Cryptomeria cases usually have a persimmon tannin or *bengara* stain under a wiped or brushed lacquer mixed with rapeseed oil.

Nihonmatsu

Lying to the southeast of Fukushima Prefecture's lacquer center Aizu-Wakamatsu, the town of Nihonmatsu was a center for small-scale production of tansu. This center was most active from the mid-Meiji era, relatively late compared to other production areas. Although Nihonmatsu chests are not well known, they are noteworthy for their uniqueness, largely uninfluenced by the surrounding tansu-producing areas. Some degree of design influence from Sendai would be expected, but a comparison of Nihonmatsu and Sendai chests indicates only two characteristics in common: a consistent width of over 110 cm and a marked preference for zelkova for the face wood.

The most outstanding feature of the Nihonmatsu chest-on-chest is its use of single-action drawer locks in combination with vertically activated slide latches, or *karajō,* both contained within a single lock plate for each drawer. The latches have a right-angle operating pattern identical to latches occasionally found on sea chests and storage boxes with drop-fit removable doors. Only the Nihonmatsu system uses two parallel exposed buttons, one for locking and one for latching on each of the four drawers.

Most Nihonmatsu tansu have a *bengara* burnt lacquer finish for hardware with *suri-urushi* wiped lacquer for the cryptomeria or pine case and a simple opaque lacquer (*tame-nuri*) on the zelkova drawers, obscuring the open wood grain. It is rare in Japanese cabinetry to find an opaque lacquer hiding the grain of a prestigious wood as in these chests. Drawer pulls are in the *mokkō* style and usually very broad in comparison with other tansu hardware from eastern Honshu.

Each half of the typical Nihonmatsu chest-on-chest has two drawers of approximately equal size with a small-door compartment, the exact height of the lowest drawer, in the lower right corner. These symmetrical features are atypical in tansu. Another point for identification, which is quite consistent, may be found in the door compartment. The face wood of the two inner drawers is usually the same wood as that used in the case, not the zelkova of the outer drawers.

Echigo

Prior to the restoration of imperial authority in 1868, the area that is now called Niigata Prefecture was known as Echigo. Sado Island, primarily because of its wealth in minerals, was under the direct control of the Tokugawa government. Echigo, in contrast to Sado, had a significantly larger disparity between wealth and poverty because of the concentration of landownership among a very few families.

In the towns of Shibata, Niigata, Nagaoka, and Murakami, only merchants involved in sakè brewing, tea distribution, and shipping could afford to own tansu in the Edo period. The economy could not support a group of professional tansu makers. Because of the severity of Echigo winters and the unavailability of cabinetry for business functions, however, merchants and landowners would keep their permanently employed house carpenters occupied with indoor work such as the construction of substantial but very simple tansu with sparse hardware for storing valuables. These *zeni to-dana,* enclosed shelves for storing money and other valuables, give an impression of disproportionate mass.

In the most substantial pieces, double tenons passing entirely through the frame members were employed, with the individual tenons secured by as many as eight hardwood wedges. With only rare exceptions, zelkova was used for both the frame and paneling.

The *zeni to-dana* configuration is found with and without wheels. When wheels are present, they are usually only to facilitate movement forward and backward from a wall recess rather than laterally as with other wheeled tansu. Double sliding doors lockable by a single-action mechanism or a detached padlock are most common. In numerous examples, both locking systems were used for one set of doors. Usually there are internal drawers with the number and configuration according to the owner's preference. A single exposed, full-width drawer in the upper third of the chest should be expected to have a square lock plate devoid of any decoration. Two pulls in the *kakute* style mounted on flat rectangular back plates and drawer corner plates, most often with the tea-seedpod motif, would complete a representative picture. An inset panel of one piece of zelkova for the top, slightly recessed between the frame members, is frequently seen on examples of exceptional quality.

Although personal tansu in one and two sections commissioned from craftsmen by farmers, using paulownia from their own lands for the trousseau of a daughter, were not uncommon in Niigata by the Taishō era, until the early twentieth century very few families could afford such luxury. Merchant families were often not much more affluent than the farmers unless they were landowners as well. If personal tansu were ordered, paulownia was the preferred wood in designs then popular in Tokyo rather than indigenous designs.

Sado

With sea chests as an experience base, craftsmen of the town of Ogi on Sado Island in the Japan Sea, thirty kilometers off the coast of Niigata Prefecture, applied their skill to creating both merchant and trousseau tansu in the late-Edo period. Whereas land-use shop cabinetry was most always by special order with the structure and proportions dependent on the customer's requirements, chest-on-chest wedding tansu adhered to a consistent design. The metalwork was inspired by the hardware of *hangai* sea chests and continued to resemble its predecessor right into the twentieth century.

Initially Ogi tansu were quite plain, with the case, face, and interior wood of paulownia. Hardware was not as extensively cut with curved embellishments as on later pieces. With prosperity stimulated by national reforms, use of zelkova burl for the face wood and cut decoration in the hardware became prominent. Two round cuts in the center vertical plate on the door in the lower section for a family crest and trademark indicate that the chest-on-chest Ogi tansu were intended for wealthy merchant families. *Warabite*-style drawer pulls set against back plates bearing the four-diamonds motif are an important identification point; however, the appearance of four small decorative studs on each major drawer lock plate, symmetrically on either side of the locking button, is the most reliable indicator of Meiji-era Ogi provenance. Most often the top and bottom sections are of equal height, especially when there are only one or two full-width drawers. Ogi chest-on-chest tansu used the *kijiro* lacquering technique to accentuate the zelkova face-wood grain with either *shunkei-nuri* (lacquer and oil) or *fuki-urushi* (wiped lacquer) for the softwood case.

Following the establishment of successful interprovincial tansu trade from Ogi, craftsmen in the neighboring town of Yahata, also on Sado Island, began producing chest-on-chest trousseau tansu of their own design by the mid-Meiji era. Emphasis on elaborately engraved hardware using Shinto symbolic motifs became by the 1920s the popular image of the Sado Island tansu. Although the chests of Ogi and Yahata are very similar in proportion, both using *warabite*-style drawer pulls and edge plates for the structural face, the origin of Ogi tansu in ship's cabinetry implies superior workmanship. Nevertheless, the Yahata tansu should be considered an important example of an early commercialization in tansu design.

Since production at Yahata was comparatively brief, pieces should be prized for their rare eccentricity rather than their excellence relative to the tansu of Ogi or Sakata. Yahata craftsmen relied exclusively on paulownia for their primary and secondary woods. The maroon finish, identical for the face, top, and sides, is oil and lacquer over a water-soluble stain of persimmon tannin. Some pieces were made with the paulownia left unstained, the close-grained wood only sealed with clay burnished to a soft patina with a stiff reed brush. The abundance of Yahata hardware makes these tansu easy to identify. Predominant use of legendary subjects adds a whimsical aspect to these chests, which evidently proved to be popular with wealthy rural families who ordered Yahata tansu for their betrothed daughters.

It is an interesting peculiarity of both Ogi and Yahata chest-on-chest tansu that the side carrying handles for both top and bottom sections are usually of the swinging type without hasp pins on the upper unit to secure the stacked sections together.

Etchū

Prior to the Meiji era, the Japan Sea coastal region was known by its geographic proximity to high mountains. The recipient of snow-laden winds off the Siberian plain, the northwest coast of Honshu is now well known by the name "snow country," popularized by Yasunari Kawabata in his most famous novel. Historically the area including today's Toyama Prefecture was known as Etchū, literally "passing through the mountains." To the north was Echigo, or "beyond the mountains." To the south, Echizen, or "before the mountains." These three terms are both specific and appropriate when used to identify ethnological objects such as tansu of pre-twentieth century origin.

As in neighboring Niigata Prefecture, the Echigo area, in Etchū the severe climate and the concentration of land ownership precluded the establishment of tansu trade until the late Meiji era. Prior to this time, salaried house carpenters were put to seasonal work in the construction of what is possibly Japan's most substantial, if not most aesthetic, mercantile cabinetry. Zelkova was usually used for the entire chest with mortise-and-tenon joinery for the framework. Only for wheeled tansu do we find chestnut, used for the wheels.

There are few obvious identification characteristics to differentiate Toyama frame-and-panel cabinetry from that of Ishikawa or Fukui prefectures. Because production was on an individual order basis, a determination of provenance must be based upon a combined consideration of hardware, choice of woods, and joinery. On Japan Sea coastal cabinetry, it was not unusual for a carpenter to identify himself, mark the completion date, place of residence, and even occasionally the construction time on the back of one of the sliding doors.

Etchū wheeled tansu often share with some of those from Kanazawa city in Ishikawa Prefecture a sliding-door design called "stone tatami" that could be used if two sets of slatted sliding doors were present. The appearance of the slats running vertically in one sliding-door set and horizontally in the other set was an Edo-period local tradition among merchants who had been designated as privileged suppliers to the daimyo. This "stone-tatami" pattern in a prominently displayed wheeled tansu indicated their special position. Although somewhat more subtle than the use in Europe of signs such as "Purveyors to the Queen," the purpose was the same. The visual effect of the "stone-tatami" pattern emphasizes the wood grain at the expense of the massiveness of the chest. The use of brace plates to cover exposed tenons, though common to frame-and-panel Toyama tansu, is also found on many similarly structured pieces from Ishikawa and Fukui prefectures.

27. *Echigoya, a clothing shop in Edo, showing merchandise drawers* (shōhin hikidashi) *and a staircase chest* (kaidan-dansu). *Illustration by Utagawa Toyoharu.*

128. Sendai merchant chest, possibly built for a merchant active in coastal trade. Zelkova case, paulownia drawer interiors. Sash hardware; hardware pattern of twelve animals of the zodiac. H. 82 x w. 97.5 x d. 46.5 cm. Late Edo period. Collection of Mr. John Gruber.

129. Sendai single-section clothing chest (ishō yarō-dansu). *Zelkova, cryptomeria case, and paulownia draw interiors.* Kijiro *finish over a* bengara *stain. H. 89.5 x w. 120 x d. 45.5 cm. Meiji era. Collection of M John Gruber.*

30. *Shōnai portable account hest (chō-dansu). Zelkova nd cryptomeria. H. 69 x w. '4 x d. 37 cm. Late Meiji ra. Collection of Mr. John ;ruber.*

31. *Cryptomeria carrying rame set into the back of the hest. Rings for straps; oval cut liminates the need for backbone ushion.*

132. *Tsuruoka trousseau chest. Zelkova face with* kijiro *finish. Cryptomeria body with wiped lacquer finish. Hardware with burnt lacquer over* bengara *stain was popular in Tsuruoka in the late nineteenth century. H. 64 x w. 62 x d. 36 cm. Collection of Mr. John Gruber.*

133. *Yonezawa chest-on-chest for clothing* (ishō-kasane-dansu). *Zelkova face with* kijiro *finish. Round lock plates engraved with cherry-blossom motif within ivy arabesque.* Mokkō *drawer pulls against back plates cut and engraved as pine boughs. Corner plates with tea-seedpod motif. H. 97 x w. 112 x d. 48 cm. Late Meiji era. Collection of Mr. Y. Takeshita.*

134. Yonezawa wheeled chest (kuruma-dansu). *Zelkova-burl face, zelkova interior-drawer faces and structure, paulownia drawer interiors.* Kijiro *finish using the full* roiro *process. H. 120 x w. 120 x d. 62 cm. Meiji era. Tonami Wa-dansu Kenkyūkai.*

135. *Sado clothing chest* (ishō-yarō-dansu). *Zelkova with cryptomeria back and paulownia drawer interiors.* Kijiro *finish over* bengara *stain on face, wiped lacquer on top and sides. H. 88* x *w. 112* x *d. 42 cm. Meiji era; Ogi. Collection of Mr. John Gruber.*

136. *Sado chest-on-ch*
for clothing (ish
kasane-dansu). *Zelk*
face with kijiro *fini*
cryptomeria case, p
lownia drawer interio
Unusual difference in s
of upper and lower che
Two openwork circles a
flower-diamond motif
small-door sash hardw
are common to Meiji-
Ogi clothing chests.
115.5 x *w. 115.5* x
43 cm. Collection of M
John Gruber.

37. *Kyoto chest-on-chest for othing* (ishō-kasane-dansu). *·ass hardware,* maki-e *·cquer.* Mochiokuri *side ındles indicate the chest was ɔt meant to be carried on a ·le. H. 107 x w. 85 x d. cm. Meiji era. Collection Mr. John Gruber.*

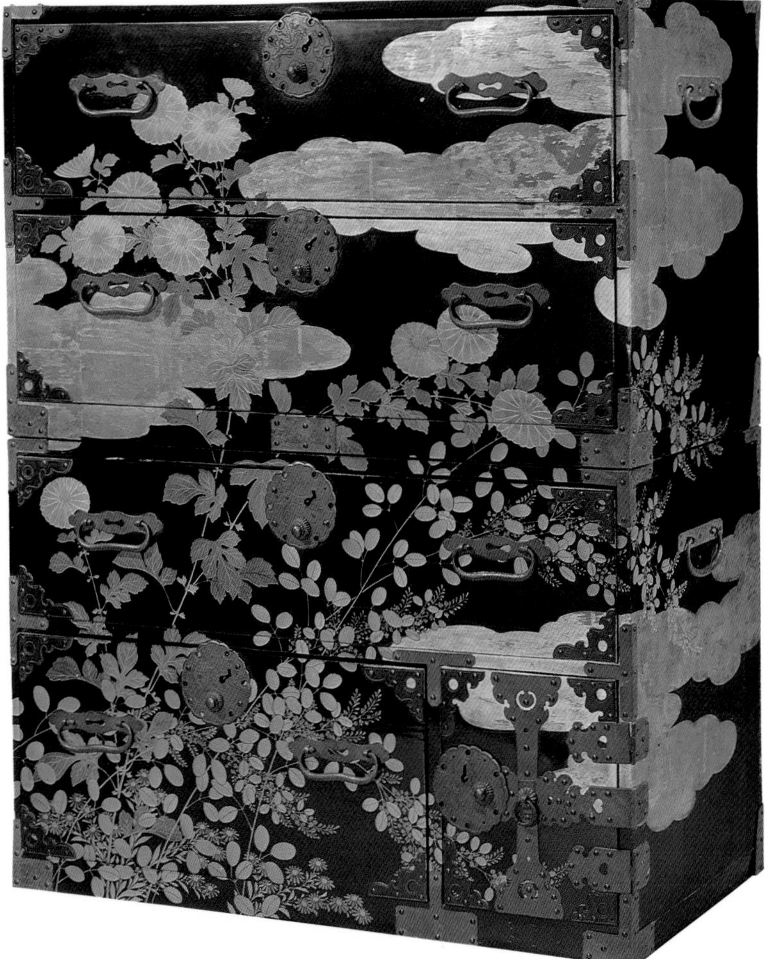

138. *Kyoto trousseau chest* (temoto). *Chased brass hardware.* Maki-e *lacquer crests of the two families. H. 69.5 x w. 73 x d. 39 cm. Meiji era. Collection of Mr. John Gruber.*

139. Double-front, free-standing serving cabinet on hidden casters. Chestnut and cryptomeria. Sliding doors wi removable panels. Top boards can be removed to insert a carving board. H. 102 x w. 106 x d. 51 cm. Co temporary. Built for Ms. Judith Fischer of Princeton by the Craftsmen's Guild of Tokyo.

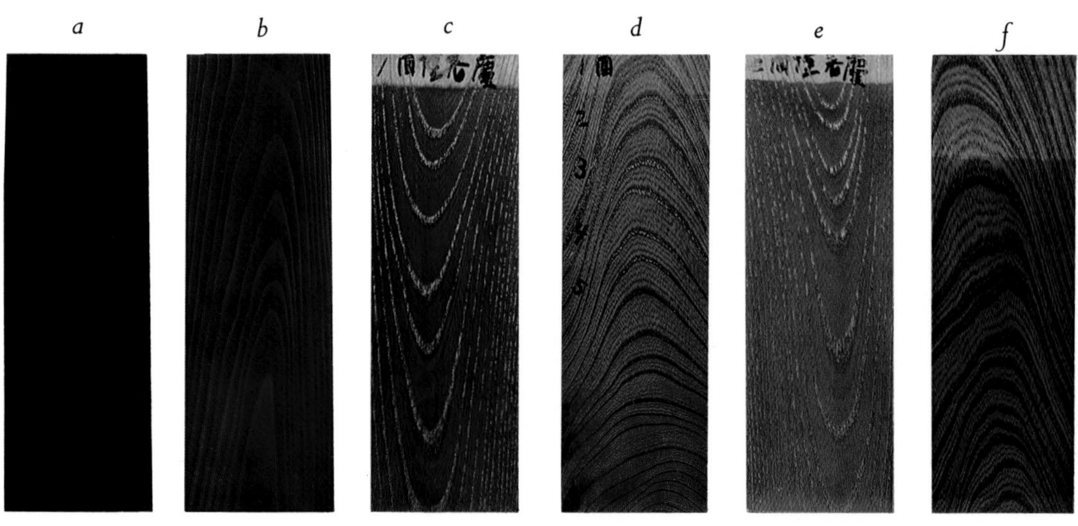

140. a) Vermilion tame-nuri *final finish on cypress. b)* Shunkei-nuri *final finish on cryptomeria. c) A mixtu of powdered whetstone, water, and* bengara *has been applied by brush as a base, followed by three coats of persir mon tannin. When dry,* shunkei *lacquer is applied. d) Raw lacquer* (ki-urushi) *applied with cloth in five stage polished after each application with powdered whetstone. e) Persimmon tannin has been applied in two coats, fo lowed by a wiped coat of raw lacquer. The final coat is* shunkei *lacquer. f) The distinctive character of* kijir *finish with carefully polished, refined pure lacquer.*

1. Sendai clothing chest for closet (oshiire ishō-dansu). *Zelkova and cryptomeria. Modified into a wheeled* *st. H. 100 x w. 174.5 x d. 55.5 cm. Late Edo or early Meiji. Tokyo Furniture Museum.*

2. Sendai clothing chest for closet (oshiire ishō-dansu). *Zelkova and cryptomeria. Fine embossed hardware* *dicates late production. H. 97 x w. 166 x d. 54 cm. Mid-Meiji era. Tokyo Furniture Museum.*

143. Sendai clothing chest for closet (oshiire ishō-dansu). *Zelkova face, cryptomeria body and interior. Sma door compartment with three drawers.* Kijiro *face finish,* shunkei *finish for body. H. 65* x *w. 183* x *d. 48 c First half of Meiji era. Tonami Wa-dansu Kenkyūkai.*

144. Heart motif found on personal chests throughout eastern Honshu. Detailed line carving or chasing of iron lock plates associated with Sendai.

145. *Sendai chest-on-chest for clothing* (ishō kasane-dansu). *Zelkova and cryptomeria. Embossed ivy flanks slightly convex, round lock plate with crest, characteristic of Sendai clothing chests from the 1880s. H. 106* x *w. 116* x *d. 43.5 cm. Second half of Meiji era. Heineken Collection.*

46. *Sendai single-section clothing* hest (ishō yarō-dansu). *Zelkova and* ryptomeria. *Cast hardware; func-* onal side carrying handles have disap- eared. Door compartment atypically ound on left side. H. 88* x *w. 83.5* x *. 48 cm. Taishō era. Collection of* Iasebeya, Tokyo.*

147. *Iwayado wheeled chest with vertical locking bars* (bō kuruma-dansu). *Cryptomeria with* shunkei *finish. Secured-case structure for large wheeled chest characteristic of area. H. 136 x w. 150 x d. 73.5 cm. Meiji era. Tokyo Furniture Museum.*

148. *Iwayado single-section clothing chest* (is yarō-dansu). *Cryptomeria with* shunkei *fini Door compartment with two simple drawers. Locki bar with large embossed drawer-pull back pla characteristic of Meiji and Taishō tansu from t area. H. 89.5 x w. 89.5 x d. 43.5 cm. Tol Furniture Museum.*

149. *Upper level for account books is not con partmentalized. Lower area has drawers an structural members of paulownia.*

150. *Yamagata wheeled chest* (kuruma-dansu) *of zelkova. H. 89 x w. 92 x d. 51 cm. Early Meiji era. Tona Wa-dansu Kenkyūkai.*

151. *Staircase chest* (kaidan-dansu) *of zelkova. Built for family storehouse in Yamagata in 1834. H. 270 w. 227 x d. 75.5 cm. Collection of the Satō family, Yamagata.*

152. Lock characteristic of Meiji-era Sakata chest-on-chests. Symmetrical, vertical staples on lock plate with extensively cut perimeter.

153. Sakata chest-on-chest for clothing (ishō kasane-dansu). *Zelkova open-grain face backed with close-grain zelkova. Cryptomeria body and paulownia drawer interiors. "Breadboard clamps" on door backed with cryptomeria show late production.* Kijiro *finish on face and* shunkei *finish on body. H. 107 x w. 87 x d. 43 cm. Late Meiji era. Tonami Wa-dansu Kenkyūkai.*

160. *Yonezawa shop chest* (chōba-dansu). *Zelkova and cryptomeria. Single* mochiokuri *side carrying handles. H. 68* x *w. 75* x *d. 45 cm. Meiji era. Collection of Mr. John Gruber.*

161. *Yonezawa single section clothing ches* (ishō yarō-dansu) *Wiped lacquer finish o chestnut face, oil-and lacquer finish on crypto meria body. Butterfl motif on lock plate rimmed in* hakudō *a compound of coppe and tin. H. 97 w. 106* x *d. 45 cm Meiji era. Collectio of the Merker family New Jersey.*

162. Nihonmatsu chest-on-chest for clothing (ishō kasane-dansu). *Zelkova grain almost hidden by* tame-nuri *finish. A lock button and a latch button of equal size on each unengraved lock plate are characteristic of most Nihonmatsu clothing chests. H. 116 x w. 105 x d. 44 cm. Late Meiji era. Heineken Collection.*

163. Echigo merchant chest (chō-dansu) *of zelkova. Thick unengraved plating indicates Japan Sea coast origin. Secured case over 3 cm thick probably built by a carpenter rather than a tansu maker. H. 63.5 x w. 91 x d. 47.5 cm. Meiji era. Collection of Mr. John Gruber.*

164. Echigo wheeled chest for storing merchant's valuables (zeni to-dana kuruma-dansu). *Zelkova with* kijiro *finish, paulownia drawer interiors. H. 81.5* x *w. 91.5* x *d. 54 cm. Early Meiji era. Tonami Wa-dansu Kenkyūkai.*

165. With double doors removed, interio appears to be five drawers. In fact, uppe left side is drop-fit door with zelkova mone box, in style of chō-bako *sea chest.*

166. Removable zelkova base with eigh recessed porcelain wheels that allow move- ment from storage alcove.

67. *Echigo portable safe* (seoi kinko-dansu). *Paulowia sealed with clay and mo*urō, *a resin wax. H. 73 x* . *45 x d. 48 cm. Meiji era.* *onami Wa-dansu Kenkyūkai.*

168. *Four interior drawers with rare corner plating.*

169. Sado merchant chest (chō-dansu)*. Paulownia, zelkova sliding-door frame. Drawer lock plates wi crane-and-tortoise motif. Crest and trademark on door sash plate. H. 67 x w. 86 x d. 43 cm. Early Meiji er Tonami Wa-dansu Kenkyūkai.*

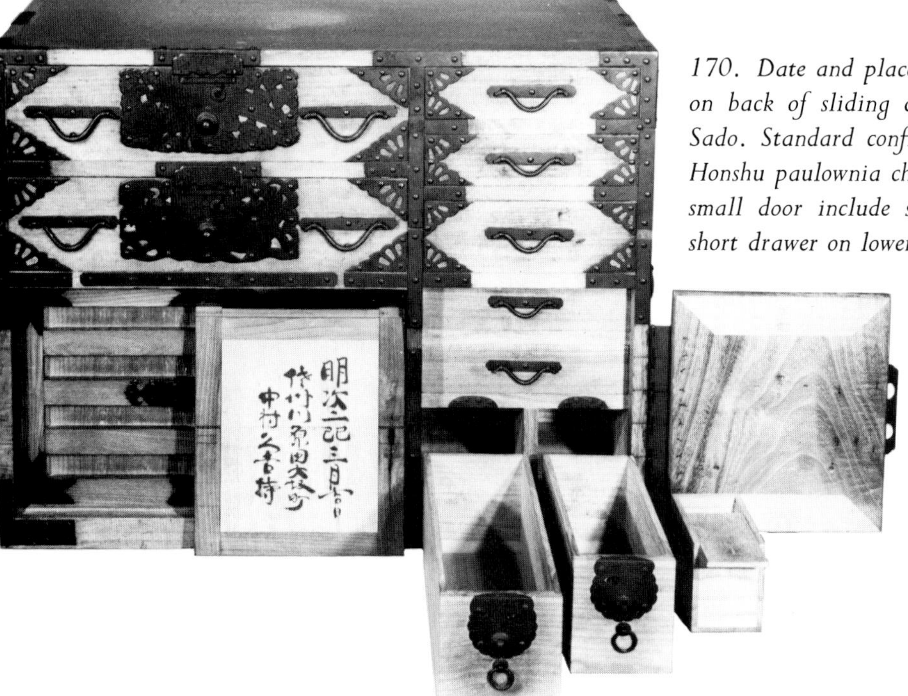

170. Date and place of purchase writte on back of sliding door: 1869, Marc Sado. Standard configuration for easter Honshu paulownia chests: drawers behin small door include seal box in back short drawer on lower right.

171. *Thin plating could be cut in broad range of Shinto and Buddhist motifs. Even drawer faces inside small-door compartment were plated.*

172. *Yahata chest-on-chest for clothing* (ishō kasane-dansu). *Paulownia with* shunkei *finish. Elaborate total face hardware typical of Sado chests from Yahata. H. 117.5* x *w. 118.5* x *d. 45 cm. Late Meiji era. Tonami Wa-dansu Kenkyūkai.*

173. *Etchū wheeled merchant chest* (chō kuruma-dansu). *Zelkova with paulownia drawers. Iron sash hardware. Originally owned by wealthy farmer. H. 86 x w. 105 x d. 56.5 cm. Late Edo period. Tonami Wa-dansu Kenkyūkai.*

174. *Upper interior open f* *storage of account books* (dai fuku-chō). *All eight drawe use plated separating rail lock jamb.*

175. *Four hardwood whee set into base rails, commo to many Etchū wheeled chest*

176. Principal mortise-and-tenon joints are protected by angular plating on many Etchū frame-and-panel tansu.

177. Etchū wheeled chest (kuruma-dansu). *Zelkova with paulownia drawer interiors. Probably merchant chest since of exact depth for account books. H. 120* x *w. 130* x *d. 56.6 cm. Meiji era. Collection of the Tanimura family, Fukumitsu.*

178. Etchū shop chest (chōb dansu). *Zelkova with wiped lacq finish. H. 91 x w. 108 x d. 52 c Early Meiji era. Tonami Wa-dar Kenkyūkai.*

179. Open interior except for six drawers, originally secured by vertical locking bar, the jamb plate of which is still visible.

180. Stacked shop shelves (chōba kasane to-dana) *used by traditional linen merchant. Cryptomeria. H. 1 x w. 184 x d. 50 cm. Meiji era. Collection of the Funaoka family, Fukumitsu.*

181. Wheeled merchant chest (chō kuruma-dansu). *Zelkova with* kijiro *finish and cryptomeria drawer interiors. Sliding-door slats in "stone-tatami" pattern, reserved for privileged merchants. Carved waves on butt ends of front base rail indicate influence from Noto Peninsula. H. 101 x w. 103 x d. 58 cm. Late Edo period. Tonami Wadansu Kenkyūkai.*

◀*182. Although usual number of drawers was four to six, this chest has ten. Inscription on back of lower doors reads: "Beginning of March, 1810, village of Shikinami. Carpenter Shichiemon received payment of 100* me *[a unit of money] for the equivalent of fifty-nine days' work."*

183. Merchant chests from Ishikawa and Toyama prefectures ▶ *often used detached double-pronged hasp to secure both sets of sliding doors.*

ɬ. *Noto wheeled chest* (kuruma-dansu). *Zelkova with* kijiro *finish. Upper two drawers secured by locking bar. aracteristic carving symbolic of waves and ivy on base rail shows influence from continent. H. 89.5 x w. 86 x 45 cm. Early Meiji era. Tonami Wa-dansu Kenkyūkai.*

186. Elaborate plating on butt ends of base rail and over wheel-axle through tenons is characteristic of nineteenth century Fukui wheeled chests.

5. *Mikuni wheeled chest* (kuruma-dansu) *from Fukui Prefecture. Zelkova and cypress with wiped lacquer finish. ulownia drawer interiors, five three-quarter-face hinges, and a depth of over 70 cm indicate Mikuni origin. 104 x w. 116 x d. 76 cm. Meiji era. Tonami Wa-dansu Kenkyūkai.*

7. *Takefu wheeled chest :h locking bar* (kuruma -dansu) *from Echizen. lkova face and cryptoria. There was often no izontal bracing on sides back of Meiji-era Takefu me-and-panel tansu. H. 9 x w. 110 x d. 55 cm. nami Wa-dansu Kenkyū-i.*

190. *Mikuni chest-on-chest for clothing* (ishō k sane-dansu). *Zelkova frame and face, cryptomer panels, and paulownia drawer interiors.* Roiro *fini over dark* bengara *stain. Recessed drawer pulls late-production style. H. 172.5 x w. 96 x d. 45 c Meiji era. Collection of the Nishida family, Oyab*

192

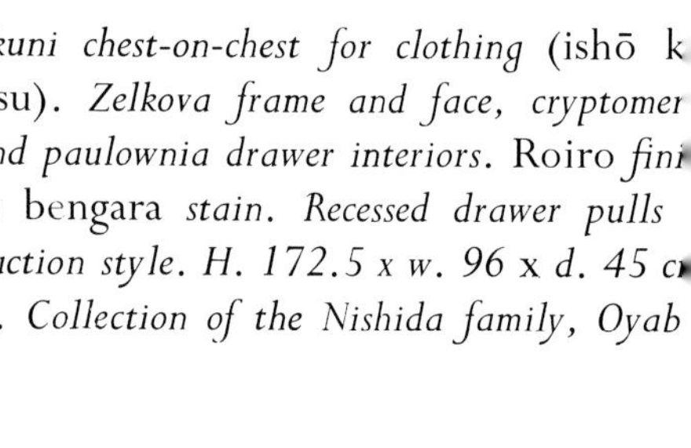

192. *With lid raised, full-width dra can be removed. Lower center doors "Kannon" style, hinged to sliding doc*

38. *Set of two clothing chests from Mikuni* (ishō yarō-dansu). *Zelkova face, pine case and interior. H. 101 x*
. *92 x d. 45 cm. Meiji era. Collection of the Hata family, Fukumitsu.*

39. *Side carrying handles*
re recessed but functional.

191. *Wheeled trunk* (nagamochi kuruma-dansu) *from Wakasa area. Zelkova frame, cypress and cryptomeria. Unusually sophisticated sectional design. H. 89 x w. 100 x d. 55 cm. Late Edo period. Tonami Wa-dansu Kenkyūkai.*

193

194

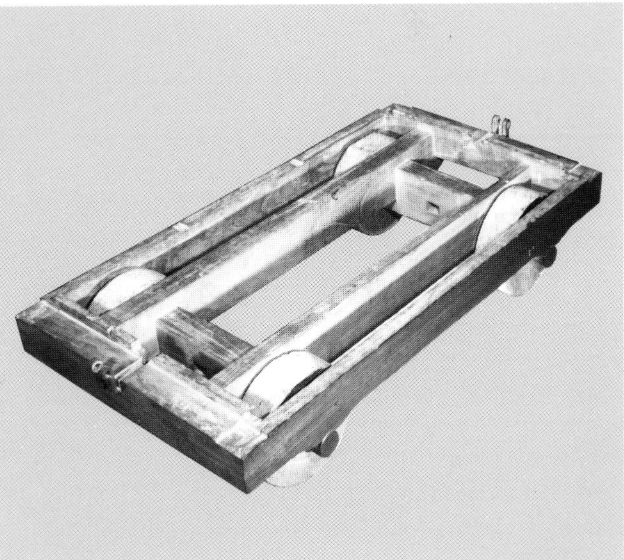

93. *With lid, drawer tray, and doors removed, ten drawers visible, three with single-action locks. Ten-link*
hains instead of side handles are characteristic of Wakasa wheeled tansu.

94. *Tansu case can be detached from wheel carriage by latch and bolt at either end.*

195. *Matsumoto shop chest* (chōb dansu). *Zelkova drawer and do faces, cypress. Ten single-acti locks and sliding-door lock use sa key.* Sao-tōshi *side carrying hand recessed into top frame. H. 105. x w. 92 x d. 42 cm. Mid-Me era. Tonami Wa-dansu Kenkyūka*

196. *Matsumoto shop chest* (chōba-dansu). *Zelkova face, cryptomeria. Lock plates with money-pouch motif. H. 99 x w. 85 x d. 36 cm. Late Meiji era. Tonami Wa-dansu Kenkyūkai.*

197. Hinged door unlatches by sliding center brace to left. Wire mesh for ventilation often backed with Japanese paper, which kept insects out.

198. Hikone chest-on-chest for kitchen area (mizuya kasane-dansu). *Zelkova drawer and door faces, cypress frame, and cryptomeria panels. H. 172 x w. 121 x d. 49 cm. Meiji era. Collection of Hasebeya, Tokyo.*

199. Kyoto small personal chest with decorative lacquer (maki-e temoto-dansu). *Black* tame-nuri *finish an brass hardware. H. 65.5 x w. 78 x d. 47 cm. Meiji era. Collection of Mr. John Gruber.*

200 201

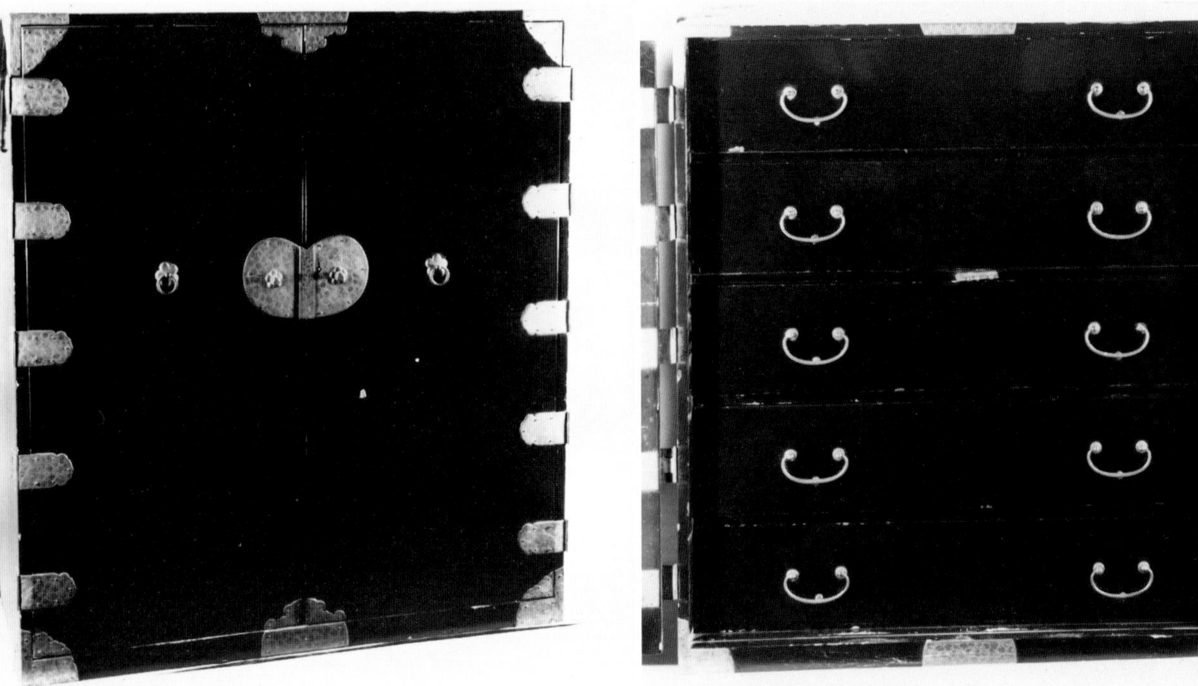

200. Kyoto clothing chest with large double doors (ōbiraki ishō-dansu). *Paulownia with black* tame-nu *finish. Chased brass hardware. H. 101 x w. 94 x d. 46 cm. Early Meiji era. Tonami Wa-dansu Kenkyūka*
201. Drawers relined with Japanese paper every year for added protection against mildew during the rainy seaso

202. *Sakai shop chest* (chōba-dansu). *Cypress face, cryptomeria body and drawer interiors. Early double-action locks. H. 95 x w. 91 x d. 39 cm. Late Edo Period. Tonami Wa-dansu Kenkyūkai.*

203 204

203. *Lower compartment for account books and documents. Inscription reads: "1849, May, Senzō, Sakai."*
204. *False, drop-fit molding conceals secret compartment.*

205. Merchant chest with large double doors (ōbiraki chō-dansu) *of zelkova from Kanto area. Three double-action locks; ones at top and bottom may have been false. H. 61* x *w. 53.5* x *d. 36 cm. Early Meiji era. Tonami Wa-dansu Kenkyūkai.*

206. Tokyo chest-on-chest for clothing (ishō kasane-dansu). *Paulownia with uneven finish resulting from deterioration of whetstone seal. H. 100* x *w. 94* x *d. 44 cm. Meiji era. Heineken Collection.*

207. *Tokyo chest-on-chest for clothing with double doors* (ryōbiraki ishō kasane-dansu). *Paulownia with persimmon-wood vertical jamb. Example of style popular in Tokyo from turn of century to Kanto earthquake in 1923. Upper section has three trays. H. 103.5 x w. 94 x d. 41.5 cm. 1898. Tokyo Furniture Museum.*

208. Three-section stacking chest for clothing (uwaoki tsuki ishō kasane-dansu). *Paulownia; cast-iron anodized hardware. Close, straight grain from careful quarter-sawing. H. 147 (43, 55, 49)* x *w. 91* x *d. 40 cm. Taishō era. Heineken Collection.*

09–10. *Recessed side car-ing handles protrude 1 cm bove top of each chest to ep them in place.*

211. *Four removable trays in center section.*

212. *Anodized factory-made drawer pulls combined handle and back plate in one unit recessed into drawer face.*

213. View from entrance foyer of Funaoka residence, Fukumitsu.

214. The Maedas of Fukumitsu having tea at the hearth (irori).

215. Tanimura residence, Toyama Prefecture.

216. Guest room of Watanabe residence, Toyam Prefecture.

Ishikawa

Wheeled chests from the Noto Peninsula at the north end of Ishikawa Prefecture are the only tansu for which decorative wood carving was used. This unique feature stems from Chinese influence, probably through the Korean peninsula. The carving, if present, always appears at both ends of the front horizontal supporting frame member in an ivy, or *karakusa,* motif. In numerous chests from the Noto area, the butt ends of both the front and back frame members are foliated without any carving on the front. It is most common to find a configuration of full-width drawers in the upper half of the chest secured by a vertical locking bar with sliding doors in the lower half. As is true of wheeled chests from all over Honshu, the appearance of wheel axles separate and below the frame members is an indication of greater age than chests where the axles have been tenoned into the frame. Zelkova is always the primary wood in a Noto tansu and usually the secondary wood as well. *Kijiro* lacquering of the entire chest was common, probably due to the availability of material and craftsmen from the local town of Wajima, a lacquer center.

Frame-and-panel tansu in the city of Kanazawa, located in the former Kaga fief, reveal the influence of house carpentry. The "stone-tatami" pattern is found on many stationary as well as wheeled merchant chests in combination with a single-action lock functioning through a vertical iron brace that secures both the upper and lower sets of sliding doors. Unfortunately, these detachable braces have often become lost, and chest owners do not understand how to restore the locking mechanism. Together with the "stone-tatami" sliding-door configuration, the vertical iron brace is a reliable indication of late Edo-period or Meiji-era origin from either Toyama or Ishikawa prefectures.

Concerning the inter-regional influence of design and technique between Ishikawa and neighboring areas, there is one structural feature that is occasionally found in merchant tansu from both Kanazawa city and the town of Tonami in Toyama Prefecture. Rather than being braced and tenoned into the supporting frame, wheels were inset into the two longest frame members, which had been carved out to receive them. The presence of angular brace plates to cover exposed tenons cannot be used to judge the quality of tansu from Ishikawa or tansu with similar detailing from the Etchū and Echizen areas. Generally, covered tenons indicate that a particular piece was the work of a tansu craftsman rather than a house carpenter.

Fukui

The town of Mikuni at the mouth of the Kuzuryū River was the most westerly of the three principal sea-chest production centers in the late Edo period and early Meiji era. Although there is some indication that sea-chest craftsmen were marginally involved with land-use tansu, there is much more conclusive evidence of an occupational crossover by cabinetmakers trained as family-altar makers.

As with family altars, Meiji-era personal tansu were designed to be set into alcoves. Therefore the face wood and finishing is often far superior to the materials chosen for the top and sides. It may be noted that personal chests from Mikuni with frame-and-panel construction, similar to most tansu from the Etchū and Echizen areas, rarely have other than face hardware except for unusual removable carrying handles inset into the upper frame members on both sides. Mortise-and-tenon joinery is consistent with personal and merchant tansu from neighboring prefectures, but in Fukui, Japanese white pine was used as a secondary wood, with zelkova as the face wood for better chests.

Personal tansu evolved from shop cabinetry with the new prosperity in the early Meiji era. At that time, a tradition of trousseau cabinetry for the bride to bring with her into her husband's home became established and has continued to the present, especially among farming families of the area. Mikuni tansu were commissioned as individual pieces, as pairs, and as chest-on-chests, both stationary and wheeled. As wheeled chest-on-chests for personal use, they are unique in Japan and are probably the tallest tansu ever produced, with a total height approaching two meters. The bat as a good-luck symbol is a recurring motif in cut hardware on many chests. With few exceptions, the upper section of Mikuni chest-on-chest tansu always has a set of sliding doors, neither slatted nor lockable. Finishing for the majority of examples does not differ from other lacquered Meiji tansu discussed so far; however, a small number of exceptional pieces reveal the sophisticated opaque-lacquering technique found predominantly in Kyoto chests.

The Mikuni merchant chest on wheels is very distinctive and representative of an indigenous style. Use of a vertical locking bar over two or three full-width drawers is a common feature but not completely reliable by itself for identification. Provenance can be established if the butt ends of the supporting front frame member are covered with an angular plate that extends at least half the distance between the ends of the frame and the axles. These plates were usually cut on the front edging in a scroll pattern. Presence of butt-end hardware and five closely grouped three-quarter-face hinges on a small door in the lower righthand corner are conclusive evidence of Mikuni origin. Zelkova should be expected for the primary frame and face, cypress or cryptomeria for secondary framing and panels, and paulownia for drawer interiors. A *kijiro* lacquer over a *bengara* stain was the preferred finish.

The Takefu area to the west produced wheeled chests that are only slightly different from those of Mikuni, principally being less deep, having some or all full-width drawers individually lockable, and having *kakute*-style drawer pulls instead of the *warabite* style prevalent in Mikuni. Wakasa at the extreme western end of the prefecture, nearest Kyoto, unfortunately did not develop an identifiable local style out of the varied range of quite unusual individual merchant wheeled chests designed and produced there in the late Edo period.

Nagano

Matsumoto, the prefectural capital and formerly the castle town of the daimyo, has been a commercial crossroads for central Honshu since the early Edo period. Zelkova, cypress, paulownia, and cryptomeria were readily available in the surrounding mountains, drawing wood craftsmen to guilds and workshops in the area. Initially shop tansu were an important status symbol, as in other prefectures. It was the local development of techniques for standardization and semi-mass production of hardware in the Meiji era that stimulated the growth of a tansu trade to other prefectures.

A small account chest is perhaps most representative because of the considerable number of these pieces made over a fifty-year period with little deviation in the structural configuration. Early Meiji examples show the influence of frame-and-panel tansu from the coast, most specifically the *zeni to-dana* chests of Niigata Prefecture. The *kakute* drawer pulls are of outstanding quality. The mounting of a pull directly into the lock plate of a small drawer in merchant tansu is unique to Matsumoto in the nineteenth century. Use of a broad staple directly under and parallel to the lock jamb plate together with lock-plate mounted pulls is a reliable indication of Matsumoto origin.

With the perfection of casting methods, the handmade *kakute* pulls were superceded by both *mokkō* and *warabite* styles, which could be purchased from a hardware maker's stock. The frame-and-panel structure disappeared toward the middle of Meiji in favor of the pegged-tenon, open-mortise corner box joint used for most personal tansu in other regions. In consort with these two changes, lock plates began to take on the shape of a tied money pouch chased on the entire surface; drawer-pull back plates for full-width drawers began to bear the openwork "four-diamonds" motif of Sado and Echigo, and the drawer corner hardware changed from an L shape to a tea-seedpod pattern without embossing.

Zelkova for the face wood continued to be favored well into the twentieth century. Secondary woods, however, alternated without any perceivable pattern between cypress and cryptomeria. In the late Meiji era, unfinished paulownia or cypress began to be used occasionally for drawer faces, perhaps to achieve a stronger visual contrast with the hardware. After the turn of the century, production reached its peak. Lock plates evolved into embossed circles covering the more advanced double-action spring mechanisms, which enabled the key to lock as well as unlock a drawer or compartment. Cutting and carving of the lock plate were eliminated in favor of embossing the entire round surface and rimming the circumference with a strip of brass. These characteristic lock plates are a reliable means of identification.

Matsumoto produced various tansu designs in the categories of personal and merchant cabinetry. By concentrating on the account chest, the prefecture's most important contribution to traditional tansu, we have perhaps implied a progression to commercial manufacture in this century through a single design. In fact, Edo- and Meiji-inspired chests were commissioned on an individual basis in Matsumoto and other centers of tansu craftsmanship well into the pre-war Shōwa era.

Shiga

The town of Hikone on Lake Biwa, near Kyoto, is associated with the largest tansu of nineteenth-century Japan. The Hikone *mizuya* were placed either in the kitchen or in an adjoining principal room. These chests were used for food and eating utensils. Initially they were made only in the vicinity of Hikone, but as their popularity grew, chests in the Hikone style were produced in numerous other locations between Nagoya and Kyoto.

Ostensibly there is little difference between Hikone style and Hikone *mizuya* chests. Face wood for drawers and door panels is almost always zelkova. Visible primary and secondary frame members were of cypress or zelkova, but less costly pine and cryptomeria were often used for the unexposed structure. Because of its large mass, the Hikone *mizuya* is always a chest-on-chest with the better examples having *hirute*-style drawer pulls. Many of the most interesting chests have a small compartment in the upper section behind either a hinged door or sliding doors covered by wire mesh, with the same function as the nineteenth-century American bread safe. Size was often determined by the tatami configuration of the main room in the house, often adjacent to the kitchen area. Whether the *mizuya* was used on the side of the wall facing the plank floor of the kitchen or the side facing the tatami-covered main room, it was backed against the same wall and was usually within an alcove determined by tatami size, approximately 186 cm long by 93 cm wide for Hikone. With a length of 186 or 372 cm for very large houses, the *mizuya* as a chest-on-chest single tansu or paired tansu provided considerable storage space rather like built-in Western furniture.

In a different functional category but rather similar in appearance, chest-on-chest tansu for bedding storage, from the Chūgoku area west of Osaka, are often confused with Hikone *mizuya*. These *yagu to-dana* always have at least one set of full-width sliding doors, a depth of over 80 cm in comparison with about 50 cm for Hikone chests, and side carrying handles one-third rather than half the distance from the front in order to compensate for the disproportionate weight caused by the zelkova face wood.

Kyoto

Kyoto has been the center of refined culture since the ninth century, when it was established as the capital. Continuing even after the political capital moved to Edo in the early seventeenth century, the manners, art, and architecture of the old capital quietly influenced Edo sensibilities. Indeed, Kyoto tansu, known for sophisticated lacquer and metalwork, were a popular status symbol.

The tansu as mobile cabinetry shows no significant developments after the Meiji Restoration. As could be expected, there was a substantial increase in production to satisfy the demand for the "Kyoto style." The degree to which the hardware was carved, the finish rubbed to an even sheen, or lacquer pictures painted over the case, was determined by how much the customer was willing to spend or, in twentieth century terms, by how much the market would bear. Fine technique was generally not compromised for the sake of lower cost until the 1930s. If a lower price was required, a different technique from a different craftsman was used, rather than requesting a highly skilled craftsman to function below the level of his ability.

A considerable proportion of Kyoto chests have brass brace and lock plates that are completely chased, indicating the pre-Edo influence of religious artifacts from China. Because the proportions of zinc and copper are different, Japanese brass was much more bronzelike than the bright yellow brass from the Asian continent. Drawer pulls, if not of brass, were often finished with the burnt-lacquer process known as *yaki-urushi*, over a vermilion *bengara* base, found extensively in Tsuruoka tansu. This technique gradually subordinated the use of brass in the early twentieth century.

In trying to establish provenance, hardware should be the primary consideration. Secondly, the opaque lacquering technique called *tame-nuri* is predominant, usually over a black base. Wood grain is rarely seen in Kyoto tansu except in the category of small personal chests or boxes for women. Men's clothing chests with a depth of over 50 cm were designed to hold the samurai ceremonial overgarment, or *kamishimo,* which should not be folded. In determining the age of a piece, the use of double-action locks is a reliable indicator of an age not older than late Edo; however, single-action locks continued to be made and used on tansu well into this century. Use of exposed side handles to facilitate carrying on a pole usually indicates construction before the twentieth century for large pieces or chest-on-chest tansu.

Osaka

Osaka is spoken of today just as it was in the early-Edo period; it is the merchant's town, the largest city, and the commercial center of western Japan. Perhaps partially because Osaka was a crossroads of commerce and popular culture, an indigenous tansu design did not appear until early in the twentieth century. Chests from every part of Japan can be found in Osaka and this has influenced the tansu made there. For this reason it is difficult to identify an Osaka style in either merchant or personal cabinetry from the Meiji era that has not been influenced by at least one of the regions described above.

The town of Sakai, the historical port for Osaka, did have a merchant tansu which, though found throughout all of the western prefectures, appears to have originated with the local wholesale merchants. Sakai reached its peak in the sixteenth century as the port for trade with Ming-dynasty China. At that time the power and independance of Sakai led a European observer to compare the system of self-government enjoyed there with that of Venice. Unfortunately for Sakai, the control of the local government by a few very wealthy merchants ran counter to the principle of strong central authority advocated by the sixteenth-century general Oda Nobunaga. In his campaign against monopolized interests separate from his own, he effectively broke the power of the city by punitive taxation. By the late-seventeenth century, embankments of the Yamato River leading to Osaka from the sea had been improved to a degree necessary to draw trade away from Sakai. This development, following on the closure of the country to foreign trade except through Dejima island in the far south of Japan, pressed Sakai away from the independent position it had once enjoyed.

The Sakai merchant tansu was used to store accounts and was usually kept on the raised area of the shop. Although the style originated in the late Edo period, it was most widely distributed and copied in the Meiji era. The cryptomeria case is most often in a four-part configuration of top drawer, upper sliding doors, middle drawer or drawers, and lower sliding doors. The hardware is always plain drawer pulls in the *warabite* style without back plates. The face wood of the high-quality chests was cypress, with cryptomeria for simpler pieces. If there are interior drawers, they are in the lower right-hand corner with the remaining open shelf space behind the two sliding-door pairs serving as storage space for accounting ledgers, or *daifuku-chō*. The lower sliding doors usually have thin horizontal slats of cypress over cryptomeria paneling. As with all traditional sliding doors, when lifted, the door will just clear the rail. With the lower sliding doors removed, the center molding is exposed. The face wood of this molding often has tight-fitting half-lapped tenons at both ends, rebated into the case. When pressed upward and lifted out, a secret compartment in the molding can be reached. A very similar merchant tansu was popular in the Tokyo area over the same period. However, the eastern version produced primarily in Tochigi Prefecture north of Tokyo was usually smaller, completely of paulownia wood, and incorporated only one pair of sliding doors in conjunction with a small-door compartment.

Tokyo

Throughout the Meiji era (1868–1912) and well into the Taishō era (1912–26), the personal chest-on-chest of paulownia with full-face double doors in the upper chest, dating from eighteenth century Edo, remained extremely popular with modification only in the size of the hardware. The internal four-drawer configuration in the door section became two full-width drawers in early Meiji and was further modified at the end of the nineteenth century to four or five full-width trays on horizontal runners without the dust-cover rail boards characteristic of all tansu until this time.

In the late-Edo period, there emerged a new style of personal chest-on-chest of paulownia wood. Overall proportions and size did not differ from the standard double-door Edo tansu; however, the upper chest consisted of two full-width lockable drawers. A compartment with a small door in the bottom right-hand corner of the lower chest, with either two or three inner drawers and a "privacy box," was characteristic of tansu popular in and around Tokyo in late Edo and early Meiji times. An identical lower section with the small-door compartment became, at the same time, the most desirable configuration for use with a traditional double-door upper chest. Indeed, when an example of a lower chest is seen without the original upper chest, it is usually impossible to determine if the missing half had double doors or drawers. One can only be certain that there was at one time an upper chest of equal size.

With the early Meiji era, craftsmen began to take advantage of the availability of precise cutting tools by cutting paulownia at a bevel for drawer faces and interiors in order to achieve a saving in materials. When viewed from above, a drawer had a thickness of 1.8 to 2.4 centimeters. By cutting at an angle from about one centimeter below the visible edge of the wood, thickness could be reduced by almost half, thereby allowing the craftsman to obtain two panels from a single board. This technique is rarely apparent unless specifically looked for. When found in tansu, it is often in combination with a similar cost-saving technique used for the top of both upper and lower chests. Generally, personal tansu of paulownia do not begin to evidence bevel cutting until the mid-1870s. Although beveling was used extensively, tansu for wealthy customers continued to be built with wood of an even thickness of up to three centimeters.

By 1890 the small-door compartment and single-action locks had been largely superceded by four full-width drawers of equal size with round locks of approximately twelve centimeters in diameter that could be both locked and unlocked by key. With the turn of the century and the end of the Meiji era in 1912, chest-on-chest styles continued relatively unchanged, a reduction in the size and quantity of hardware being the most prominent modification. The appearance of *gumpai*-style drawer pulls of iron or copper of uniform thickness and without horizontal back plates is a reliable indication of twentieth-century production probably in the Tokyo area as a personal chest-on-chest tansu.

CHAPTER FOUR

TAISHŌ ERA: MASS PRODUCTION

The new leaders of Japan after the restoration of the emperor were well-educated young pragmatists, acutely aware that the colonialist fervor of the Western nations could easily destroy the fragile structure of the feudal government left by the Tokugawa shogunate. One-sided commercial treaties forced upon China thirty years earlier were a frightening example. Although the trade treaty reached with the United States in 1858 and subsequent treaties with other major powers signed during the last ten years of the shogunate opened Japan to technology and overseas market opportunities especially for silk, the double standard inherent in the extra-territoriality that the Western nations insisted upon was seen as a dangerous imposition.

Accepting that Japan could not negotiate except from a position of parity, the Meiji-era government leaders began in 1868 to build their own westernized nation based upon Japanese principals. Great Britain became the model for government organization. The Napoleonic legal code was adopted. Military organization emulated a German model. Engineering followed from the Scots, who established Japan's first railroad in 1872. Hokkaido, the northernmost main island, became an agrarian image of Pennsylvania. By the end of the century, Japan had elevated itself to a position of respect theretofore never achieved by a non-Western nation. Japan had learned much in a short time, including the push and shove of regional power politics. The defeat of China on the Korean peninsula in 1895 and Russia in Manchuria in 1905 gave Japan a self-confidence by the end of the Meiji era, which continued to grow without restraint during the early Taishō era. During this time the West was involved in World War One. As an imperialist power at peace while its competitors were at war with each other, Japan enjoyed an unparalleled prosperity. The consolidation of private business interests to achieve political influence was especially pronounced at this time. The omnipresent military, steeped in Edo reminiscence, remained aloof from most commercialism. Significantly, their elitist attitude was enforced by their sole responsibility to the emperor. Japan's new national constitution promulgated in 1889 did not require the military to be accountable to the electorate. The industrialists who represented the zaibatsu cartels were primarily concerned with a stable raw-material supply and reliable markets. Their special interests were a stabilizing, conservative counter-influence to the military in a government increasingly democratic in appearance.

Several developments in tansu during the Taishō era were the result of trends in motion since the Meiji years. Three of these developments were particularly important in stimulating a return to a generalization of design, away from the regionalism that had persisted since the late-Edo period.

From the middle of the Meiji era there had been a gradual tendency, especially among people serving in the government bureaucracy, to adopt Western clothing, which was considered more convenient and efficient than traditional costume for daily use. The prestige resulting from the successes of Japan's Western-style warriors against the Chinese and the Russians accelerated this trend. As a natural consequence of this use of Western clothing and general westernization, tansu for personal use in the large cities began to become stationary furniture in function.

There was initially little modification in traditional design to indicate a change in use; however, the side carrying handles were gradually reduced to recessed hoops quite incapable of any serious function. The appearance of separate framed bases of five to seven centimeters in height in the very late nineteenth century for use under chest-on-chest pieces was for the practical positioning of tansu on tatami, which would need an air space between the chest and the mats in order to inhibit the growth of mold during the annual rainy season. Another change, particularly evident in Tokyo just prior to the 1920s, was the introduction of recessed drawer pulls, usually of iron and very similar in design to the pulls found on British campaign chests from the nineteenth century.

Expanding urban demand placed pressure on tansu craftsmen to seek economies in their scale of production. Specialization in labor was but one result of their need for greater efficiency. By adhering to a standard size, tansu siding could be pre-cut, planed, and glued at a rural mill with cheap labor, then sent on to the city to be assembled and individually fitted by a joiner, and finally finished by a craftsman specifically trained for that function. Such semi-manufacture with numerous variations did not replace the tansu maker, but permitted small groups of craftsmen-entrepreneurs to function as manufacturers with fixed costs, capital overheads, and inventory depreciation now to be taken into consideration.

National distribution might have logically been considered a predictable result from the introduction of manufacture in a Western national economy. In the case of Japan however, a maze of subtlely interconnected obligations and responsibilities based upon historical, social, and financial relationships hindered development of national distribution sixty years ago as it still does to some degree today. There was significant success in rationalizing distribution within the vertically integrated trading empires such as Mitsui where forests, mills, and retail outlets were under the influence of a central management. Unfortunately, it took a natural calamity to create a conducive climate for wide-scale experimentation with inter-regional tansu distribution.

On September 1, 1923, a massive earthquake and ensuing fire obliterated much of Tokyo and Yokohama, taking more than 130,000 lives. As with the Meireki fire of 1657, response from outside regions was immediate and indirectly stimulating to the national economy. Because the possessions of great numbers of people as well as the stock and productive capacities of local tansu craftsmen had been destroyed, great quantities of three-piece stacked tansu of paulownia wood in a new style popular in Osaka were sent in from the western provinces. The timely introduction of this *uwaoki-tsuki* chest combining face drawers, hinged double doors, and double sliding paneled doors in three stackable sections was very successful. There is no doubt that the good fortune of the few enterprises that perceived the needs of the distant Tokyo consumer market ameliorated the fear of failure felt by many provincial tansu craftsmen. The years following the Kantō earthquake witnessed a rapid cross-fertilization of local tansu styles due to the maturity of nationwide distribution. Although tansu did not become national furniture in the minds of most Japanese, they did offer excellent commercial marketing potential because of their long association with the bride's trousseau. On the basis of tradition, convenience, and use, tansu gradually passed from the craftsman to the manufacturer, continuing to meet cultural and practical needs. In this way, tansu continue in the curious balance between art and commercial expediency that pervades many facets of Japan.

PART TWO

TECHNIQUES

CHAPTER FIVE

WOOD

The Japanese islands run in a northeast-southwest tangent north of the Tropic of Cancer; seasons are distinct and there is a great variety of vegetation. Japan is also fortunate to have vast mountain forests where trees of the same species today as in the eighth century grow in profusion. In contrast to China, where a scarcity of hardwoods stimulated considerable trade from Malaysia, Burma, Thailand, India, and the Celebes during periods of colonialism in the T'ang dynasty, the Japanese aristocracy relied almost exclusively upon indigenous woods. At the Shōsō-in, an imperial storehouse of the Nara period, there are very few small objects in which imported woods have a structural function, most of these being musical instruments and games. None of the cabinetry uses imported wood structurally. However, for marquetry, compartment liners, or decorative facing, numerous sub-species of sandalwood, ebony, rosewood, betel palm, camphorwood and aloewood were incorporated by Japanese Nara-period craftsmen.

A classification of Japanese cabinetry woods into two categories of evergreen and broad-leaved trees is more accurate than a reference to softwoods and hardwoods. For primary structure, cryptomeria and Japanese cypress are most common among the evergreens; zelkova, chestnut, and paulownia are most prominent among broad-leaved varieties.

Seasonal variances, especially in northeast Honshu, are evident in the spring and autumn sapwood-growth characteristics of trees in both categories. Partially in consideration of growth variation but also the functional demand each tree's timber must serve, a log was quarter-sawn along the radial longitudinal surface in order to reveal a straight grain for maximum strength, or flat-sawn along the tangential surface to bring out the beauty and spirit of the wood.

In this consideration of cabinetry, structural woods for the case, exposed frame members, and drawers will be considered as primary. Indigenous woods for paneling, decorative facing, and interior framing will be called secondary woods. This simplification for convenience is not however without exceptions and additions, which though rare are occasionally found in pre-Edo and late-Meiji pieces.

CRYPTOMERIA (*sugi; Cryptomeria japonica* D. Don) The most prevalent evergreen on Honshu, cryptomeria is only rarely found outside Japan. With few exceptions, secured-case tansu for personal use in which either zelkova or chestnut have been used for the drawer face woods rely upon cryptomeria for the case top, sides, back, and drawer sides, back, and flooring. The drawer interior wood is most always left natural and may still emit a characteristic piquant aroma even after many generations of use. These trees also figure in Japanese history. The magnificent cryptomeria that line the ancient approach road to the Tokugawa Ieyasu mausoleum in Nikkō were the gift of an impoverished provincial samurai lord. After three hundred years, his cryptomeria thrive with heights approaching sixty meters. The sapwood is white with a slightly pinkish hue when taken from a deep snowfall area. Heartwood can be as red as American redwood.

JAPANESE CHESTNUT (*kuri; Castanea crenata* Sieb. et Zucc.) Because the density of .53 is not appreciably different and the grain rather similar to zelkova, though without feathery grain shadow, chestnut was often chosen as an economical alternative, especially for drawer face wood in Meiji-era tansu. To the unpracticed eye, it is very difficult to discern a difference under a finish. A reliable double check is to examine the inner unfinished drawer face. If zelkova has been used, the wood will have a honey cast with grain lines a brownish red. Chestnut is visibly gray in hue with the vein color much less distinct.

JAPANESE CYPRESS (*hinoki; Chamaecyparis obtusa* Sieb. et Zucc.) In the evergreen category, Japanese cypress is the most stable wood, traditionally preferred as the base for opaque lacquer. It is drier and more finely grained than the North American species, closest in character to Port Oreford cedar. The aroma of the raw wood is quite distinctive, more pungent than cryptomeria and of longer duration. Trees from the Kiso valley in Gifu Prefecture are particularly prized for the clarity, strength, and aroma of the timber that has for centuries been shaped by coopers into the best Japanese bathtubs.

PAULOWNIA (*kiri; Paulownia tomentosa* Steu.) Although a broadleaf tree, paulownia is as light in weight as fir with a density of only

.35. It is also exceptionally fast-growing, attaining a height of seven meters in only three to four years. The wood is both stable and strong with an excellent expansion-contraction ratio under atmospheric change. The unique ability of paulownia to flex made it especially desirable for drawer and compartment interiors. Even though favored with a consistently straight grain and high percentage of clear sapwood, nuance in quality difference has kept paulownia, since the mid-Edo period, at a price level comparable to oak in England or black walnut in the United States. Korea, China (Chinese *kiri* is *Paulownia fortunci*), and North America now farm paulownia for export to Japan; however, because their wood tends to have various undesirable hues and a wandering grain, it is used principally for veneered plywood.

PINE (*Ezo matsu; Picea jezoensis* Sieb. et Zucc.) Perhaps because the sapwood resin continued to be secreted even after long periods of air drying, pine was generally not favored as a tansu wood. The only noteworthy exceptions were among late-Edo and early-Meiji farmer's *mizuya* and wheeled chests from Iwate and Yamagata prefectures, where zelkova or chestnut, used for the front stiles, door frames, and face rails, was occasionally substituted with pine for the less exposed sides and back. A similar practice is evident in many personal-use tansu from Fukui Prefecture made during the second half of the Meiji era.

ZELKOVA (*keyaki; Zelkova serrata* Makino) Among the broad-leaf cabinet woods, zelkova is the most dense at .68 and prized for its grain strength and warm amber color. Although a member of the elm family and even referred to as Japanese gray-bark saw-tooth elm in North America, the delicate shading of the zelkova flat-sawn grain is more analogous to the leguminous hardwoods found in the fine furniture of Ming-dynasty China.

There were a large number of secondary woods with uses varying according to period, purpose, and region. In particular, framed door panels of prized woods for *temoto* chests and shelved display stands were sought by the upper classes. Three trees in this category have been especially popular since the eighth century:

MULBERRY AND PAPER MULBERRY (*kuwa; Morus bombycis* Koidz. and *kōzo; Broussonetia Kazinoki* Sieb.) Leaves of the *Morus bombycis* species were the traditional food for commercially raised silkworms.

PERSIMMON (*kaki; Diospyros kaki* Thunb.) A rare wood in the ebony family. The presence of orange, yellow, or brown streaks in the black surface has been particularly valued and given the name *kurogaki*, literally black persimmon. At the Shōsō-in in Nara, the double-sided cabinet known historically as *kurogaki ryōmen zushi* is the earliest surviving example of this wood used in cabinetry.

SANDALWOOD (*wabyakudan; Santalum album* Linn.) Available from a small group of islands off the coast of Honshu, indigenous sandalwood is equally as aromatic as South Asian varieties. Although incorporated occasionally for special use in cabinetry, it was more extensively used for carving.

Woods of secondary use, favored by both samurai and merchant, include several trees that are also respected in Europe and North America:

MAGNOLIA (*hō; Magnolia obovata* Thunb.) As with Japanese cypress, this wood is stable, fine-grained, and an excellent base material for urushi, Japanese lacquer.

FIR (*momi*; *Abies firma* Sieb. et Zucc.) In the pinaceous family and related to North American fir, this wood can be found in tansu from very isolated provinces as an alternative to cryptomeria or pine, but only as paneling and never in a structural capacity.

YEW (*ichii; Taxus cuspidata* Sieb. et Zucc.) Within the same taxaceous family, nutmeg wood was used similarly.

CHAPTER SIX

JOINERY

The fundamentals of Japanese cabinetry are consistent with the principles underlying traditional Japanese architecture: both manifest an explicit appreciation of nature and the inherent flexibility of wood. In contrast to European cabinetry, few rigid joints have been employed. Changes in humidity according to the season were an acknowledged variable recognized by skilled craftsmen in many countries. Problems of lateral and vertical stress in an earthquake, cyclone, or typhoon were of equal concern to the Japanese. This resulted in wooden buildings and cabinetry dependent upon joints to act as shock absorbers.

Perhaps more in Japan than in any other country, the condition of a wood craftsman's tools reflects his professional abilities. Steel blades are always honed after use, not with one stone but with several in a progression according to fineness. It is not unusual for the average craftsman to spend two out of every eight hours of work in sharpening, always by hand and in a kneeling position for maximum strength and control. Saws are an exception to this rule. Because the angle of the saw teeth is essential to cutting accuracy, saw blades are usually handed over to professionals for feather filing.

The sketch (Fig. 225) by the eminent nineteenth century physician and botanist Philipp Franz von Siebold is an accurate rendering of the categories of woodworking tools in use in the 1840s for all stages, from the rough-cut log to the finished surface. Japanese saws differ from their Western counterparts principally in being drawn toward the body rather than being pushed away. Beams in Hōryū-ji, a temple in Nara founded in A.D. 607, indicate the use of a crosscut saw. The kerf from an ancient blade indicates that the saw was approximately 5 mm thick, quite the same as today. Although there is archaeological evidence that crosscut (*yokobiki*) saws, later refined to *dozukibiki* saws for crosscutting tenon shoulders, were in use as early as the fourth century, tangential ripping was not possible until the introduction of the two-man saw (*oga*) in the Muromachi period (1336–1568). The one-man (*kobiki*) saw came into use in the Edo period and is well documented by Japan's famous celebrant of the human condition, the printmaker Hokusai.

The Japanese rarely pinned tansu joinery with iron; instead, various kinds of gimlets were used to drill holes for the multitude of wooden pegs needed to secure panels and lock tenons. These pegs were made of *utsugi* wood (*Deutzia crenata* Sieb. et Zucc.). Possibly the earliest woodworking tool in many cultures, the adze was used to work timber even before saws were developed. The presence of a long-handled version of this ancient tool in the von Siebold sketch might be misleading in that its use was limited by this late date to the shaping of logs into structural beams. More importantly, the adze gave rise to a broad range of chisels that enabled the cabinetmaker and the finishing carpenter not only to cut accurate joints but also to shape the wood as if by a molding plane with infinite adjustments.

The *sumi-tsubo,* or line-marking gauge, in which a cotton cord on a spool can be drawn through cotton or silk floss soaked with *sumi* ink and then snapped to mark a straight line much as the Western chalk line is used, was necessary to cut logs into boards of an even thickness. This tool became something of a status symbol in the early Meiji era, the zelkova-wood body frequently being carved with a tortoise and crane to invite a long and happy life.

Introduction of the plane from the Asian continent in the sixteenth century was a significant development. Prior to this time, Japanese cabinetmakers had relied upon chisels and *tokusa* reed, called Dutch scouring reed in Europe, to smooth wood surfaces. The plane with its adjustable blade eventually made it possible to finish a surface to a nearly perfect level with a succession of progressively finer blades. The finishing plane (*nimai-ganna*) with two blades is capable of very thin cuts of .02 to .025 mm in skilled hands. Whereas Western planes are pressed away from the body, Japanese planes are drawn toward the craftsman. The wood mallet illustrated by Dr. von Siebold was essential to seat tenons and to adjust the degree of exposed blade on planes.

Not pictured, but applicable to the traditional techniques of a cabinetmaker, the *kebiki,* a bladed gauge for marking parallel lines to the edges and ends of boards, is the last of the categories of tools that a craftsman would need to have at hand. There are other tools for very specific functions that were popular regionally. Some of them, such as the indigenous inshaves used by house-carpenters-cum-tansu-makers of the Echizen area, are quite fascinating, but their limited regional use precludes their consideration here.

The range of joints employed by tansu craftsmen was not dissimilar to those found in cabinetry around the world. It is in examining the preference for one particular type of joint at the expense of another that a distinctly Japanese conception of joinery becomes recognizable. Before considering several representative joints in the general categories of parallel, mortise and tenon, miter, housed, butt, and clamping, it may serve for a better understanding to begin with a few observations regarding the Japanese craftsman's approach to the materials:

1 The grain of the wood must be respected. Wherever possible, the grain must be in harmony by either book-matching a log, as was done for the eighth century *zushi* cabinet at Shōsō-in by cutting drawer faces from a single board with flat-sawn grain.

2 Tansu joints were intended to be functional without detracting from the chest's total appearance. There was no attempt to have them appear decorative through excessive complexity. If a joint is hidden, the purpose was to create a flush surface without exposing a joint's butt end grain so that an opaque lacquer finish could be more perfectly applied. Secret joints are most common in tea-utensil shelves and round-cornered tea chests made in the twentieth century.

3 Metal nails were not used to pin the tansu case or drawers. Handmade square-shank iron nails for attaching iron hardware are common to all tansu except lacquered pieces with chased brass or copper hardware. If a nail is used structurally, it is quite certainly a repair.

4 No attempt was made to disguise one wood by staining it to resemble a more desirable wood.

5 Panels in frame-structured tansu were not floated as in Chinese cabinetry. However, the "mirror-board" panels of many framed sliding doors are not only floating but removable, especially if the board panel is a single piece of wood.

The parallel edge joint is perhaps the most common of all joints used in tansu. In that wide boards were considered unstable unless very

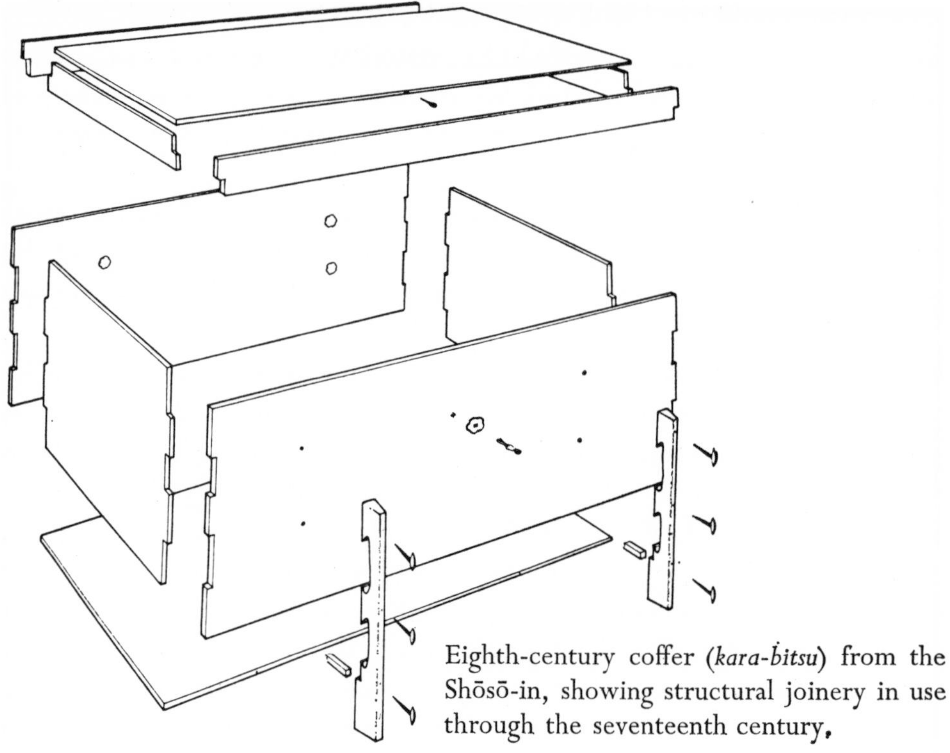

Eighth-century coffer (*kara-bitsu*) from the Shōsō-in, showing structural joinery in use through the seventeenth century.

thick, secured-case tansu usually had tops made of two boards and sides made of three boards. Drawer flooring could be up to ten boards; the back of the case could be five to seven. Although parallel connections were normally glued and rubbed for long boards so that the glue would penetrate into the wood pores, craftsmen knew that shock and atmosphere could eventually break even the best bond. As a precaution consistent with the need for maximum flexibility, "slip-feather" bamboo dowels were inserted before clamping the joint, with a spacing of twenty to thirty centimeters between dowels.

The halved joint in which a rabbet or lengthwise groove has been cut to a half depth in each of the two woods to be joined is most commonly found in frame-and-panel tansu for the horizontal rails. It was often used for the vertical or horizontal rails over the removable panels of sliding doors in both stationary and wheeled frame-and-panel tansu as well.

As the parallel edge joint was the most prevalent, the mortise-and-

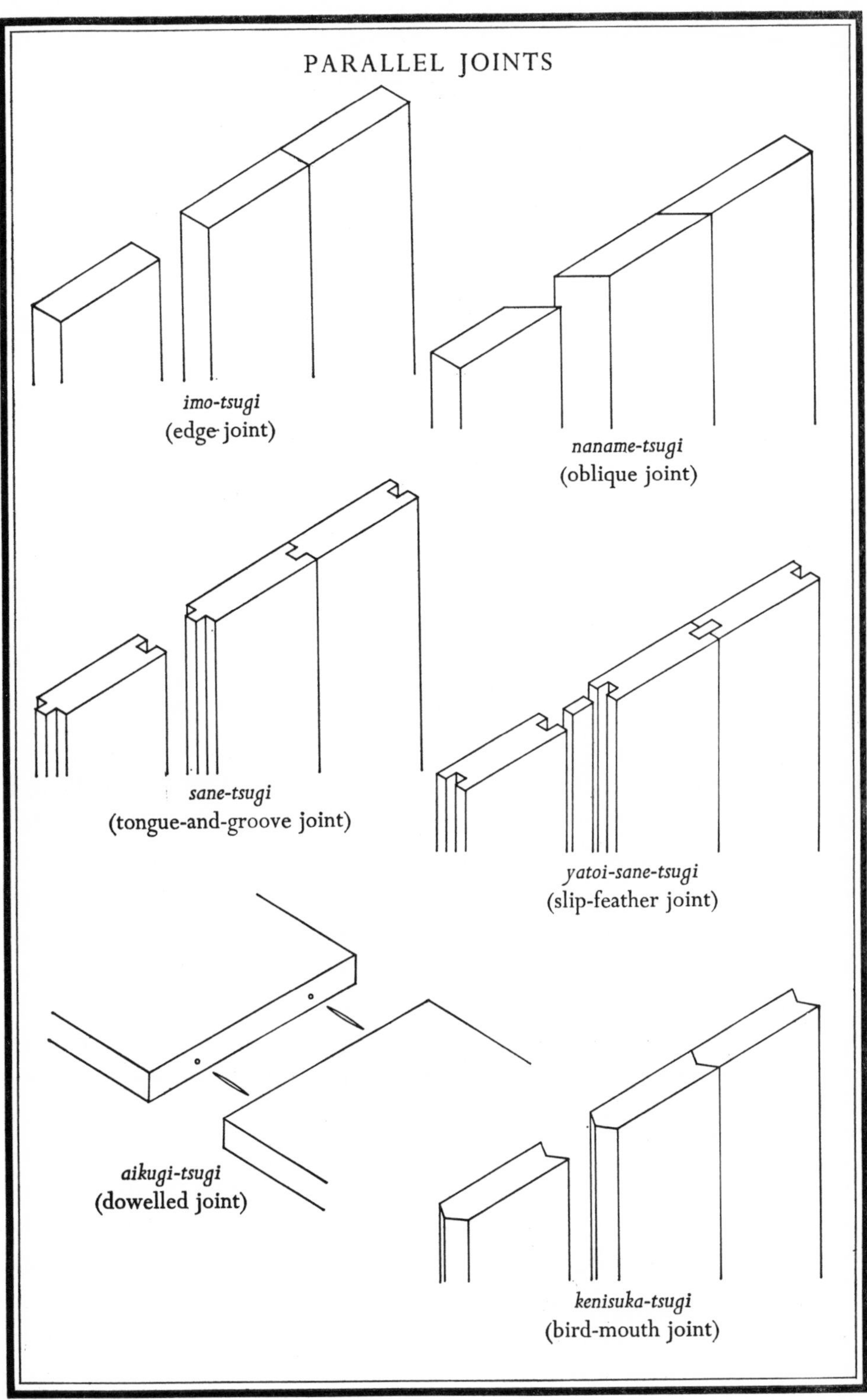
PARALLEL JOINTS
imo-tsugi
(edge joint)
naname-tsugi
(oblique joint)
sane-tsugi
(tongue-and-groove joint)
yatoi-sane-tsugi
(slip-feather joint)
aikugi-tsugi
(dowelled joint)
kenisuka-tsugi
(bird-mouth joint)

MORTISE-AND-TENON JOINTS—I

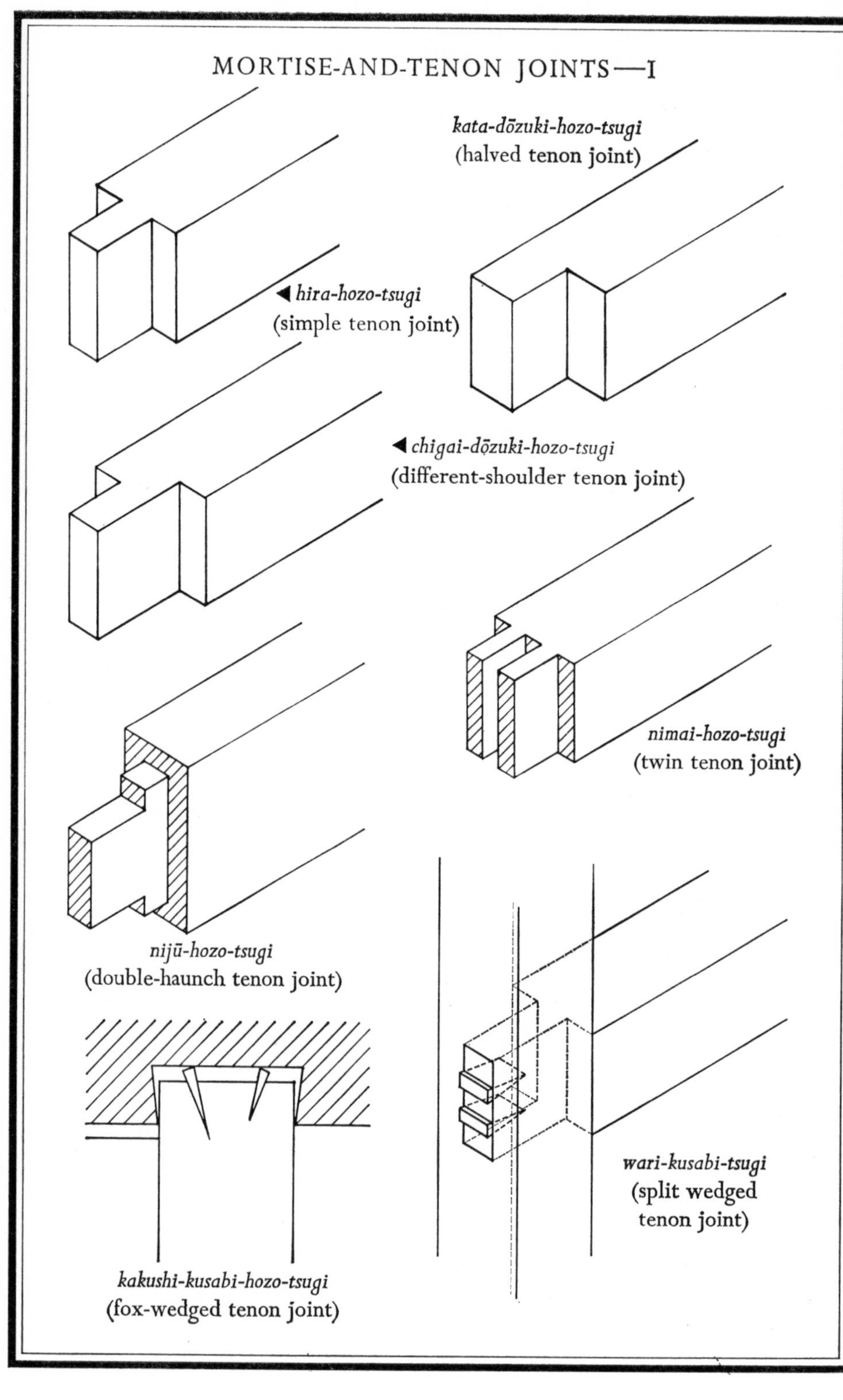
kata-dōzuki-hozo-tsugi
(halved tenon joint)
◀ *hira-hozo-tsugi*
(simple tenon joint)
◀ *chigai-dōzuki-hozo-tsugi*
(different-shoulder tenon joint)
nimai-hozo-tsugi
(twin tenon joint)
nijū-hozo-tsugi
(double-haunch tenon joint)
wari-kusabi-tsugi
(split wedged tenon joint)
kakushi-kusabi-hozo-tsugi
(fox-wedged tenon joint)

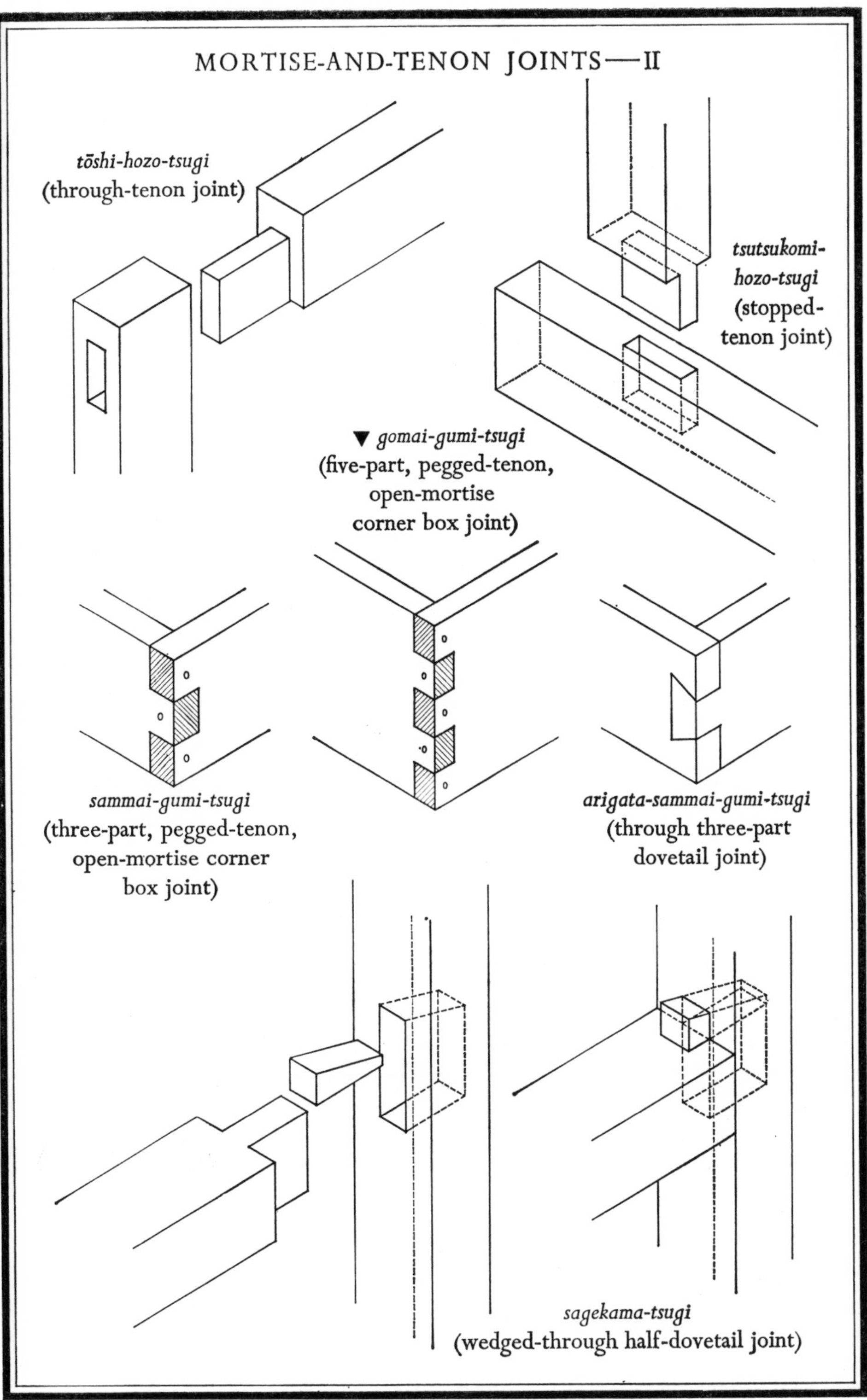
MORTISE-AND-TENON JOINTS—II
tōshi-hozo-tsugi
(through-tenon joint)
tsutsukomi-hozo-tsugi
(stopped-tenon joint)
▼ *gomai-gumi-tsugi*
(five-part, pegged-tenon, open-mortise corner box joint)
sammai-gumi-tsugi
(three-part, pegged-tenon, open-mortise corner box joint)
arigata-sammai-gumi-tsugi
(through three-part dovetail joint)
sagekama-tsugi
(wedged-through half-dovetail joint)

LAP JOINTS

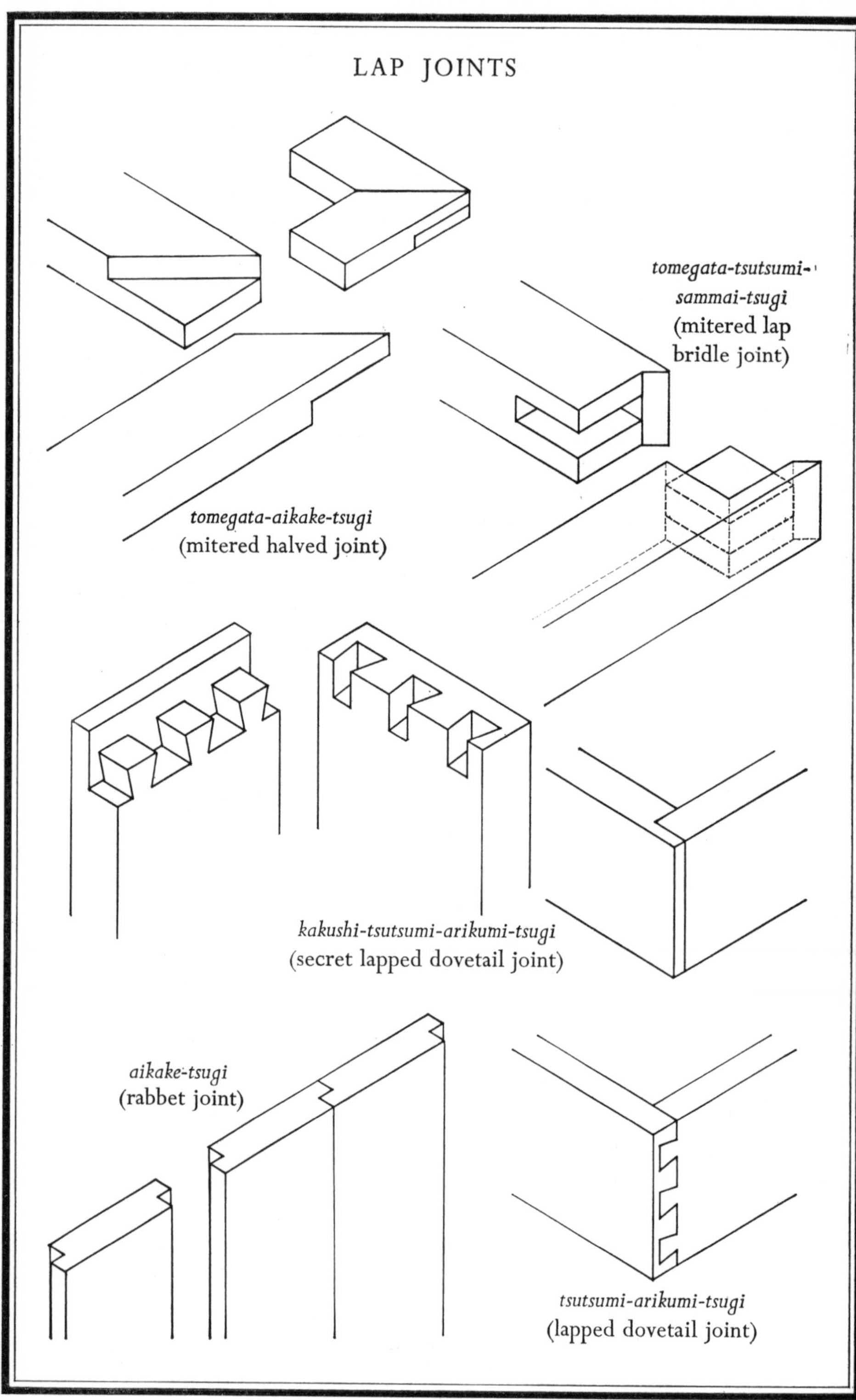

tomegata-tsutsumi-sammai-tsugi
(mitered lap bridle joint)

tomegata-aikake-tsugi
(mitered halved joint)

kakushi-tsutsumi-arikumi-tsugi
(secret lapped dovetail joint)

aikake-tsugi
(rabbet joint)

tsutsumi-arikumi-tsugi
(lapped dovetail joint)

BUTT JOINTS

sumi-uchitsuke-tsugi
(plain butt joint)

tsutsumi-uchitsuke-tsugi
(stopped butt joint)

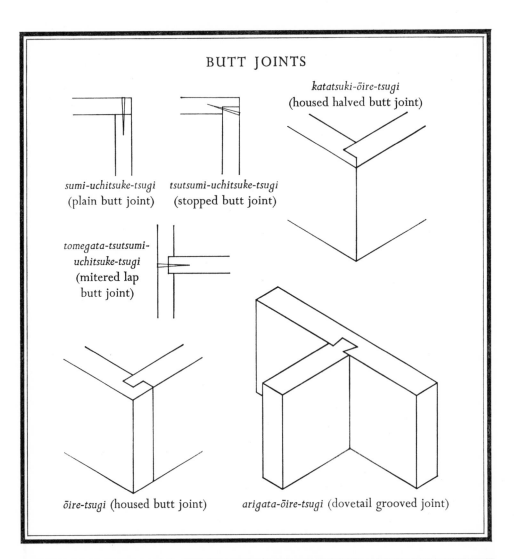

katatsuki-ōire-tsugi
(housed halved butt joint)

tomegata-tsutsumi-uchitsuke-tsugi
(mitered lap butt joint)

ōire-tsugi (housed butt joint)

arigata-ōire-tsugi (dovetail grooved joint)

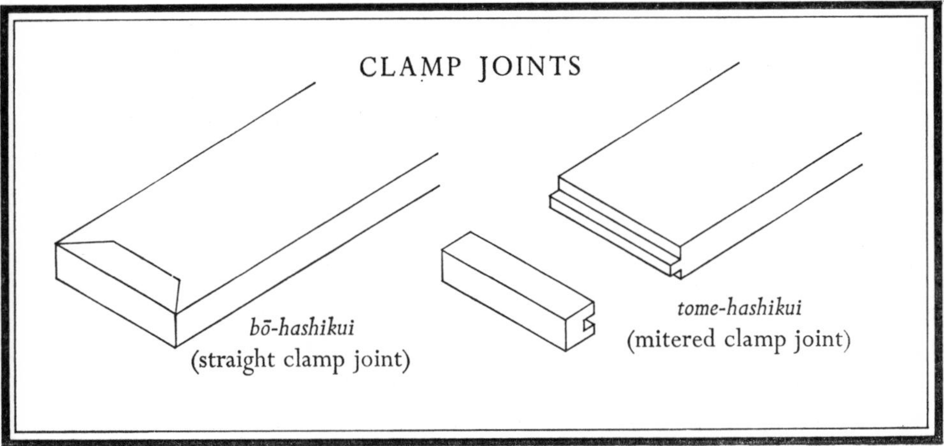

MITERED JOINTS

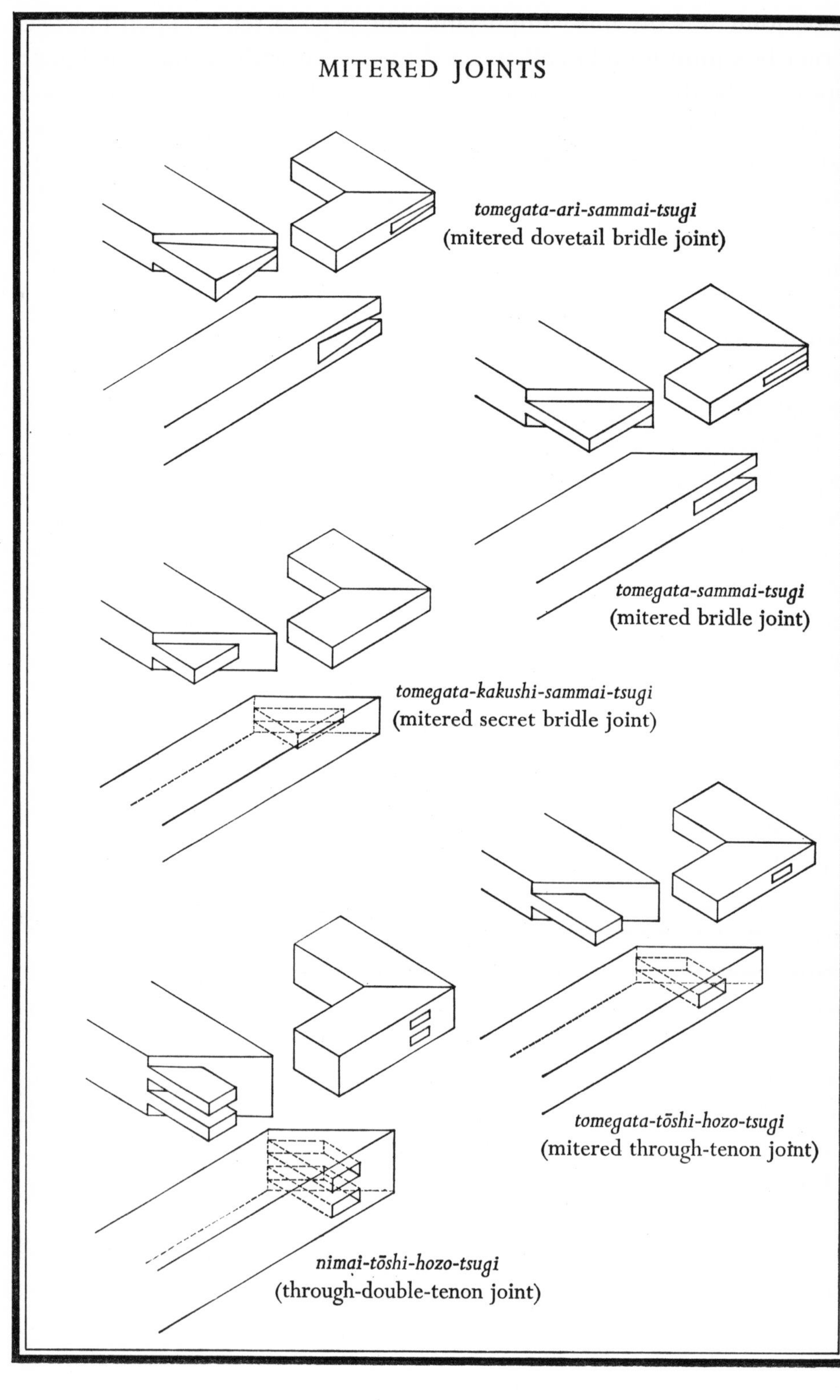

tomegata-ari-sammai-tsugi
(mitered dovetail bridle joint)

tomegata-sammai-tsugi
(mitered bridle joint)

tomegata-kakushi-sammai-tsugi
(mitered secret bridle joint)

tomegata-tōshi-hozo-tsugi
(mitered through-tenon joint)

nimai-tōshi-hozo-tsugi
(through-double-tenon joint)

tenon joint was the most important. The pegged-tenon, open-mortise, corner box joint found in all secured-case tansu with visible wood grain appears to be distinctly Japanese and is in evidence on numerous pieces of seventh and eighth century cabinetry at the Shōsō-in. In the frame-and-panel structure, tansu made by house carpenters from the Japan Sea coast tended to favor the full mortise and through tenon. Examples from professional tansu craftsmen often combine the wedged through tenon with the more sophisticated fox-wedged blind tenon, which has been used in Japan for at least 1,200 years. It is interesting and perhaps significant to the frame structure that Japanese through tenons could be locked with as many as eight key wedges. The wedged through haunched tenon with double shoulders became by the middle of the Meiji era the preferred joint for securing the juncture of three perpendicular rails in frame-and-panel tansu, especially in Yamagata Prefecture.

The full miter was not particularly common in Japanese cabinetry until the late Meiji era. Mitering in corner joinery for tansu is most frequently seen in the connecting of the frame members for small sliding doors in which the mirror-board panel is not removable and no covering rails are present. The mitered lap-butt joint, found primarily on small pieces of high craftsmanship for the samurai class and aristocracy, may be considered obscure in tansu; however, this joint has some significance in this presentation since it is represented in cabinetry at the Shōsō-in.

The housed joint was used primarily for shelf boards that ran from side to side parallel to the face and functioned as drawer rails. Most usually, the shelf board for a full-width drawer was three full-width parallel boards joined with dowels and glue, housed as a straight butt or dovetailed and stopped five to ten centimeters from the face of the tansu. The housed shelf board was then further secured by a row of three long pegs inserted through the sides of the chest. It is interesting to note that in North America, early Shaker chests also used through shelf boards, called "dust boards" or "dust panels."

Tansu craftsmen believed that the butt joint, if correctly pegged, was the most effective way to build a flexible drawer. With few exceptions, the drawer face and drawer sides were so joined, with the side board stopped into the face wood rebated to receive it. The drawer backboard and sides were usually joined by a plain pegged butt; however, there are numerous examples of both two- and three-part pegged-tenon, open-mortise construction here.

The last representative joinery category is well known in Western cabinetry as the tenoned and mitered clamp, used for large table tops before the introduction of plywood to prevent the longitudinal movement of parallel joined boards. This "breadboard" end, as it is often called in North America, has been in use in Japan since at least the eighth century, specifically for doors of all sizes. In tansu, doors on hinges and flush-faced sliding doors were invariably constructed in three parts with the top and bottom parts functioning as a mitered clamp on the central part. In very late tansu, straight clamps joined by tongue and groove into the center section began to be used occasionally.

The foremost considerations implicit in tansu construction were mobility and flexibility. Just as a Japanese wooden house incorporated flexible joinery and rooms for multiple functions, the tansu likewise served its owner only rarely as stationary furniture capable of obstructing movement. Most frequently, tansu were convenient mobile storage to be kept in a detached storehouse or storage room within the main house, inside a sliding-door closet, or set into a room alcove.

Frame-and-panel tansu, if not on wheels, are often mistaken for the Japanese equivalent of the Western breakfront or buffet. Although there are parallels in function, the "horn handle" overhanging structure of the exposed rails shows that these chests are mobile, and it thus establishes such cabinetry as the Hikone *mizuya* as true tansu, with or without iron side handles. It is a further unfortunate misconception that there are numerous similarities in the structuring and woods of Chinese and Japanese cabinetry. Although the eighth century Japanese aristocracy admired T'ang culture, there is no free-standing cabinetry in the Shōsō-in that indicates other than Japanese origin through either primary wood or structural joinery. In terms of design, however, the famous zelkova cabinet does indicate Chinese influence in the base and in the use of a movable mullion functioning as a detachable jamb for paired doors, well documented in *Chinese Domestic Furniture* by the late Dr. Gustav Ecke. Beginning before the introduction of the tea-ceremony culture, shelves for utensils exhibited a recognizable influence from China continuing well into the twentieth century.

As mentioned previously, panels were not floated between frame members with the exception of some mirror-board panels in sliding doors. The reason for this was two-fold. First, pinning of the frame and panels with soft, well-dried wooden pegs assured flexibility. Secondly, the grain of the panels, usually of cryptomeria, intentionally ran perpendicular to the grain of the covering rails, thereby creating a control over any tendency of the wood to move.

Construction of the carriage frame for wheeled chests is a reliable indicator of age. With very few exceptions, if the wheel axle is a separate member with the butt ends exposed under the front and back supporting rails, the chest is from the Edo period, probably before 1850. If the axle is tenoned into the rails, origin during the Meiji era is indicated. Generally speaking, the use of a through tenon covered by protective hardware for axles implies greater age than a blind tenon housed into the rails.

Secured-case cabinetry enjoys an ancient origin, as the schematic drawing of the legged coffer from the Shōsō-in testifies. The principal differences between this eighth century coffer and the seventeenth century *nagamochi* lie in the use of iron pins to secure legs to the case and an early preference for one solid board for each of the six sides. Certainly, this continuity over nine hundred years is remarkable.

Construction in the secured-case style required approximately four hundred *utsugi*-wood pegs for a personal-use chest-on-chest tansu. The *utsugi*-wood pegs had to be thoroughly dry before being dipped in rice paste and inserted into holes drilled by a gimlet. Peg lengths in typical tansu are as follows: 106 mm for the case; 85 mm for shelf boards and inner stiles; 67 mm for drawer sides and back; 55 mm for drawer flooring and case back; and 32 mm for small inner drawers. It is widely believed that these exposed pegs were bamboo. In fact, bamboo pegs were only used for the dowels in parallel joint connections. If used for an exposed surface, the hard bamboo would chip the blade of a craftsman's finishing plane. Another common misconception is that animal glue was not used in tansu construction. Although it is true that rice paste (*sokui*) was used for the exposed joints because an excess could be easily cleaned off, animal glue (*nikawa*) was preferred for internal blind joinery.

Drawer construction, especially for secured-case structures, was rather unique. Instead of drawer rails, as found in most cabinetry, the Japanese preferred a shelf cover running from one side of the tansu to the other on which the drawer could rest. Drawers of better tansu were constructed with an imperceptible bevel in height running downwards from the face to the back. As the drawer closed, height clearance was progressively reduced, thereby trapping air inside the chest. Cuts at the back of each shelf board allowed the trapped air to pass from the closing drawer to one already closed, consequently forcing the other drawer to open slightly, usually with a pleasant whistling sound. The subtlety of this phenomenon is distinctly Japanese, but widely appreciated by many who recognize fine craftsmanship.

By the late Meiji era there was a growing tendency to back a hardwood, flat-sawn drawer or door facing with an equally thick, straight-grain board of the same wood for strength. These laminations were not necessarily cost saving, but were rather a conservative approach to wood with unpredictable characteristics. In flush-faced doors, whether hinged or rabbeted, lack of an exposed clamp joint, either mitered or straight, indicates the use of a lamination probably in the twentieth century.

Tansu, especially after the Edo period, usually have drawer flooring of parallel boards perpendicular to the drawer face, which extends beyond the drawer backboard as a stop. This consideration was intended to allow for an easy adjustment should the flooring expand in a longitudinal direction after the chest was finished. In North America, this technique was also employed by the Shakers.

Perhaps one of the most enjoyable aspects of tansu for the collector is the secret compartment which is sometimes present. Usually incorporated within a small-door compartment, these secret compartments can be structured as boxes behind an inner drawer, a false drawer floor, a false back panel behind a short inner drawer, or a removable hollow inner stile. The purpose was always related to the function of the tansu. In merchant chests, secret compartments were for money and important notes of obligation. For personal tansu, compartments are most often simple boxes behind a short inner drawer intended for private papers or some personal mementos.

CHAPTER SEVEN

METALWORK

When tansu are seen through Western eyes that are familiar with and receptive to decorative embellishment, the apparently excessive use of hardware seems to be more visual than functional, as is the case with Korean furniture. Although excesses unrelated to function are occasionally evident, particularly in urban pieces produced since the late nineteenth century and intended to reflect the owner's status, there was for the most part a direct correlation between function and the placement of hardware on tansu.

The introduction of Buddhism from the Asian continent in the mid-sixth century brought with it various religious accoutrements that incorporated both bronze and brass. As protective plating on the corners of altar tables, scroll rails, and boxes for artifacts, brass was the preferred material in Japan just as it had been in China. Brass could be fashioned into very thin sheets and worked easily with line carving and chasing at a low cost in comparison with gold; it thus became popular among the Heian aristocracy for use on a range of secular furnishings. This early, positive association with privilege and elegance continued to the end of the Edo period among samurai families, especially in or adjacent to Kyoto. With the Meiji era and new prosperity, some exploitation of such an elegant image was inevitable, resulting in the excessive use of nonfunctional brass plating on all manner of cabinetry. Perhaps because it is fabricated rather than being the recognizable extension of a natural state, brass was never used on a broad scale in Japanese society and continued to be considered a "foreign" material.

Copper, on the other hand, has persisted as a desirable metal for boxes, small tansu, and peddler's portable cabinetry since the mid-Edo period. Although often confused by the unfamiliar eye with brass because of patination, copper (*akagane* or *dō* in Japanese) will usually reveal a slight reddish cast along the edge. In addition, most brass hardware was subjected to considerably more fine line engraving and chasing than copper.

Iron sheeting, the traditional material used in Japanese hardware, had to be pounded out from ingots until barely one hundred years ago. This laborious process resulted in hardware that was uneven in thickness, rusted easily, and was expensive to make. Toward the middle of the Meiji era, a factory was established in the town of Kamaishi in northern Honshu to produce sheets using a pressing method. The advantages of the mechanical process were many: even thickness, a hard, smooth surface, more corrosion resistance, lower cost, and, for the first time, iron sheeting thin enough to be cut with shears rather than

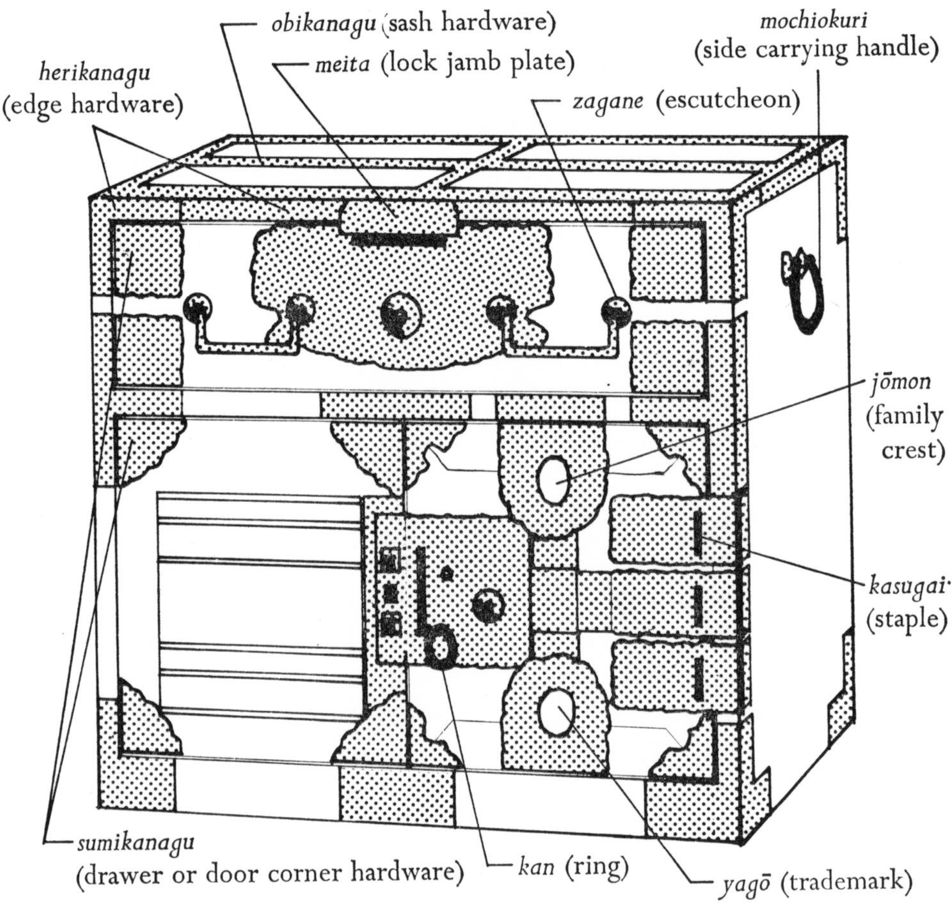

This sketch and the one on the facing page show all major kinds of tansu hardware.

chisels. Ultimately, the availability of thin iron sheets made it possible for hardware makers to greatly expand their output by this change in cutting methods for secondary hardware, which could be thin and decorative without sacrificing function. Examples from this category include drawer-pull back plates, lock jamb plates, T and L flat brace plates for covering exposed butt joints, and drawer corner plates. By reducing the sheet thickness to one millimeter or less, cutting could be done quickly, without chisels. The convenience of mechanically made, thin iron sheeting permitted craftsmen to cut an outline with shears, then finish the plain hardware using chisels for engraving or openwork. This also facilitated the addition of occasional decorative

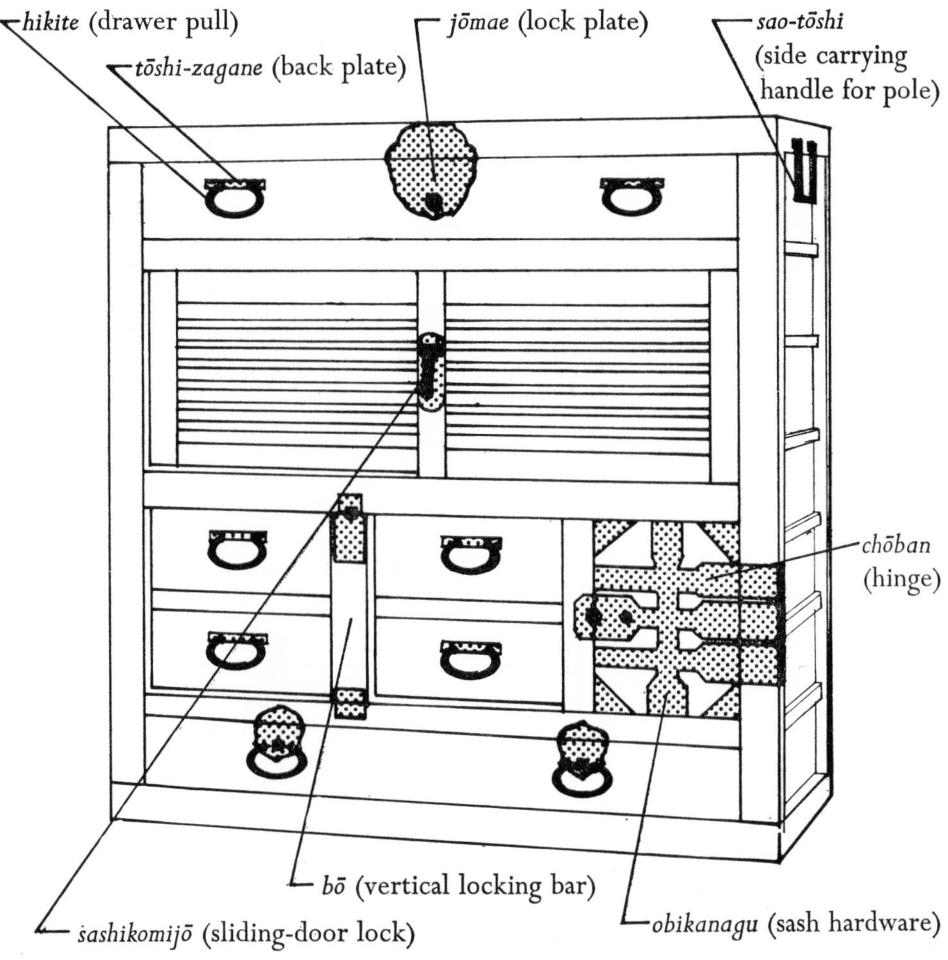

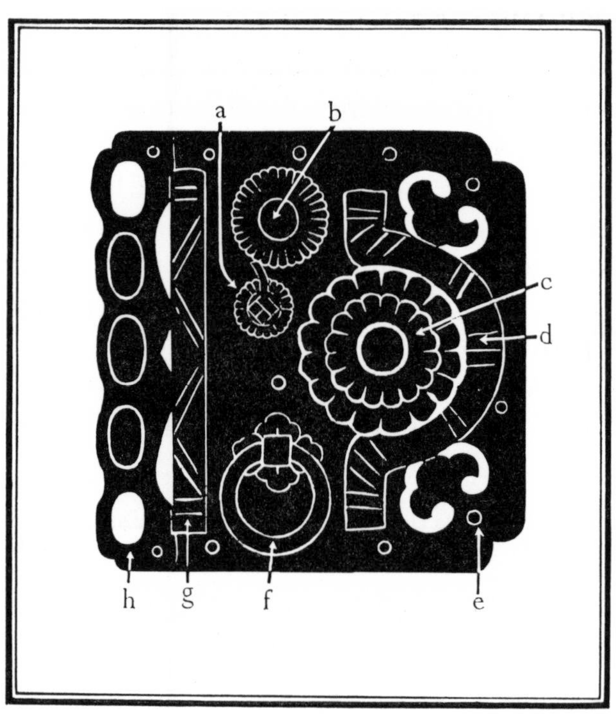

Single-action lock (*omotejō*), exterior view.

a. *zagane-tsuki kagiana* (keyhole with collar)
b. *karajō* (slide latch)
c. *kikuza-tegakejō* (floriate button)
d. *kasugai* (staple)
e. *byō* (pin)
f, *kan* (ring)
g. *kasugai* (staple)
h. *meita* (jamb plate)

Single-action lock, interior view.

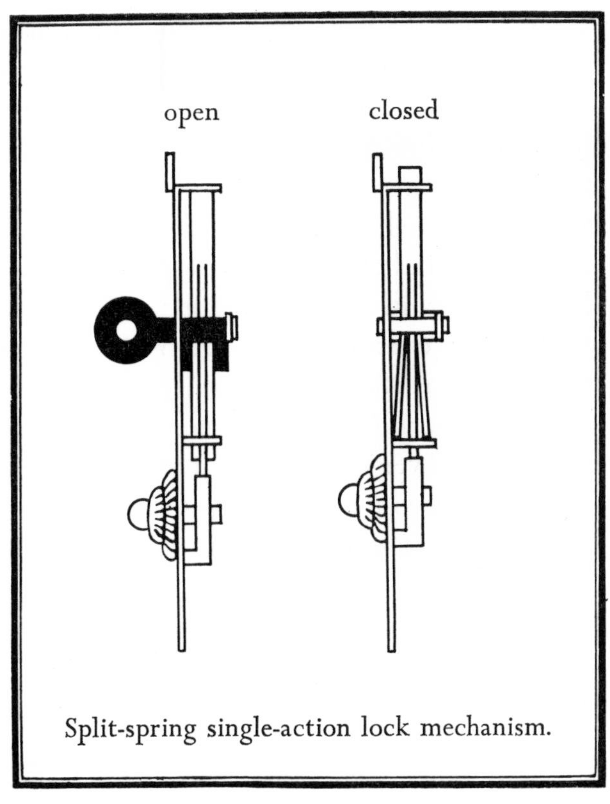

Split-spring single-action lock mechanism.

plates and braces of questionable function, particularly evident in personal chests from Yamagata and Miyagi prefectures between 1890 and 1915.

Hardware may be conveniently categorized into four groups: locks, drawer pulls and handles, hinges, and surface plating. Locks as systems housed within the wood structure of tansu appear to date from the late seventeenth century. Prior to that time, the flared-spring slip-bolt padlock with a flange key in the Chinese style was relied upon. From the Shōsō-in inventory it is known that these locks were in use at least as early as the eighth century. The earliest housed tansu lock has persisted into the twentieth century and may be unique to Japan. The single-action lock, or *omotejō,* locks by pressing an exposed button in the direction of the lock-plate jamb, thereby extending the bolt and liberating a flared spring. Keys were intended only for unlocking. By turning counterclockwise, the two prongs of an inserted key catch the spring and press its flared ends together while forcing the exposed button and the bolt away from the jamb.

The double-action lock, or *urajō,* in which a single-prong key both locks and unlocks a curvilinear spring, thereby eliminating the exposed button, was first used in the mid-nineteenth century and by the 1920s had largely superceded the single-action system.

Another lock type, a kind of slide latch, is called a *karajō*. This system can be found together with split-plate locks in the upper half of paulownia, double-door, chest-on-chest personal tansu made during the Edo period and Meiji era. Many small, hinged doors in merchant and personal chests also incorporated the slide latch within a key-activated system for the convenience of frequent access. When used for both sides of a drop-fit *kendon-buta* detached door, as in many *chō-bako* and *hangai* sea chests, the slide-latch pattern was often at right angles instead of straight. This touch of intentional complexity combined with the use of false keyholes was probably responsible for the descriptive term *karajō*, literally empty lock.

Handles and drawer pulls are iron, with a few exceptions found primarily in the personal chests of samurai families. There are five dominant drawer-pull styles. The oldest, *warabite,* literally "bracken-hand," derives its name from the young bracken plant in spring and was thought to be analogous in shape to a fist. The *kakute,* or square pull so common to sea chests, and the *hirute,* or leech-shaped pull, appear to have originally been used on chests in the mid-Edo period. The *mokkō,* or melon, and *gumpai,* or military-fan, shapes were not popular for tansu until the middle of the Meiji era. The construction methods varied: *warabite* were always forged, and *mokkō,* if flat or faceted, were always cast. Flat *hirute* were usually forged, but those with a two-faceted face were cast. Forged *kakute* have slightly rounded corners, while later examples with sharper corners indicate cutting from manufactured iron sheeting after 1880. Rings, backed by round escutcheons, for small drawers, both internal and external, have been in use since the seventeenth century and quite possibly pre-date the *warabite* pull.

Iron handles for carrying a tansu on a pole, whether of the lift or swing type, were always forged and their designations, *bō-tōshi* or *sao-tōshi,* are interchangeable. The *warabite* style was also used sporadi-

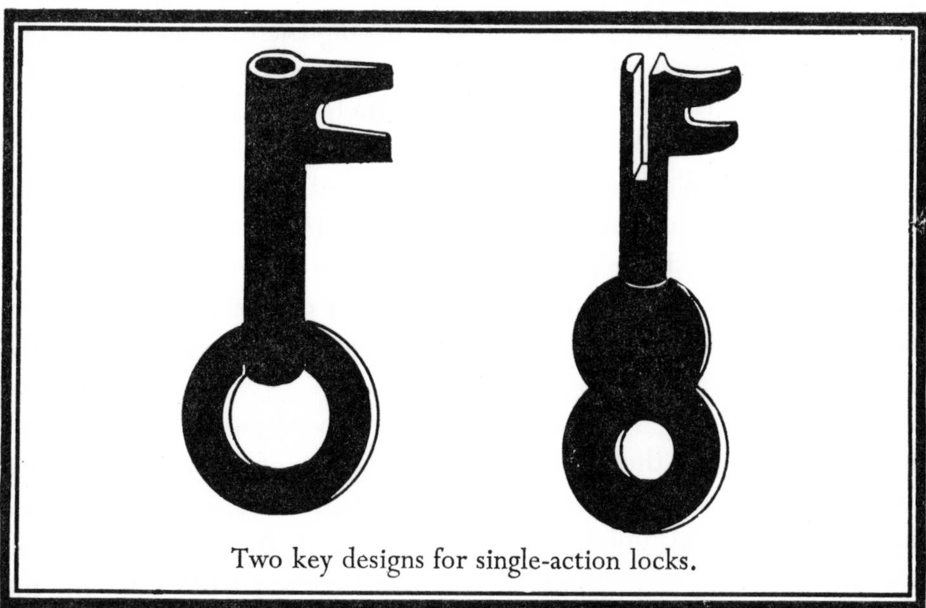

Two key designs for single-action locks.

Popular keyhole and collar designs for nineteenth century tansu.

cally for two handles arranged in a horizontal line at mid-level, under a *sao-tōshi* handle, on either side of large secured-case tansu. This style also appears as an individual handle in the top center of a *kakesuzuri* chest; as single handles on either side of a sea chest, either *chō-bako* or *hangai;* as single handles on either side of a large chest crafted in a tansu style probably within the last hundred years; and as single handles on either side of small personal tansu for women. When functioning as a handle for lifting, but designed in one of the five predominant drawer-pull styles, side handles are properly termed *mochiokuri*, and top handles, *totte*.

Protective plating was used to secure exposed end-grain and joints, as well as to cover the vulnerable face corners of drawers and doors. These pieces were each a single plate cut by chisel or shears from sheeting. Their two-fold function was to prevent theft and to lend a nonstructural rigidity since tansu were often moved from one place to another. Lateral bracing across one or even all six of the sides of a chest is called *obikanagu*, literally sash hardware. Although associated primarily with sea chests, these iron bands have been an integral feature of mitered clamp doors since the seventeenth century.

Tansu door hinges were initially copied from those used in the cabinetry of the aristocracy, and they in turn had been influenced by the wooden cases, probably from T'ang-dynasty China, which held images of Kannon, the bodhisattva of mercy. The doors of these cases used full-face or three-quarter-face hinges and subsequently came to be known as Kannon doors. In time, a half-face hinge with the hinge-pin fulcrum precisely on the case edge became popular. When used for double-door, front-opening, chest-on-chest personal tansu, particularly in the Tokyo style, they are called *ryōbiraki* hinges, literally both-opening hinges, but have become known colloquially as Kannon hinges for Kannon doors, or doors that open in the style of a Kannon case. Hinges in one continuous plate or in separate groupings of two, three, and five are all known as Kannon or *ryōbiraki* hinges.

Subordinate to the four categories mentioned, but nonetheless essential, the square-shank iron nails used to pin the hardware were handmade well into this century. Regardless of whether the head is rounded or faceted, the taper and shape of the shank can often be relied upon to indicate either the age of the chest or the quality of the repair. Nailheads usually found under a drawer pull or a handle function as bumper stops to keep the hardware from damaging the wood when the tansu was carried.

The most traditional hardware technique employs a chisel and hammer for iron forging, carving, and openwork. Early chests with plating ranging in thickness from 1.2 mm to over 3 mm, cut by chisel from forged iron sheeting, relied upon engraving, cutting, and filing. Embossing at different levels was not used until the middle of the Meiji era. The techniques employed for sea-chest hardware represent the highest levels achieved by the Japanese tansu-hardware craftsman. An iron sheet, either forged or pressed mechanically, was allowed to rust slightly before a pattern outline was marked with an "iron pencil." Compass, ruler, and calipers were used to achieve correct proportions. Details were drawn freehand. For openwork (*sukashibori*) and line carving (*sembori*), approximately three hundred different chisels were necessary. The presence of some rust on the iron sheet helped keep the chisels from slipping. Even with hardware of considerable thickness, some distortion occurred in the rough openwork. This was corrected by hammering the plating from the back with wooden mallets and filing the perimeter and openwork cuts to a bevel in order to emphasize the thickness of the hardware. Perhaps the highest skill is shown in the precise and delicate working of keyhole collars, escutcheon plates, and lock-plate staples by sea-chest craftsmen on the Japan Sea coast. It is estimated by one of Japan's foremost hardware craftsmen that he would require eighty hours to complete the full complement of locks, drawer pulls, handles, nails, clamps, and plates for a *chō-bako* sea chest in the traditional manner.

Embossing of thin iron sheets of 1.2 mm or less is most closely associated with the personal tansu of Sendai and the Iwayado area in northern Honshu, where this technique was highly refined in the late nineteenth century. Because of the intricacy of many of the patterns, a stencil, or a sketch on "linen paper" (*azafu-gami*) for a new design, was used to mark out the iron sheet before drawing on the metal with an "iron pencil." Cutting of outlines and general openwork then proceeded in exactly the same way as the traditional technique without embossing. From this point, however, the desire for embossed detail resulted in sophisticated techniques. The stencil or sketch was pasted to the rough-cut plating and worked with both line-carving and ring-head chisels. The latter, used occasionally on flat iron lock plates for repetitive incising of small dots or stars, were more commonly used for brass hardware. In order to achieve an illusion of detail and depth for scales on a dragon's tail, for example, this technique (*nanakobori*) was combined with embossing (*uchidashi*). Portions of a pattern desired for embossing were hammered from the reverse side with hammers of various shapes and sizes, producing an even, impacted surface. Molten lead poured into the embossed pattern hardened just enough to allow the pattern to be worked in detail using ring-head as well as fine-line chisels without collapsing the embossment. The correction of distortion and finishing by file for embossed hardware is essentially identical to the traditional procedure discussed above for two-dimensional hardware.

Samurai personal cabinetry from the Edo period, and subsequent pieces that affected an upper-class elegance, favored brass hardware extensively chased in the techniques described above. This urban style was misinterpreted by people in the provinces as Edo high taste. A *bengara* stain under a burnt lacquer finish on hardware was used to imitate brass. This is most commonly found on chests from Tsuruoka, and came to be considered an acceptable Japanese alternative in the Meiji era to the "foreign" brass.

Processes to darken hardware varied according to the level of craftsmanship and the availability of raw materials. The process for fine iron hardware, called *yaki-urushi*, used urushi filtered through linen paper and thinned, if necessary, with castor oil. Applied to the hardware, urushi will become a light brownish color when almost dry. Then the hardware is heated from the back, and the lacquer will smolder slightly and turn to a matte black. A repetition of this process three times will fuse the lacquer and make it quite impervious to wear. A more simple but quite effective process popular in the late Meiji era utilized the special nature of silk and raw cotton for the coloration. When applied to red-hot iron, silk gauze or unbleached long-fiber cotton saturated with rapeseed oil will turn the metal surface to a matte black. If silk gauze is used, the process is called *mawata-migaki*, if cotton, *tetsu menshoku abura-migaki*. When this process is repeated several times, the surface color will become quite even and stable.

These hardware-finishing processes were properly followed by several applications of resin wax to the warmed iron, which was then polished with wadded rice straw to a slight sheen.

One of the most fascinating aspects of tansu hardware is the abundant use of motifs from mythology and religious symbolism. The variety and interrelationships of such motifs alone could fill many volumes. Some comments on the more prevalent themes encountered on chests crafted in the nineteenth century serve as an introduction to this fascinating corner of Japanese ethnology:

BAMBOO Together with the pine and blossoming plum, bamboo is known as one of the "friends of the deep cold" (*saikan sanyū*) since it flourishes even in the dead of winter. The flexibility and resilience of bamboo were considered particularly admirable traits for a person to develop, especially during Japan's feudal period.

BAT A common theme for brass drawer-pull back plates in China and Korea, and subsequently borrowed by British and colonial cabinetmakers, the bat was most always rendered in iron plating in Japan. The bat symbolizes good fortune and prosperity on the basis of a pun in Chinese.

BUTTERFLY The butterfly was a popular theme with the Nara-period aristocracy and appears frequently in family crests. Favored for its elegance, it was employed in round lock plates of Meiji-era personal tansu from Yamagata Prefecture, usually rimmed with a bright compound of copper and tin (*hakudō*).

CHERRY BLOSSOM This indigenous subject is associated with the changes in nature and the transiency of life. It is a common image in both literature and the visual arts. The cherry blossom was a dominant pattern in Yonezawa round locks during the Meiji era.

CHRYSANTHEMUM An embellishment borrowed from T'ang-dynasty China, the leaf is rarely used alone and always represents the elegant flower. The sixteen-petal chrysanthemum was chosen by the late twelfth century Emperor Gotoba as the principal imperial crest. The chrysanthemum was believed to have special powers to sustain good health based upon a Chinese fable concerning hermit-monks who could live to be one-hundred-years old merely on a diet of the flower. The chrysanthemum-diamond pattern (*kiku-bishi*) is a recurring adaptation of the classic flower used as an openwork pattern in flat braces, hinges, and drawer-pull back plates, especially on chests from Yamagata Prefecture and Sado Island during the last half of the nineteenth century.

CRANE AND TORTOISE Originally borrowed from Chinese folklore, the crane and the tortoise are associated with longevity and often appear together, representing one thousand years and ten thousand years respectively. The tortoise is sometimes depicted with the head of a dragon, considered to be one of the four most auspicious creatures in ancient China. What appears to be a shaggy tail on the tortoise is actually seaweed that has accumulated over hundreds of years according to legend.

DAIKOKU One of the Seven Gods of Fortune borrowed from Chinese mythology, Daikoku is usually depicted standing on two bales of rice with a magic mallet in one hand and a bag over his shoulder. Daikoku always wears a cap.

DRAGON The dragon is an ancient mythological subject borrowed from China. Although ferocious in appearance with two horns, four legs, five claws and 9,981 scales, the Asian dragon is an auspicious creature unlike the scoundrel St. George slew.

EBISU Also one of the Seven Gods of Fortune, Ebisu is called "the laughing god" even though he is the patron of honest dealing. He is also the patron of fishermen and the god of the harvest as well, usually rendered with a large red snapper under one arm and a fishing pole in hand, and seated with his legs crossed. The bearded Ebisu is most often depicted in the company of his friend Daikoku either on a large lock plate or on separate but complementary hardware.

FALCON Emblematic of the warrior's spirit of preparedness, the hunting falcon was carved or rendered in openwork as either a kite or a peregrine. Crossed falcon feathers engraved on lock plates were a popular provincial theme for personal tansu in the early Meiji era.

FLOWER DIAMOND Interchangeable with the chrysanthemum diamond mentioned above, the more popular flower diamond (*hana-bishi*) can be differentiated by its uniform angularity. The origin of this pattern appears to lie in an ancient textile pattern called China flower (*karahana*), probably from the continent.

FLOWERING PLUM Probably the most popular Heian-period motif imported from T'ang China, the plum blossom is symbolic of constancy in adversity since it is the first spring flower to challenge the snow. It appears frequently in embossed hardware on women's personal tansu from the Shōnai plain during the Meiji era. The plum is usually seen together with the other "friends of the deep cold," bamboo and pine, as mentioned above. The plum was especially popular on the Japan Sea coast, partly due to the fact that the Maeda family, lords of the wealthy Kaga fief, used a plum-blossom family crest.

IVY Both Chinese-style *kara kusa* and Japanese *tsuta* ivy were widely used as decorative motifs during the Edo period. The resulting arabesques are somewhat more suited to engraving than openwork with the exception of some simple ivy-pattern outlines on mid-nineteenth century single-action locks from Yamagata, Miyagi, and Iwate prefectures and on door hardware of *kakesuzuri* sea chests.

KAGUYAHIME A traditional fairy tale about an elderly bamboo-basket craftsman who found a baby girl emitting a wondrous glow inside the bamboo he was felling. Kaguyahime grew to be a woman of great beauty sought by samurai from all over Japan. Finally, even the emperor came to seek her favor. Although greatly honored, she explained that she was indeed a daughter of the moon and was now commanded to return to her parents. Before leaving the Earth, she left several presents for her imperial suitor. Angered by her rejection, he cast them into Mount Fuji, causing the mountain to smoke from that day on.

Magic Mule An eighth century Chinese legend about a magic mule was incorporated into Japanese folklore. It concerns a wise old man who refused imperial honors in order to pursue a nomadic life with his magic mule, which was kept in a gourd when it was not needed.

Money Pouch A late motif for tansu in Japan, the money-pouch pattern on lock plates is found only on merchant chests, usually from Nagano Prefecture. The relationship of a pouch or bag with good fortune is based on associations with riches and is traceable to Daikoku, one of the Seven Gods of Fortune from China, always depicted with a large bag over his shoulder.

Mount Fuji Mountains figure prominently in Japan's animistic symbolism. For samurai families in particular, Mount Fuji, the highest mountain in Japan, was always associated with unyielding domination.

Paulownia Flower The paulownia flower is a symbol of prestige only slightly lower than the chrysanthemum. It was closely associated with the brilliant peasant-general of the sixteenth century, Toyotomi Hideyoshi, who was granted the right by the emperor to use the paulownia as his personal crest, and he in turn extended the right to many of his most loyal supporters. By the late Edo period, use of the paulownia as a decorative motif was only sporadically controlled by the government, and many families that were not true descendants of either Hideyoshi or a designated liege family adopted the flower as their family crest.

Peony Initially a Buddhist symbol, the peony as a decorative subject was considered prestigious, though not quite to the level of the chrysanthemum, paulownia, or hollyhock. Used as a medicinal tea, this flower was also associated with good health.

Pine Because legend taught that pine sap turns to amber after a thousand years, the tree has been popularly associated with long life, strength, and endurance. The pine-nut nailhead found on many Yonezawa wheeled chests has similar associations.

217. *Cryptomeria* (sugi).

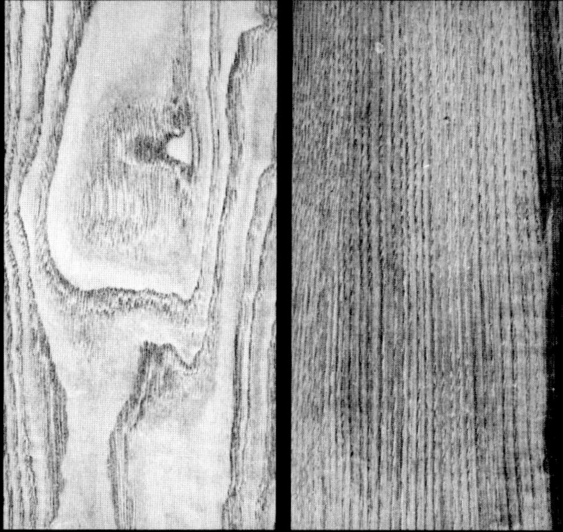

218. *Japanese chestnut* (kuri).

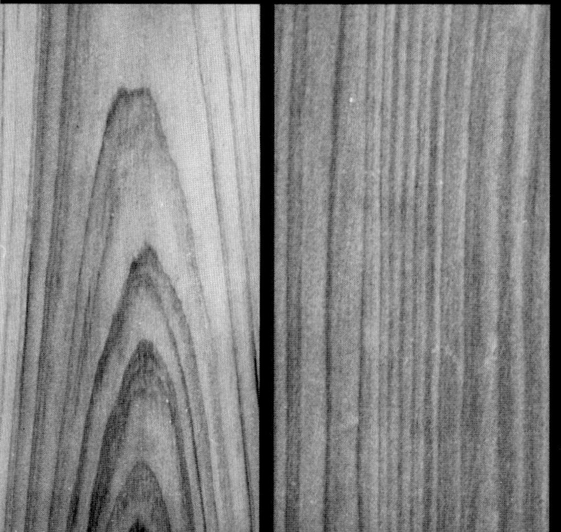

219. *Japanese cypress* (hinoki).

220. *Paulownia* (kiri).

221. *Japanese pine* (Ezo matsu).

222. *Zelkova* (keyaki).

223. *The workshop of a contemporary tansu maker only appears disorganized.*

224. *The blade is the soul of a cutting tool; not to keep it sharp is disrespectful.*

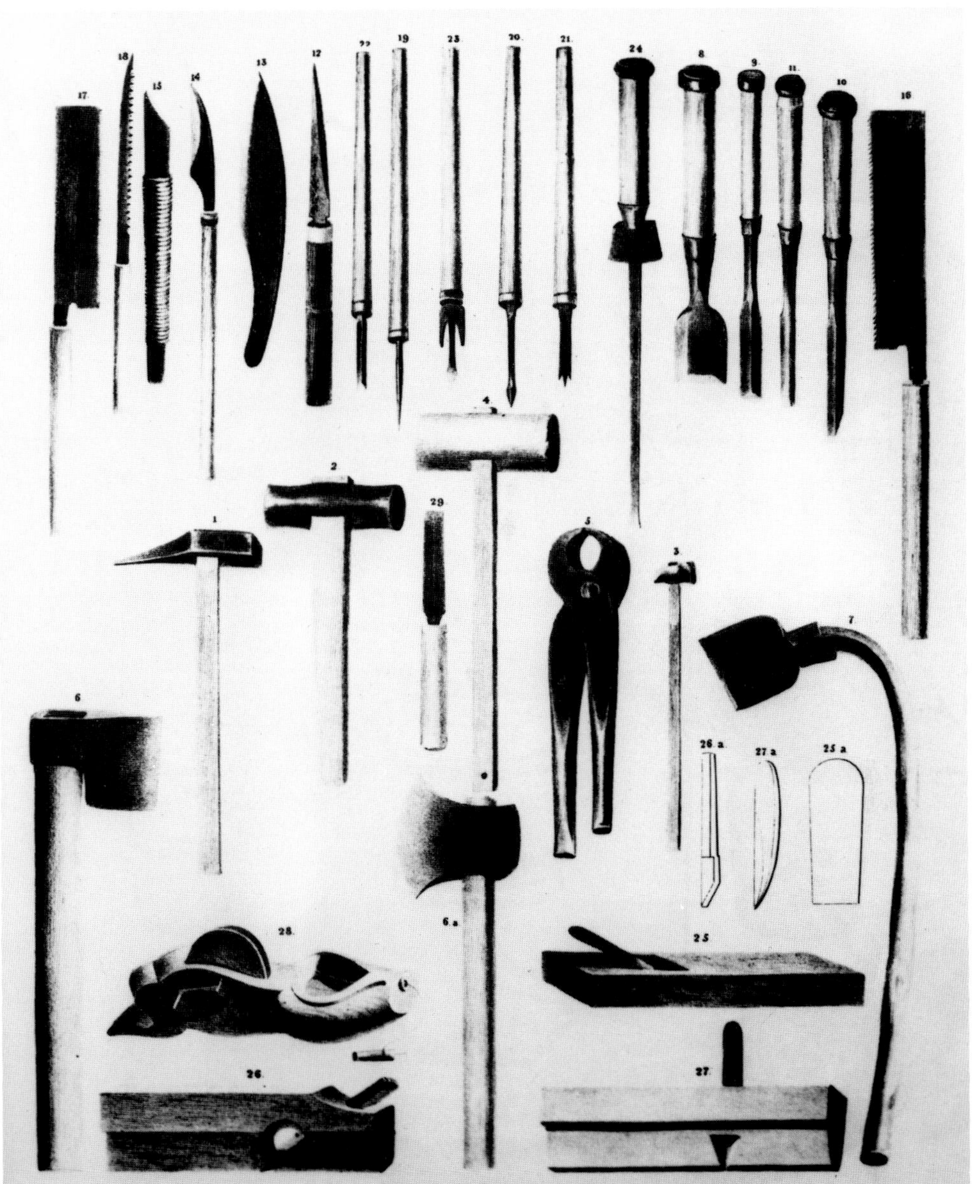

225. Illustration of Japanese woodworking tools drawn in the late Edo period by Philipp Franz von Siebold and published in 1897 under the title Nippon.

1. *tongari kanazuchi* (tack hammer)
2. *kanazuchi* (flathead hammer)
3. *shibuichi kanazuchi* (quarter hammer)
4. *kizuchi* (mallet)
5. *emma* (pincers)
6. *nata* (ax)
7. *chōna* (adze)
8. *shinogi-nomi* (ridge chisel)

9–11. *mukōmachi-nomi* (mortise chisel)

12. *kuri-kogatana* (inshave)
13. *kiridashi-kogatana* (pointed knife)
14. *yari-ganna* (spear plane)
15. *mae-ganna* (drawknife)
16. *kataba-noko* (rip or crosscut back saw)
17. *dozuki-noko* (tenon back saw)
18. *mawashibiki-noko* (keyhole saw)
19. *yotsume-giri* (four-sided gimlet)
20. *mitsume-giri* (three-sided gimlet)
21. *nezumiba-giri* (mouse-tooth gimlet)
22. *tsubo-giri* (circular gimlet)
23. *mitsumata-giri* (three-pronged gimlet)
24. *tsuba-nomi* (guarded chisel)
25. *hira-ganna* (smoothing plane)

25a. *kanna-ba* (blade)

26. *shakkuri-ganna* (shoulder rabbet plane)

26a. *kanna-ba* (blade)

27. *gara-shakkuri-ganna* (plough plane)

27a. *kanna-ba* (blade)

28. *sumi-tsubo* (line-marking gauge)
29. *yasuri* (file)

226 227

226. Ryōba *saw, which rips and crosscuts on the pull stroke, did not come into common use until the Meiji era. 227. Planing is done by using the body motion to draw the blade toward the craftsman. 228. Traditional tools, such as this hammer and chisel, are preferred to electric tools for all but the roughest work. 229. The marking gauge* (kebiki) *is a relatively recent tool.*

230 231

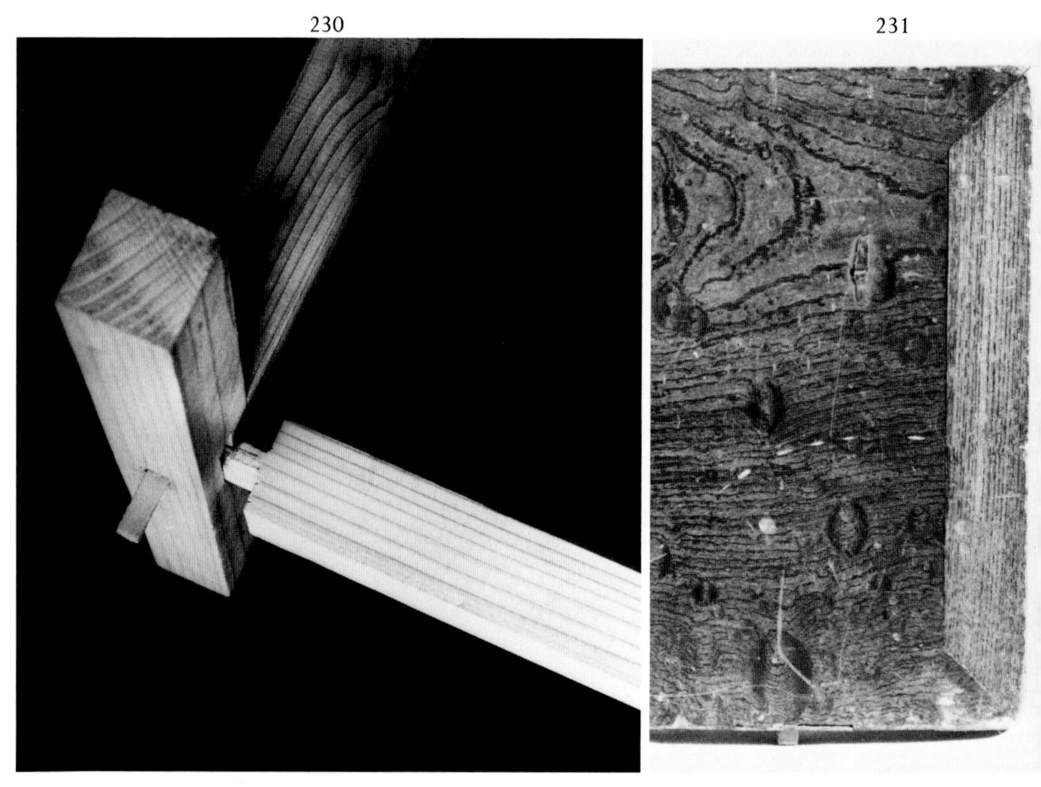

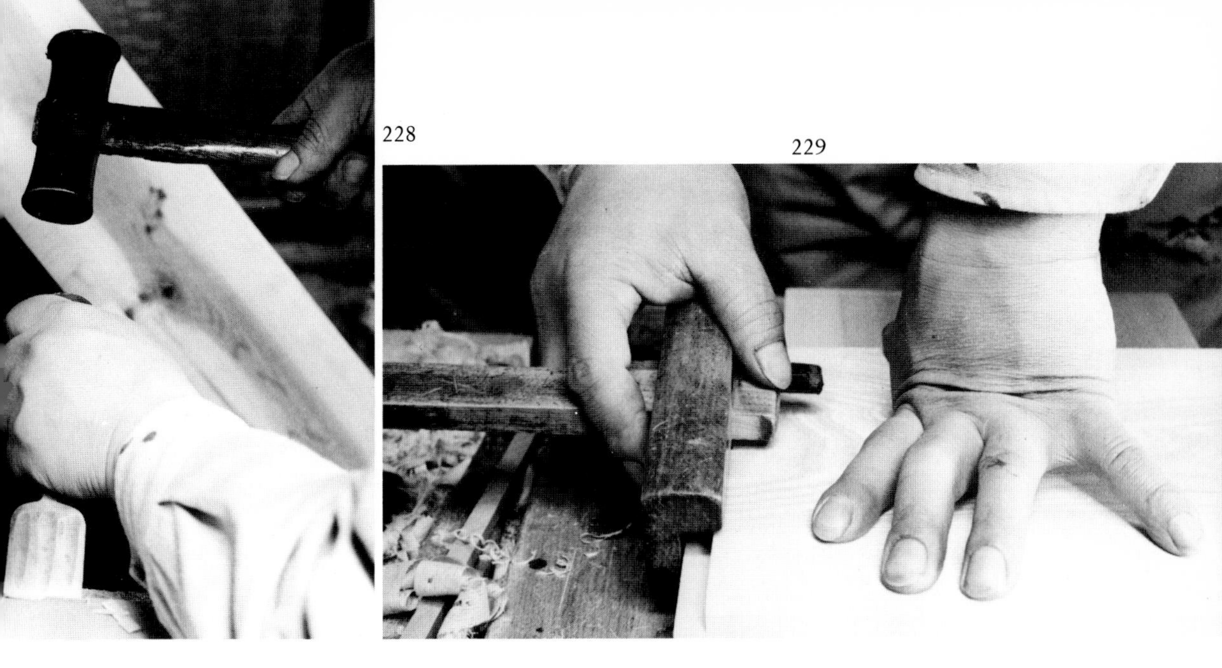

228

229

30. *Wedged-through, haunched d shouldered tenon.*

31. *Mitered clamp joint (ha- ikui) for tansu doors, also ed for eighth century Shōsō-in ffer.*

32. *Measuring a door to fit is ne with an eye trained to rceive minute variations.*

233 234

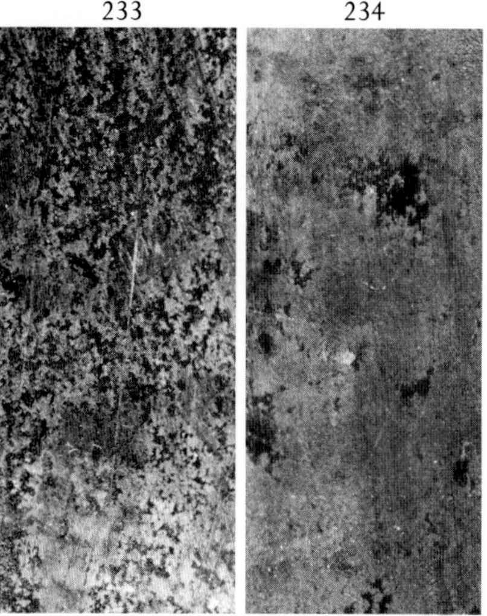

233. Forged iron, beaten from ingots.
234. Pressed iron.

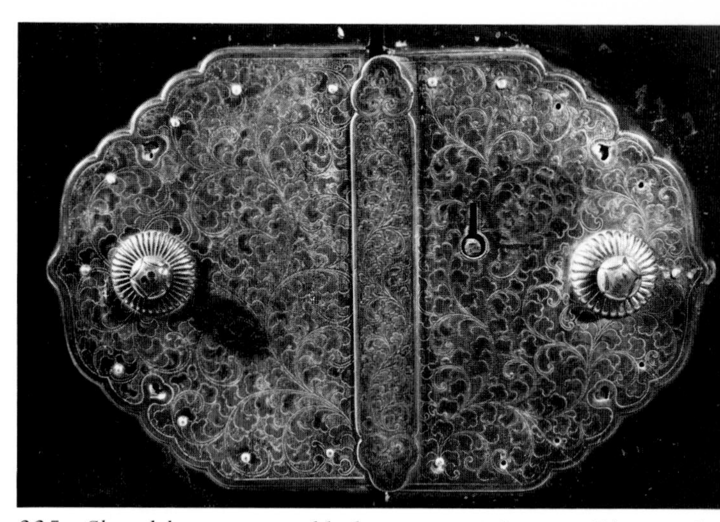

235. Chased brass against black tame-nuri *lacquer. Edo period.*

236. Sash hardware (obikanagu) *on tansu vertical locking bars is both decorative and functional, keeping the wood from warping. From left to right: Iwate, Iwate, Shōnai plain, Sendai, and Tsuruoka.*

237. Ring; used on small inner drawers, tool chests, shop chests, and hinged doors. 238. Warabit *(bracken) drawer pull. Edo period. 239.* Kakute *(square) drawer pull. Edo period. 240.* Gump *(military fan) drawer pull. Probably the most recent of pulls used during nineteenth century. 241–42.* Hirut *(leech) drawer pull; rounded type older than faceted. 243–44.* Mokkō *(melon) drawer pull. Both faceted an flat-face styles date from the Meiji era.*

7
239
238
240
241
242
243
244

245

246

245. Hasami *(scissors) handles for a pole from Edo-period medicine peddler's box.*
246. *Squared handle swinging on two fulcrum pins may be as old as* hasami *(scissors) handle.*

247

248

249

247. *To secure upper and lower chests, a combination of swinging and lift* sao-tōshi *were used. Two inset pins* (sashibō) *on each side of upper chest received swinging* sao-tōshi *in raised position.*
248. *In this large chest-on-chest, each unit combines* mochiokuri *side carrying handles with* sao-tōshi *for a pole.*
249. *Lift handles, rather than swinging ones, were often used on frame-and-panel, single-section tansu, and for the top chest of many Meiji-era chest-on-chests for clothing.*

250. Tool box for chisels.

251. A variety of chisels are needed, especially for embossing.

252 253 254

252. Iron for plating and pins can be cut with shears if less than 1.2 mm thick. If not, cutting is done with a hammer and chisel.

253–54. Hardware craftsmanship requires a long apprenticeship and is usually passed on within a family. Craftsmen today are as skilled as their ancestors, but fewer than five families remain.

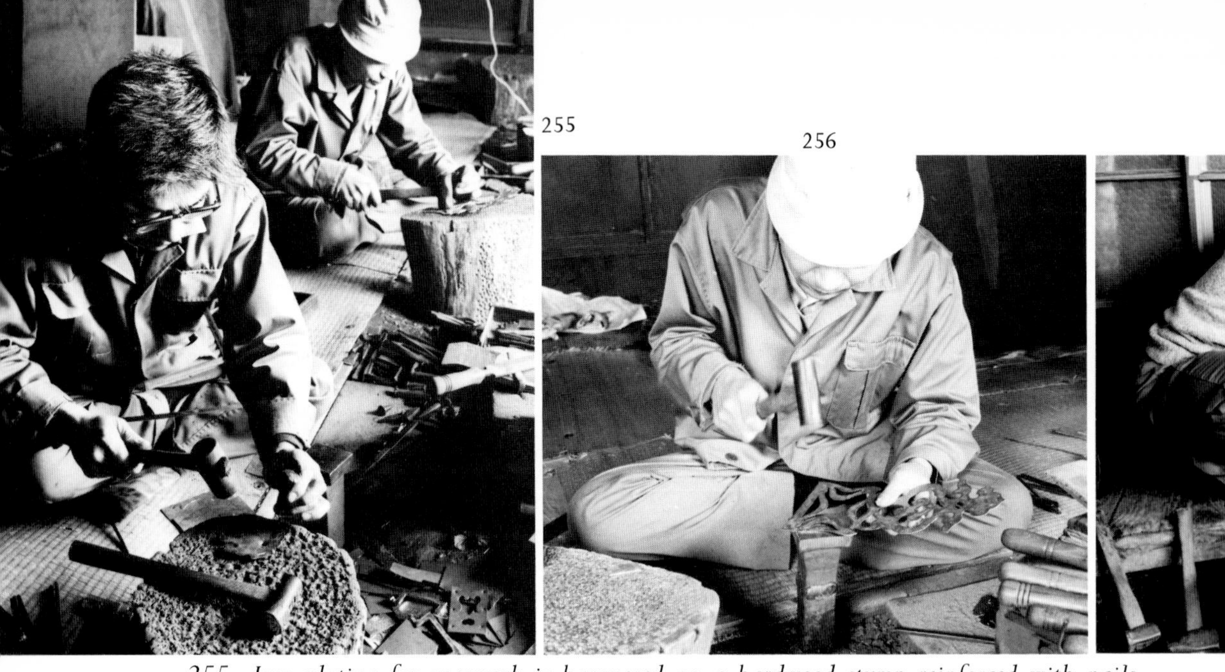

255 256

255. Iron plating for openwork is hammered on a hardwood stump reinforced with nails. 256. After cutting openwork, proportions are corrected on an anvil. 257. Bellows operated with left hand while craftsman holds iron bar in bed of coals, slowly bringing it to a forgeable temperature. 258. Superheated iron bar then hammered into warabite *drawer pull on anvil within which the god of fire is thought to visit. 259. Rough edges filed to smooth bevel. Sharp angles are characteristic of unfiled cast hardware.*

260. Workshop open on one side, separated by shoji doors from street. Craftsman's wife ready at porcelain hibachi to prepare green tea.

257 258 259

261   262 263 264

261. Crane and tortoise. *262. Cherry blossom.* *263. Butterfly.* *264. Rabbit and waves.*

265. *Dragon.* 266. Shishi (*lion-dog*). 267. *Peony.* 268. *Magic mule.* 269. *Falcon.* 270. *Bat.* 271. *Mount Fuji.* 272. *Chrysanthemum.* 273. *Chrysanthemum diamond.*

274. Tiger and bamboo. 275. Paulownia. 276. Money pouch. 277. Flower diamond. 278. Above: sparrow with bamboo. Below: Takasago. 279. Tea seedpod. 280. Above: Shōjō. Below: crane and tortoise. 281. Bamboo, flowering plum, and pine; falcon.

282. Quarter-sawn paulownia brought to a tan to light-brown glow by sealing with powdered whetstone, waxing with resin wax from the lacquer tree, and then burnishing surface with dried eulalia roots.

286

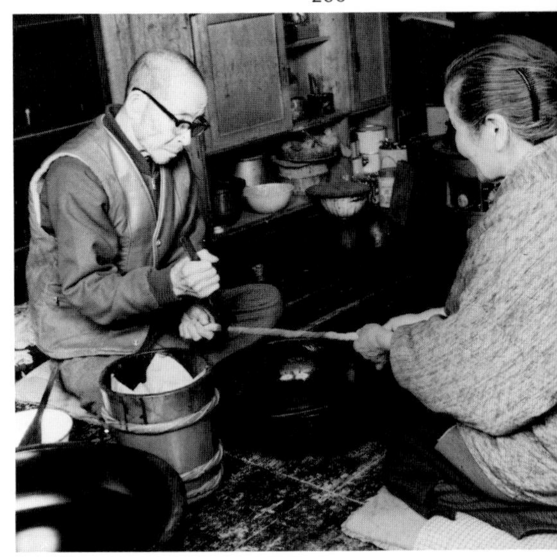

283

284

283. Trees are tapped for urushi rather as sugar maples are for syrup. In the case of lacquer, however, it would take about four years to fill this bucket.
284. Urushi straight from the tree is a milky gray, syrupy substance. First it is filtered to remove foreign particles.

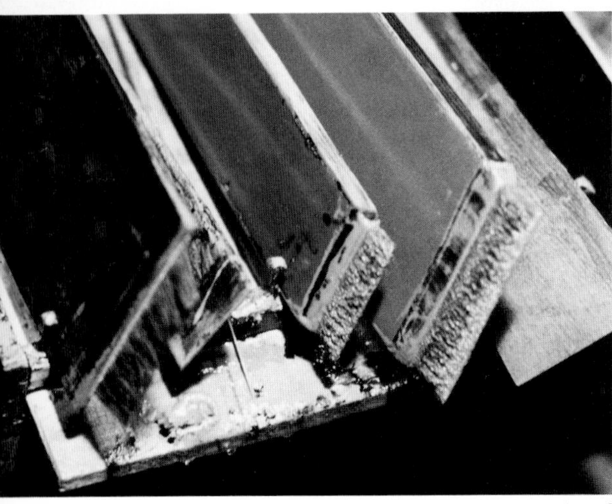

285. Fine brushes for applying urushi are made of human hair laid the full length of two cypress slats.

289

287

288

286. Particles are removed from natural urushi by filtering through finely woven cotton. 287. For perfect consistency, raw urushi is stirred in a shallow wooden bowl. 288. A brazier of hot coals suspended over raw urushi for six to ten hours causes excess water to evaporate. 289. Urushi mixed with powdered whetstone and a certain amount of water is used for the base preparation of a wood surface. 290. Raw lacquer filtered through Japanese paper into a small porcelain bowl is used for the final finish. 291. Refined urushi is applied with straight and circular strokes, at a speed depending on the humidity, and using several brushes.

290

291

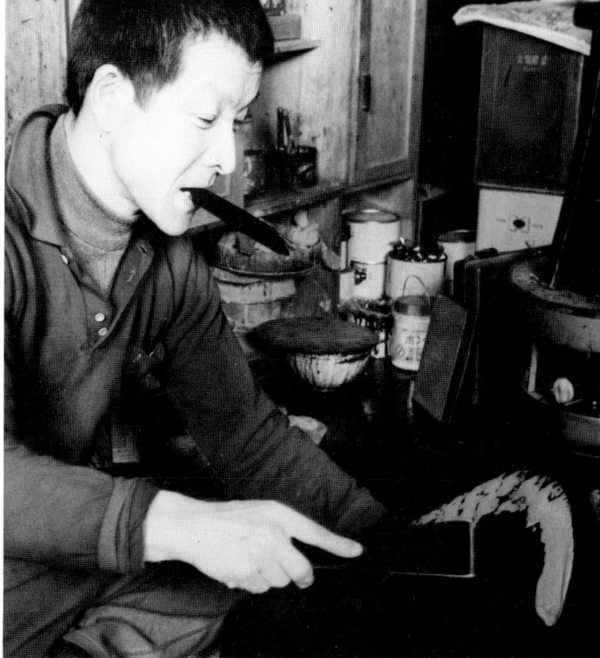

292 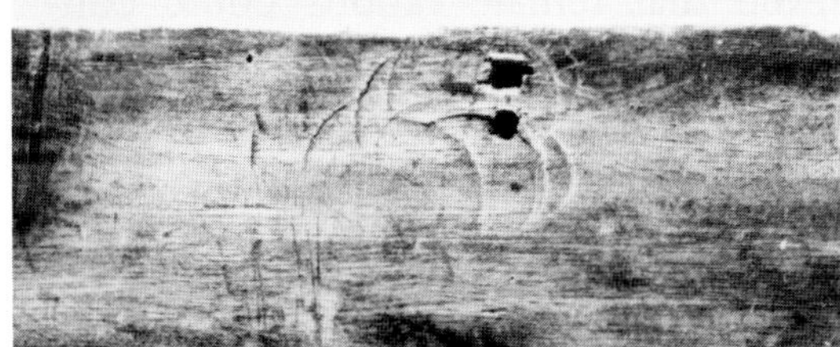

293 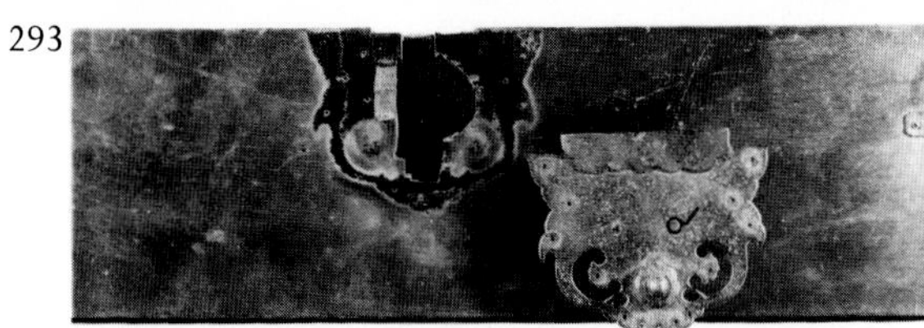

292. In the late nineteenth and twentieth centuries, paulownia exterior wood was stained with yashabushi*-seed dye mixed with powdered whetstone. Oxidation gives a purplish, muddy appearance, but, with regular oiling and waxing, can result in a beautiful patina.*

293. With lock removed after 120 years from drawer face with kijiro *finish, combined result of urushi phenol changes and surface oxidation presents contrast to area covered by lock plate.*

294 

 295

294–95. Tansu with two small drawers in lower corner. When viewed from side, nail holes and discoloring indicate original presence of door.

296 

296. Zelkova back boards of this tansu show normal parallel joint opening, recognized by the straightness of the opening and the presence of dowels. Uneven splitting to left and right results from excessive dryness.

297. Thin wood, such as that used for drawer flooring, relied upon parallel joints with bamboo dowels to absorb the expansion and contraction of the wood.

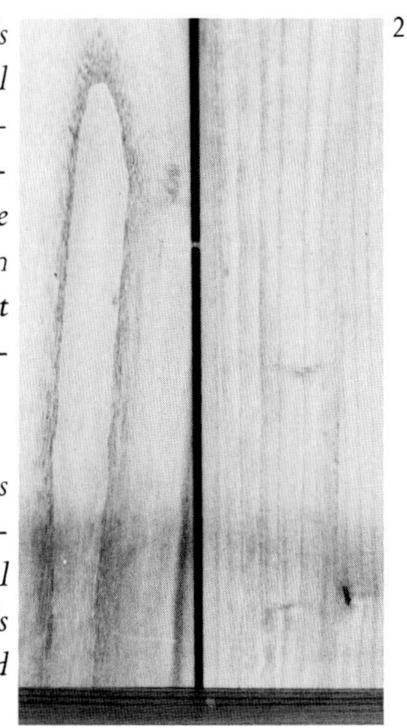 297

Rabbit and Waves It was believed that female rabbits could conceive by running over the waves on the eighteenth day of the eighth moon if the sky were clear. For the Etchū-area towns on the Japan Sea where it was most prevalent, this motif was meant to ensure fertility for the women of the house.

Shishi Another mythical beast borrowed from the continent, the *shishi,* or lion-dog, is associated with courage and strength since a popular legend relates that these creatures tested the vitality of their young by throwing them off a high cliff to "sink or swim." When used in conjunction with a peony, rocks, waterfalls, or with one paw resting on a ball, the *shishi* become guardians of Buddhism.

Shōjō The *Shōjō* are two mythical creatures with long hair who dance around a large urn of sakè. The Shōjō were believed to live near the sea and to have enormous appetites for rice wine. They are usually depicted carrying a dipper for the sakè and dancing with open fans in the company of a tortoise. This motif is associated with the pleasures of comradery.

Sparrow with Bamboo Depicted in winter, the two motifs together represent gentleness and friendship. The famous Uesugi family, originally from Niigata Prefecture, adopted the sparrow with bamboo as one of their formal crests, and, through intermarriage, spread the use of this crest rather extensively during the Edo period. Use of these paired motifs on personal tansu during the Meiji era probably had no direct relationship to the Uesugi clan, but was more likely motivated by the family's reputation for pragmatism and tenacity.

Takasago An old couple are pictured in a pine forest called Takasago, where, according to legend, they gathered pine needles for their living. It was believed that the couple lived happily as husband and wife until they both died at the same hour on the same day at a very old age. They are always shown with a rake, a broom, and a fan, and symbolize long life and fidelity in marriage.

Tea Seedpod Before becoming a tansu motif for drawers disseminated through Mogami River trade from the Japan Sea, this design appears to have spread with the popularity of the tea-ceremony culture beginning in the Momoyama period. Although there seems to have been influence on the tea-seedpod design from the older and very similar mandarin-orange motif, there is as yet no conclusive proof.

TIGER AND BAMBOO A tiger walking among bamboo represents the ability of the weak to serve the strong and be protected in return.

ZODIAC ANIMALS Of the twelve animals that are associated with the twelve-year cycle first developed in China, each animal represents both positive and negative characteristics in the plan of nature. Representation of the entire group of twelve is probably symbolic of the cycle of life within the five elements of nature: wood, fire, earth, metal, and water. Use of any single zodiacal sign in hardware might indicate the sign of the birth year of the tansu owner.

CHAPTER EIGHT

FINISHING

Tansu finishes may be categorized for convenience as dry or lacquer. With very few exceptions, the kind of wood determined which category of finish was appropriate. Although the protective function of a finish was a key consideration, the ability of a finish to either enhance the natural beauty of the wood or entirely supplant it was of equal importance for tansu.

Finishes on the Shōsō-in cabinetry, dating from the eighth century and earlier, are prototypes for tansu finishes popular in the late nineteenth century. Even though lacquer as a bonding medium predates its use as a finishing material by many centuries, both functions are in evidence in the imperial-storehouse cabinetry. With the development of inexpensive animal and vegetable glues, lacquer's function as a bond, except for porcelain repair, had passed from general use by the Edo period. As a finish, lacquer appears on the famous *zushi* cabinet of zelkova burl attributed to Emperor Temmu's collection of A.D. 673. Oil was added to the lacquer used over a sapanwood stain. This technique, known as *shunkei-nuri,* which eliminated the need to polish the final finish, came into widespread use in the Edo period and continued into the twentieth century. For softwood finishing, oyster or clamshell chalk as well as various powdered clays used in early times are still preferred by contemporary craftsmen for paulownia wood.

Before examining dry and lacquer finishes, it should be understood that there are many tansu that have no finish whatsoever. Shop inventory chests kept in storehouses and *mizuya,* used in the kitchen area, are two kinds of tansu that often had no finish, yet through time, use, and care could develop an exquisite patina. Pieces with or without a finish that were kept near the cooking hearth were in time tinted by the smoke of the charcoal, often itself a product of oily mountain paulownia or resinous pine. The resulting patina has been instinctively prized by the Japanese. Drawer interiors of either cryptomeria or paulownia were always unfinished. Even the occasional eccentric tansu with a zelkova interior would have no finish. The reason for this preference for natural wood is found in the characteristics of the woods used. Cryptomeria has a delicate aroma disliked by moths, and the unique ability of paulownia to expand and contract with humidity changes made it an effective mildew deterrent. The only exception to the unfinished drawer would have been the use of black lacquer for a rare *temoto* chest of unusual quality.

The term "dry finish" is more accurate than "natural finish" because the latter cannot be applied to stained wood, whereas the former correctly implies simply the absence of oil. In that paulownia tansu were practically the only tansu that used a dry finish, we shall confine our consideration to this wood only.

The earliest dry finish from the Edo period was *yakigote,* or burning with a hot iron. Although the popularity of this process to accentuate the wood grain gradually declined for tansu, it has not only persisted into our century but expanded in the last ten years as a technique for finishing cryptomeria siding and fencing. In the late Edo period, *yakigote* was modified to a softer appearance by the application of powdered whetstone worked into the scorched wood with bundled, dried eulalia roots, bringing the surface to a dull sheen.

With the Meiji era, tansu with a still softer look were in demand. The ancient product *gofun,* chalk from clam or oyster shells, or powdered whetstone, was used to create this effect. The technique involved combining either of the mentioned ingredients into a paste with water-soluble animal glue and applying it to the wood surface. After drying, the application could be brought to a soft sheen by rubbing it with *mokurō,* a wax preferably derived from the lacquer tree.

In 1897 an entirely new approach to dry finishing was introduced. Though unrelated to past traditions, this new technique was in harmony with the Japanese respect for natural materials. By quarter-sawing paulownia to achieve a perfectly straight grain, then smoothing the wood with a double-blade finishing plane, the need to use the overly abrasive traditional scouring reed was eliminated. For a delicate tint, seeds of the *yashabushi* tree from the Izu Peninsula in Shizuoka Prefecture were boiled to produce a reliable finishing dye. The new technique was a marked success and has influenced both the wood-grain configuration and the finishing of paulownia chests throughout the twentieth century. The wood surface was first sealed with a mixture of powdered whetstone and water applied as a paste with a brush. When absorbed, the excess was wiped off with a cotton cloth. As soon as it had dried in the sun, the chest was moved into shade. Liquid from boiled *yashabushi* seeds was then applied in a thin coat, dried in the sunlight, and the chest was again returned to shade. By working the grain with a eulalia-root brush, any lingering excess of the powdered whetstone then could be removed and the grain of the wood finely embossed. To assure even coloration, a second coat of *yashabushi* liquid mixed with powdered whetstone was then applied to the smoothed surface and allowed to dry in the shade. A final polishing with eulalia root to bring out an even sheen had to be done with great care so as not to destroy the prepared surface. Sealing of the finished surface could then follow using *mokurō* wax applied with the fingertips, using very little pressure.

The name lacquer is unfortunately synonymous in the West with any opaque varnish used to create a shiny appearance. The nature of the lacquer tree, *Rhus verniciflua* of the anacardiaceous family, is not clearly understood outside Asia.

Techniques using indigenous lacquer as a bonding medium are in evidence as early as Japan's neolithic Jōmon culture. From the Yayoi culture beginning in the third century B.C., potsherds indicate that iron pigments were mixed with lacquer for decorative coloring. During the Asuka period (552–646), the influence of Chinese lacquer techniques for religious objects was considerable. This infusion of refined craftsmanship in combination with native rudimentary technique formed the basis of Japanese artistic secular lacquering in the following centuries, firmly established as a mature tradition by the late Heian period (897–1185). Although the wild lacquer tree had been tapped in China, Korea, Vietnam, Burma, Thailand, and India for untold centuries, the Japanese were the first people to attempt cultivation of the tree. Beginning in the Nara period (646–794) and persisting until the seventeenth century, lacquer was accepted as a tax base by the government with the same status as rice. When the quality of lacquer craftsmanship for small objects and the quantity of output relative to the demand from the samurai and emerging merchant classes are considered in historical perspective, it is easy to understand why the Dutch traders in Nagasaki during the sixteenth century found Japanese lacquer unprofitably expensive as an export commodity.

The lacquer tree is deciduous and identifiable as male or female by the bark texture. It favors mild weather, fertile soil, good air circulation, and consistent sunshine to reach, in Japan, a circumference of thirty centimeters over twelve years, at which time tapping the tree begins to be feasible, yielding approximately 250 grams of lacquer in a year. The lacquer trees of tropical countries such as Thailand and India are much larger than those of Japan and achieve a circumference of over three meters in some areas. The principal difference in the sap from tropical and temperate areas lies in the percentage of latex present. Japanese lacquer on the average contains eighty percent urushiol (a complex-acid hydrocarbon), and twenty percent water, latex, and impurities. Tropical lacquer has a much higher proportion of water and latex, causing the raw substance to have a natural black color in contrast to the grayish beige hue of Japanese urushi lacquer. Lacquer dries through the reaction of the urushiol with oxygen in the air, forming an impervious bond with the latex and a uniform surface. This process is at its most efficient in an atmosphere of high humidity and a temperature within a range of 0° to 40° C. Between 40° and 80° C, drying is inexplicably difficult; however, above 80° C it will accelerate even without the presence of humidity.

Possibly one of the reasons urushi lacquer is so highly respected in Japan relates to the strength and unusual character of the natural substance. Although urushi lacquer in a capsule from a Heian-period tomb was found to be in its original liquid state, pigment added to urushi even a short time before the period of application will completely prevent drying. The rash from undried urushi is justifiably notorious, with blisters and itching rather like poison oak but of longer duration. Some people of exceptional susceptibility have acquired the rash by breathing the air in the same room with a not-quite-dry lacquer object. The classic antidotes only increase the mystique of urushi: raw river-crab flesh and cryptomeria leaves. Once dry, lacquer is harmless. The smooth bark of the female lacquer tree makes it easy to tap, but the volume of sap is much less than that from the rough-bark male tree. Lacquer can be collected from June through November with tapping of an individual tree optimally spaced over alternating four-day periods, but lacquer collected during the first six weeks of the season often contains a high percentage of water. Lacquer collected from mid-July through August is the best and most suitable for the critical final finish, or *uwa-nuri*. September lacquer has a somewhat lower percentage of water and is most suitable for the base finish, or *shita-nuri*. With cooler weather, the lacquer of the final two months in the season becomes thick and sticky, making it difficult to use. Lacquer direct from the tree must be filtered to remove dust and dark particles, thereby creating *ki-urushi,* or "raw lacquer." The water content is then evaporated by either exposing the raw lacquer to sunlight or by suspending a hot charcoal brazier over the lacquer held in a large shallow bowl. This refining process is critical to the final stage of stirring to a perfect consistancy, thus creating *kijiro-urushi,* a clear, even-textured, syrupy substance with a marked ocher tint suitable for final finishing.

In Japan, lacquer was traditionally applied with a cypress spatula when used as a base sealer and with a brush of human hair if intended for one of the finishing processes. It was thought that the long hair of women abalone divers was especially well suited because it was not oily. The hair should be dried ten years before being tightly bundled and pressed between two strips of flat cypress which serve as a handle.

Lacquer was usually applied to wood that had been carefully examined to determine its tendencies to move and to warp after its surface had been sealed with a mixture of raw lacquer and powdered whetstone or powdered baked earth in a water paste. This sealer was reapplied numerous times with progressively finer powders until the base was deemed ready for refined lacquer. An imitation of this basic process came into wide use in the late Edo period during a time of lacquer shortage. Persimmon tannin, animal glue, rice paste, and pine soot carefully mixed were a clever substitute for the traditional base. This was not initially evident but became apparent to the discerning eye as the wood aged.

For small, opaque lacquer pieces with a flat surface, a covering of linen or more rarely Japanese handmade paper, to insure against any tendency of the wood to move, was a fairly common practice beginning before the Edo period. This technique was not normally used for tansu unless the structural wood was for some reason inferior.

Prior to discussing each of the several lacquering techniques employed in tansu finishing, an introduction to the application of color, the use of oils, and the importance of polishing is in order. Because the temperate-zone lacquer of Japan contains a low percentage of latex in contrast to the lacquer from most other areas in Asia, black lacquer had to be obtained by adding iron oxides and/or *sumi,* a charcoal, to the raw lacquer. For this reason, Japanese black tends to develop a brownish hue through years of exposure to light, while most non-Japanese black lacquers remain absolutely black. Black pigments obtained from pine soot, rapeseed oil, or burnt urushi were also very effective initially, but the phenols present in urushiol without the presence of a higher proportion of latex ultimately brought out some hint of the natural lacquer color through a reaction with sunlight. The various blacks, vermilion from cinnabar, yellow from orpiment, and green, blue, yellow-red, and green-red from natural mineral pigments could be added as delicate hues to the raw lacquer during the base coat if desired. Oils were never used as conventional tansu finishes but were often added to the final lacquer coat in order to eliminate the tedious task of final polishing. This approach is referred to broadly as *nuritate,* and relied upon seed oil from the perilla, a flowering annual in the mint family. The classic lacquer finish of the highest standard always involved many polishings. This total process, or *roiro-nuri,* is by all criteria the ultimate measure of tansu lacquer finishing, and can best be appreciated by tracing the craftsman's task from bare wood to a weary smile.

Wood Sealing

1 If there is a crack or flaw in the wood surface, the defect must be carved out with an inshave or drawknife so that the filler material will adhere well.

2 Apply raw lacquer lightly to the crack or flaw to seal any open grain, thereby minimizing shrinkage of the filler material.

3 Apply filler, a mixture of raw lacquer, water-soluble paste, fabric lint, and powdered baked clay, with a bamboo spatula.

4 After the filler has dried, it will form a concave surface that must be filled again. For this use a mixture of powdered baked clay, powdered whetstone, water, and raw lacquer is applied with a spatula.

5 When the second filler has dried, it need only be polished with a whetstone and water.

If steps four and five are eliminated, step three should be repeated using powdered sawdust instead of baked clay. After drying, any excess filler should be removed with a drawknife.

Base Finish

1 Apply mixture of powdered baked clay, water, and raw lacquer to the surface with a cypress spatula.

2 After this mixture has thoroughly dried, smooth the surface with a dry whetstone and apply a second coat.

3 When this second coat becomes firm, smooth the surface with a fine whetstone and water.

4 Apply raw lacquer alone or with water as a thin coat to seal and bond the filler.

5 Apply mixture of baked clay, powdered whetstone, water, and raw lacquer. Allow to dry.

6 Repeat the previous step in order to assure that the depth and texture consistency are perfect.

7 Polish to a uniformly smooth surface with a fine whetstone and water.

8 Apply raw lacquer alone or with water to seal the highly polished surface.

9 Apply a thin mixture consisting of powdered whetstone, water, and raw lacquer with a base-finish brush or cypress spatula. This final sealing is critical to the pure-lacquer final finishing.

10 After the surface has thoroughly dried, polish with great care using a superfine whetstone and water.

If an absolutely smooth surface is not required, steps one through eight could be eliminated, providing step nine is repeated and followed by step ten.

Base Finish Variations I: Persimmon tannin

1 Apply mixture of unripe-persimmon tannin (*kaki-shibu*) and char-

coal powder once or twice according to the depth of color required.

2 After drying, follow with pure tannin polished while still wet with a whetstone.

3 Mix pine soot or rapeseed-oil soot into tannin and apply by brush. Immediately polish with a whetstone using the mixture as a medium. Repeat application.

4 Apply tannin only by brush.

If the surface is still not smooth enough, apply a mixture of raw lacquer, water-soluble paste, lint, and powdered sawdust, followed by a mixture of powdered whetstone, water, and raw lacquer.

5 Apply tannin and immediately polish with a whetstone. Repeat the process with a thinner coat of tannin followed immediately by polishing before the tannin dries.

6 Polish with dry *tokusa* scouring rush.

The persimmon-tannin base finish is less time-consuming than the traditional process with ten steps outlined previously. This alternative base finish has been extensively used in the famous lacquer of Aizu in Fukushima Prefecture.

Base Variations II: Animal Glue

1 Apply mixture of powdered whetstone and water with animal glue (*nikawa*) and water.

2 Polish with a whetstone and water.

3 If a certain color is desired, it should be added at this point. Black is obtained by mixing animal glue dissolved in water with rapeseed-oil soot and applying the mixture over the polished first coat. If either vermilion *shu-nuri*, or rust-red *benitame-nuri* are sought, ferric oxide may be substituted for the rapeseed-oil soot.

Animal-glue techniques, with or without tinting of the wood surface, are economical for large-scale production, but do not stand up against time and wear.

Final Finish

The classic process from which most variations in final finishing proceed is called *roiro-nuri*, traditionally a pure-lacquer black finish only.

1 Apply refined black lacquer without oil to the finely polished surface. The lacquer should be dried in a sealed room at 25° to 30°C in 80 to 85 percent humidity.

2 Polish with magnolia-wood charcoal or hackberry-wood charcoal, using water as a medium.

3 Apply refined black lacquer.

4 After it is thoroughly dry, polish with wood charcoal as in step two.

5 Apply *roiro* lacquer made from the best quality raw urushi with non-oxidized iron powder or rapeseed-oil soot added to produce a black color.

6 Polish with wood charcoal as in step four, followed by polishing with soft *egonoki* (*Styrax Japonica* Sieb. et Zucc.).

7 Using water mixed with *egonoki* powdered charcoal or rapeseed oil mixed with powdered whetstone, polish with a soft cloth.

8 Rub raw lacquer into the surface with a cloth and wipe off excess with soft Japanese handmade paper. Repeat this process.

9 Rub the surface with soft Japanese handmade paper or absorbent cotton impregnated with rapeseed oil, occasionally dipped in powdered deerhorn, to remove any excess raw lacquer.

10 Repeat step eight using a thinner coat of raw lacquer. One application only.

11 Repeat step nine.

12 Repeat step ten using raw lacquer in a still thinner coat.

13 Repeat step nine.

If a vermilion finish is desired, ferric oxide should be added to the refined natural lacquer in step three, and cinnabar pigment should be added to the lacquer in step five. Tansu finishes were not always done precisely in the traditional process outlined above: wood sealing, base finish, and final finish. All variations were, however, rooted in this three-tiered approach.

Other Variations I: Kijiro-nuri

The *kijiro-nuri* technique specifically emphasizes the beauty of open, tangential wood grain. It was used extensively for the zelkova and chestnut of tansu, either untinted or with a red or yellow hue.

1 Seal wood surface by rubbing well with a whetstone and water.

2 Apply mixture of raw lacquer, powdered whetstone, and water by spatula. Repeat two or three times, letting the surface dry completely between applications.

3 Polish surface and remove excess filler with a fine whetstone and water.

4 Apply tint, if desired, with a brush and wipe off excess before drying.

5 Apply mixture of ten parts dehydrated lacquer and five parts turpentine with a cotton cloth.

6 Apply *kijiro-urushi,* the best quality of refined lacquer obtained after water has been evaporated from the raw lacquer and the dehydrated substance has been brought to an even consistancy by stirring until smooth. Use a hair brush.

7 Apply a thin coat of *kijiro* lacquer and allow it to dry completely.

8 Polish with magnolia- or hackberry-wood charcoal and water followed by polishing with soft *egonoki*-wood charcoal.

9 Polish with rapeseed oil and powdered deerhorn.

If no color tint is desired, eliminate step four. In step five, raw lacquer should be applied thinly with a spatula followed by polishing with a whetstone and water. Step five may be repeated several times to improve the surface for a final finish. Step six is then unnecessary, but steps seven, eight, and nine remain unchanged.

Other Variations II: Suri-urushi-nuri

The technique *suri-urushi-nuri,* which is popularly called *fuki-urushi-nuri,* literally wiped lacquer, was used on any of the primary tansu woods, often in complement to the *kijiro* finish on the drawer and door face wood.

1 Apply mixture of powdered whetstone and water to seal the wood surface. Not necessary for needle-leaf tree woods.

2 Apply color pigment or dye, if required, over the dried, sealed surface.

3 Apply three coats of raw lacquer mixed with turpentine, using a cotton cloth. After each application, the excess must be removed with Japanese handmade paper.

Ratio of lacquer to turpentine:
First application: ten parts to five to ten parts
Second application: ten parts to two to five parts
Third application: ten parts to zero to two parts

4 Polish twice with a mixture of rapeseed oil and powdered whetstone.

For cryptomeria panel and case finishing, raw lacquer, applied directly to the unsealed surface, produces an attractive contrast of light and dark shading according to the absorption of the lacquer into the grain of the wood.

Other Variations III: Shunkei-nuri

Shunkei-nuri, like the *kijiro* technique, has as its primary purpose enhancing the beauty of the wood grain. However, by the addition of perilla oil to clear, raw lacquer, the need to polish was eliminated, thereby saving considerable time without compromising the durability of the finish.

1 Apply mixture of powdered whetstone, water, and persimmon tannin or persimmon tannin and ferric oxide, with a brush, wiping off excess before drying.

2 If powdered whetstone, water, and persimmon tannin have been used in step one, then ferric oxide and persimmon tannin should be used for step two, again applied with a brush.

3 Apply three coats of pure persimmon tannin with a brush.

4 Apply *shunkei-urushi* with a brush, once only.

In Yamagata Prefecture, the sealer is a mixture of powdered whetstone, water, and ferric oxide, followed by steps three and four. Generally, persimmon tannin with ferric oxide was the most common *shunkei-nuri* color base; however, if a yellowish shade was desired, instead of the familiar reddish orange black, gardenia-seed dye could be substituted.

Other Variations IV: Tame-nuri

The predominant opaque lacquer finish on tansu was *tame-nuri,* a technique relying upon contrasting tinted lacquers under a translucent final finish. *Tame-nuri* with a red hue has been considered quite sophisticated since the early Meiji era for personal tansu. The critical difference between true *tame-nuri* and other opaque-lacquer tansu finishes lies in the use of a clear, final urushi finish giving an illusion of three-dimensional transparency.

1 Apply black lacquer. Persimmon tannin was sometimes used as an alternative in step one with a raw lacquer overcoat in imitation of red *tame-nuri*.

2 Apply raw lacquer to which ferric oxide has been added if a normal red is preferred or cinnabar-derived vermilion for a dark red.

3 If the final finish is pure lacquer, polishing with the final *roiro-nuri* steps will assure an extremely hard but not brittle surface resembling fine porcelain.

Perilla oil was often added to the final-finish lacquer in the manner of *shunkei-nuri* in order to avoid polishing. Lacquer is unique in Japan where it has enjoyed a position as a fine art as well as a craft for objects of daily use.

CHAPTER NINE

BUYING AND CONSERVING

The single most important consideration is whether you want to buy an antique, a piece of furniture, or both. If you wish to buy simply a piece of furniture, make sure you are not paying for an antique. By our criteria, an antique tansu is older than the end of the Meiji era, 1912; has no replaced structural wood; has the original hardware and the original hinged door or original sliding-door frame; and has either the original finish or a refinish following the original precisely. The replacement or repair of drawer interiors and case backboards was common, often with iron nails after the 1920s. This is unfortunate but does not greatly diminish the value. Frame-and-panel tansu that have had a panel replaced present a gray area, which should be considered case by case, as should tansu with mirror boards or attached panels in frame-and-panel doors. The use of modern or Western techniques in a restoration —lacquering with a technique not original to the chest, use of oils not indigenous to Japan, use of polyurethane, and use of oil-base stains or "scratch covers"—destroys an antique's value.

Three other frequently encountered irregularities are not so easy to detect and should be pointed out by the dealer when you are considering a purchase. If a small hinged door is missing, the two or three inner drawers and the separation rails may have been brought forward to make them appear flush with the original exposed-face drawers. In this case, traces on the wood where the door hinges were once located and nail holes may be evident on the side of the chest. Another clue is that the small drawers will be 3.5 to 5 cm shorter than the depth of the case. If a vertical locking bar is missing, the originally recessed drawers may have been brought forward as in the previous example. The receiving plates for the missing bar and foot prongs are usually still in place. It may be helpful to keep in mind that if a one-section clothing storage tansu were designed without a locking bar, either all or none of the large drawers would have individual locks. This is a general rule with only rare exceptions. The third common irregularity is found only in chest-on-chest tansu. If the receiving pins on the top chest do not precisely engage the swing side handle of the bottom chest when in a raised position, a hardware replacement has been made.

Unless you are buying from someone both knowledgeable and reputable, it is best to assume that you are not buying an antique but actually an old chest of great character, very usable as a piece of furniture. In the long run it is perhaps wisest to either buy the costly authentic antique or a new tansu made without compromise by one of the few craftsmen who have chosen to carry on the tradition. The former would be a wise investment. The latter may prove to be an antique of the future.

The following discussion will present both ideal and practical methods of tansu conservation. Professional care of a tansu is possible provided the appropriate conservation materials are available. Outside Japan, although wood conservation is quite well developed, Japanese materials are not always readily at hand.

Tansu were designed for traditional Japanese buildings, which are not centrally heated. This presents a particular problem when a chest is transferred to a contemporary Western house in a temperate climate. If the absolute humidity is 15 percent while the house is 70° F (21° C), the relative humidity would be 49 percent. This is a comfortable minimum for most tansu. In humidity consistently below this level, the air-dried wood of the drawer flooring and the case backboards may contract or even split. Expansion in the form of a parallel joint opening is an indication that the tansu has merely made a seasonal adjustment. A split, on the other hand, often indicates a structural problem. A good humidifier will make cabinetry of any origin as well as the occupants of the house or apartment more comfortable. In addition, tansu should be kept out of direct sunlight, not only to protect the wood, but also to prevent the always active phenols in a lacquer finish from becoming overactivated and thereby creating an uneven tone.

Excessive dryness alone is not usually harmful to paulownia case pieces, but parallel joints in other woods are particularly subject to separation. A straight opening between two boards is often considered a split when in fact it is only the shrinking of a parallel joint, recognizable by perpendicular dowels between the boards originally bonded together. If such a separation occurs in the drawer flooring or the case backboards, repair can be effected by removing the entire section, moving the boards together, regluing the parallel joints, and then adding a new parallel strip of wood on one side to correct the shrinkage. This process, however, should only be considered after determining the limits of expansion and contraction by which the tansu will adjust to its current environment. An uneven parallel opening resulting from the splitting of a single board, especially in the case top or sides of an authentic antique, should be left untouched or corrected only by a professional conservator with the proper materials. Thus, parallel openings and splits appear essentially the same, but are in fact very different in character.

If a joint is still pegged rather than having been repaired at some point in time with iron nails, it is preferable to continue using pegs. As an alternative to *utsugi* wood pegs, wooden matches with the heads removed, which have been dried out in a pan over low heat, are acceptable as substitutes. After drilling out the old peg with a gimlet, the match, dipped in water-soluble glue, should be inserted as far as possible and seated carefully with a mallet; snip off any protrusion after the glue has dried.

Assuming that original woods are not available, the following North American woods may be substituted for minor repairs:

Japanese wood	*North American wood*
zelkova and chestnut	red oak
cryptomeria	white cedar or Eastern white pine
cypress	Port Oreford cedar
paulownia	Tennessee Princess tree (a North American variety of paulownia)

Traditional wood care was very simple in Japan: never wax, never oil, never chemically cleanse, only rub again and again with a soft dry or damp cloth and in twenty or thirty years the tansu will develop a natural patina. Although this approach is still appreciated in Japan, it is understandably difficult for contemporary Westerners to accept. And the dryness problem inherent in most Western homes makes feeding the wood, though not traditional, good preventive maintenance in addition to increasing the beauty of the wood. For unlacquered finishes such as those found on many paulownia and cypress tansu, boiled linseed or tung oil applied every six months will give vibrancy to the dry wood. The oil should be warmed to increase its penetration properties and applied with a cloth. Then the wood surface is wiped dry of excess oil after thirty minutes. This process may be repeated two or three times followed by brisk buffing with a lint-free cloth after removal of excess oil to prevent stickiness. If a water- and fingerprint-resistant finish is required, the dried, oiled wood may be given a coating of paste wax.

For a stained finish over which lacquer with oil has been used in the *nuritate* process, as found on the cryptomeria top and sides of most secured-case tansu, application of several coats of one-third boiled linseed oil, one-third apple-cider vinegar, and one-third turpentine will enhance a neglected finish, provided any excess of the mixture is removed before drying. A clear lacquer finish under which the wood grain is easily visible, as found on the drawers, doors, and frame members of fine zelkova and chestnut tansu, can be cleaned of surface dirt with warm water and a pure soap or denatured alcohol applied carefully. Above all, thenatural patina resulting from oxidation over many years must not be disturbed. Use of a wood-derived paste wax such as Butcher's Amber Boston Polish or Antiquax from England, or the microcrystalline Renaissance wax also from England, are recommended. It is always best to apply the wax with the fingertips and then buff with a two-centimeter pure-bristle brush.

An opaque lacquer can be lightly cleansed of surface dirt with alcohol or a volatile thinner, but oil or wax streaking cannot be buffed out, so these steps are not recommended. Just rub the wood again and again and in twenty or thirty years. . . .

If color matching is required, never use a petroleum-base dye. Water-soluble inorganic colors may be time consuming, but they are the most compatible to the original dyes and pigments.

Most important in the care of hardware is to use the iron oxidization rather than to remove it. Superficial flaking rust is unstable and therefore should be removed with 0000 steel wool. The under layer of oxidization can be fed with light machine oil applied with the fingertips and buffed, building over a fairly short period of time to a proper patina. If a piece of hardware needs to be darkened, the *tetsu menshoku abura-migaki* technique using raw cotton and rapeseed oil should be more than adequate.

When a piece of hardware has come off or come loose, the nail holes should be filled with the matchstick pegs described above in order to ensure that the nails will seat securely.

BIBLIOGRAPHY

English-language Publications

Basillvov, Norman. *Japanese Daily Life from the Stone Age to the Present.* New York: Carlton Press Inc., 1976.

Beardsley, Richard K.; Hall, John W.; and Ward, Robert E. *Village Japan.* Chicago: University of Chicago Press, 1959.

Dower, John W. *The Elements of Japanese Design.* Tokyo: Weatherhill, 1971.

Ecke, Gustav. *Chinese Domestic Furniture.* Tokyo: Charles E. Tuttle Co. and Hong Kong University Press, 1962.

Hall, John W. and Jansen, Marius B., ed. *Studies in the Institutional History of Early Modern Japan.* Princeton: Princeton University Press, 1968.

Hirai, Kiyoshi. *Feudal Architecture of Japan.* Tokyo: Weatherhill/Heibonsha, 1973.

Itoh, Teiji. *Kura: Design and Tradition of the Japanese Storehouse.* Tokyo: Kodansha International Ltd., 1973.

Itoh, Teiji. *Traditional Domestic Architecture of Japan.* Tokyo: Weatherhill/Heibonsha, 1972.

Kaempfer, Engelbert. *History of Japan.* 1906. Reprint. New York: AMS Press, 1971.

Kodama, Kota. *Agricultural Life History of the Edo Period.* Tokyo: Yoshikawa Kyobunkan, 1958.

Joly, Henri L. *Legend in Japanese Art.* Tokyo: Charles E. Tuttle Co., 1967.

Latourette, Kenneth Scott. *The Development of Japan.* New York: The Macmillan Co., 1926.

Meader, Robert F.W. *Illustrated Guide to Shaker Furniture.* New York: Dover Publications Inc., 1972.

Munsterberg, Hugo. *The Folk Art of Japan.* Tokyo: Charles E. Tuttle Co., 1958.

Murdoch, James. *A History of Japan,* vols. I, II, III. London: Kegan Paul, Trench, Trubner, & Co., Ltd., 1925.

Ohwi, Jisaburo. *Flora of Japan.* Edited by Frederick G. Meyer and Egbert H. Walker. Washington, D.C.: Smithsonian Institution, 1965.

Reischauer, Edwin O. *Japan Past and Present*. New York: Alfred A. Knopf, 1964.

———. *The Japanese*. Cambridge, Ma.: Harvard University Press, 1977.

Sansom, G.B. *Japan: A Short Cultural History*, revised edition. New York: Appleton-Century-Crafts Inc., 1962.

Shively, Donald H. "Sumptuary Regulation and Status in Early Tokugawa Japan." *Harvard Journal of Asiatic Studies*, vol. 25 (1964–65).

Takekoshi, Yosaburo. *The Economic Aspects of the History of the Civilization of Japan*, vols. I, II, III. London: Dawsons of Pall Mall, 1967.

Taut, Bruno. *Houses and People of Japan*. London: John Gifford Ltd., 1937.

Toyoda, Takeshi. *A History of Pre-Meiji Commerce in Japan*. Tokyo: Kokusai Bunka Shinkōkai, 1969.

Turk, F. A. *Japanese Objets D'Art*. New York: Sterling Publishing Co. Inc., 1962.

Yanagida, Kunio, ed. *Japanese Manners and Customs in the Meiji Era*. Translated by Charles S. Terry. Tokyo: Ōbunsha, 1957.

Japanese-language Publications

books

Arakawa, Hirokazu, et al. *Shikkō*. Nihon no Kōgei, vol. 6. Kyoto: Tankōsha, 1978.

Ishida, Hisatoyo. *Nihon no Bijutsu · Shokunin Zukushi-e*. Tokyo: Shibundō, 1977.

Ishida, Ryōsuke. *Ofuregaki Hōreki Shūsei; Kampo Shūsei; Temmei Shūsei; Tempo Shūsei*. Tokyo: Iwanami Shoten, 1958.

Koizumi, Kazuko. *Kagu to Shitsunai Ishō no Bunkashi*. Tokyo: Hōsei Daigaku Shuppan-kyoku, 1979.

———. *Nihon no Tansu*. Tokyo: Kagu no Rekishikan, 1973.

———. *Wa Kagu*. Tokyo: Shōgakukan, 1977.

Kuroki, Takashi. *Meireki no Taika*. Tokyo: Kōdansha, 1977.

Makino, Ryūshin. *Kitamaesen no Jidai*. Tokyo: Kyōikusha, 1979.

Makino, Ryūshin, Nishikubo Kenzan, Tone Yūtarō. *Nihon no Funa-ema—Kitamaesen*. Tokyo: Kashiwa Shobō, 1977.

Matsuda, Gonroku. *Urushi no Hanashi*. Tokyo: Iwanami Shoten, 1964.

Matsumoto, Asanosuke. *Nihon Tansu Ishō to Sono Seisaku no Shiagehō*. Tokyo: Chūō Kōgakkai, 1934.

Matsumoto, Sekizō. *Kiri Tansu no Dezain to Seisakuhō*. Tokyo: Kōsakusha, 1960.

Morita, Tadashi. *Ki no Komingei*. Tokyo: Kōgei Shuppan, 1975.

Muramatsu, Teijirō. *Daiku Dōgu no Rekishi*. Tokyo: Iwanami Shoten, 1973.

Okada, Jō. *Nihon no Bijutsu · Chōdo*. Tokyo: Shibundō, 1966.

Ōta, Hirotarō. *Shintei Zusetsu Nihon Jūtakushi*. Tokyo: Shōkokusha, 1971.

Rokkaku, Shisui. *Tōyō Shikkōshi*. Tokyo: Yūzankaku, 1932.

Sawaguchi, Goichi. *Nihon Shikkō no Kenkyū*. Tokyo: Bijutsu Shuppansha, 1966.

Terajima, Ryōan. *Wakan Sansai Zu-e*. 1713–15.

Yanagi, Sōetsu. *Funa-dansu*. Tokyo: Shunjūsha, 1974.

REFERENCE WORKS

Fūzoku Jiten. Tokyo: Tōkyōdō, 1957.

Kokawa-dera Engi. Nihon Emakimono Zenshū, vol. 6. Tokyo: Kadokawa Shoten, 1977.

Mokuzai Kōgei Yōgo Jiten. Tokyo: Rikōgakusha, 1976.

Nihon Bijutsu Jiten. Tokyo: Tōkyōdō, 1952.

Nihon Bijutsu Taikei. Tokyo: Kōdansha, 1961.

Nihon Bijutsu Zenshū. Tokyo: Tōtobunkasha, 1953.

Nihon Bunkashi. Tokyo: Chikuma Shobō, 1965–66.

Nihon Kenchikushi. Kenchikugaku Taikei, vol. 4. Tokyo: Shōkokusha, 1957.

Nihon kodai. Sekai Kenchiku Zenshū, vol. 1. Tokyo: Heibonsha, 1961.

Sanjūniban Shokunin Uta-awase Emaki. Nihon Emakimono Zenshū, vol. 28. Tokyo: Kadokawa Shoten, 1979.

Shōsō-in. Tokyo: Mainichi Shimbunsha, 1954.

Shōsō-in no Hōbutsu. Tokyo: Asahi Shimbunsha, 1965.

Shōsō-in no Mokkō. Tokyo Nihon Keizai Shimbunsha, 1978.

Urushi Kōgei Jiten. Tokyo: Kōgei Shuppan, 1978.

Zusetsu Nihon Bunkashi Taikei. Tokyo: Shōgakukan, 1956–58.

GLOSSARY

bengara: in ancient times, a pigment imported from Northern India, but since the Edo period derived by processing iron oxide (Fe_2O_3) in Japan. Widely used traditionally as a wood stain.

bō-dansu: a general term for any tansu that relies on a vertical locking bar (*bō*) to secure the drawers. This is one of the very oldest of tansu designs. The bar is sometimes referred to as a *kannuki,* or closing bar.

byō: general term for straight pinning, whether with iron nails to secure hardware, or with wooden pegs to pin an open mortise, stopped butt, etc. When used as bumpers for drawer pulls, to protect the finish, called *atari-byō.*

Cashew: brand name of a synthesized lacquer with characteristics similar to urushi.

cha-dansu: a chest for tea utensils. Finely crafted pieces made in the twentieth century have lost their mobility and therefore cannot be considered tansu in the strict sense of the word. Chests specifically intended for use in the tea ceremony are called tea-ceremony tansu.

chako: a commercially available, water-soluble dye widely used in Japan for traditional wood stains.

chō-dansu: a general term for shop tansu, originally used to store account books, also called *chōba-dansu* if intended for use on the raised platform (*chōba*).

Dewa: a historical district on the Japan Sea coast encompassing modern Akita and Yamagata prefectures.

fuki-urushi: popular name for a wiped lacquer finishing technique also known professionally as *suri-urushi-nuri.*

funa-dansu: sea chests, tansu used on the "thousand-*koku* ships" and on land by ship owners and captains. Mostly built between 1716 and 1907 at the Japan Sea towns of Ogi, Sakata, and Mikuni in three styles: *kakesuzuri,* for the ship's papers; *hangai,* for clothing; and *chō-bako,* for account books, money, and documents.

goyō-dansu: *goyō* designates some official function. These chests were most commonly used to transport and store documents.

gyōshō-bako: cabinetry carried by itinerant craftsmen and peddlers. Also referred to as *senda-bitsu.*

hako: literally a box but occasionally applicable to tansu as in the *chō-bako* sea chest and the *gyōshō-bako. Hako* is pronounced *-bako* in compounds. In that tansu makers were often referred to as *hakoya,* or boxmakers, it is still common for the older generation to speak of the tansu craft as *hakomono,* literally box things.

hakudō: compound of 70 to 80 percent copper and 20 to 30 percent tin, used as lock-plate edging on many clothing tansu from the northern provinces in the Meiji era, primarily from Yamagata Prefecture.

hikidashi: drawer, whether external or internal, with or without hardware.

hiki-do: sliding doors in a pair used in cabinetry.

hikite: tansu drawer pulls as opposed to rings.

hinoki: aromatic cypress used for the framework of some merchant tansu from western Honshu, as well as for objects of daily use.

hitsu: any number of free-standing cabinetry styles were once grouped within this broad category. Two examples mentioned in the text are *tate-bitsu* and *kara-bitsu*. The *hitsu* may generally be considered a free-standing coffer. When used in a compound, *hitsu* is pronounced *-bitsu*.

Hokuriku-dō: historical route and the surrounding district, comprising parts of Fukui, Ishikawa, Toyama, and Niigata prefectures.

imono kanagu: cast hardware.

ishō: general term used to denote clothing storage.

itame: flat-sawn grain resulting from tangential ripping. Most tansu drawer-face hardwood is cut this way so that the lacquer will show off the grain to best advantage. The open-grain pattern is popularly called *mokume*.

jō: general word for lock. The *omotejō* is the older, single-action lock, the *urajō* is the double-action lock, and the *karajō* is a slide latch.

kaidan-dansu: built-in staircase tansu, most always in two or three sections for mobility. Popular with merchants in urban areas of Honshu during the Edo period for use in shops and storehouses.

kaki-shibu: persimmon tannin, used as a wood stain under lacquer for the secondary wood of many Meiji-era tansu.

kanagu: hardware

kasane: stacked chest, or chest-on-chest, in either two or three sections. The individual sections may have different heights.

katabiraki-do: side-hinged door, most commonly exposed, with one or more drawers set in behind it. When quite small in proportion to the chest, it is sometimes called a *kobiraki-do,* or small-door compartment.

katana-dansu: tansu for storing sword blades without the hilts and scabbards. Usually of paulownia wood with one or several small lockable drawers to accommodate sword fittings.

kendon-buta: drop-fit removable door. Such doors are most often found in book tansu (*sho-dansu*) and used to secure compartments for tea utensils. When found inside sea chests, they often function side to side rather than top to bottom.

keyaki: zelkova, a hardwood related to the elm with a bold grain and used in tansu as both a primary and a secondary wood.

kijiro: refined finishing lacquer made by evaporating the excess water from raw lacquer. Colloquially, the term *kijiro* is used to describe both the translucent lacquer over stained wood and the honey to reddish tone of the finish itself.

kiri: paulownia, a softwood highly prized by the Japanese for cabinetry because of its flexibility, tone, and texture.

kosode: short-sleeved kimono. When used as a tansu designation, this term indicates a chest of multiple drawers for the storage of these kimono, probably from the Edo period, often with a vertical locking bar.

kuri: Japanese chestnut, quite similar to the North American tree. *Kuri* is used interchangeably with *keyaki* in tansu, but has a less pronounced grain.

kuruma-dansu: wheeled chest

masame: straight grain achieved by quarter-sawing a log. Wood cut in this way is resistant to splitting and warping even if thin.

mizuya: the term *mizuya* is associated with the preparation area of a tea-ceremony room. The *mizuya* chest is usually a frame-and-panel chest-on-chest for food and utensil storage, found within or near the kitchen.

nagamochi: trunk with a hinged lid, usually detachable, for the storage of personal belongings. An extension in design of the *hitsu,* the *nagamochi* was a coffer with wheels (*kuruma nagamochi*) or iron handles (*tōshi nagamochi*) for easy mobility, common in the Edo period.

-nuri: when used as a suffix, this is a general term for finish, i.e., *kijiro-nuri, shunkei-nuri,* and *tame-nuri.*

rō: wood-resin Japanese hard wax similar in appearance to paraffin. Also called *mokurō,* which correctly refers only to a by-product of the lacquer tree.

ryōbiraki-do: exposed double doors that open on hinges, the hinge plates being at right angles to each other. *Kannon-biraki-do* (Kannon doors) is often used interchangeably but correctly indicates double doors on hinges with either both plates on the front surface or one plate and only half of the other on the front, as in many wooden boxes constructed for statues of Kannon, the bodhisattva of mercy.

sho-dansu: book chests, usually small, with drop-fit *kendon-buta* doors. These chests are sometimes referred to as *sho-bako.*

Shōnai: a fertile plain on the Japan Sea coast of Yamagata Prefecture divided by the Mogami River and including the cities of Tsuruoka and Sakata.

shu: brownish red tint used in opaque lacquering, derived originally from cinnabar.

shunkei-nuri: lacquering technique for final finishing. The use of oil in the lacquer makes this technique less demanding than the building up and careful polishing of multiple layers of *kijiro* lacquer.

sugi: cryptomeria, a non-resinous conifer used extensively as a secondary wood for the tops and sides of case pieces with hardwood-faced drawers.

tana: free-standing shelving. When used in a compound, *tana* is pronounced *-dana,* i.e., *to-dana:* shelves enclosed by sliding doors, *zeni to-dana:* merchant *to-dana* for money and valuables, *yagu to-dana:* bedding storage shelves.

tamamoku: a swirling grain or burl. Zelkova burl was widely used for drawer, door, and panel wood, especially from the Meiji era.

tame-nuri: general term applied to the various techniques used to achieve opaque lacquer finishes using contrasting tinted lacquers under clear lacquer.

tansu: Japanese cabinetry that allows for mobility by either structural design or hardware. When used in a compound, *tansu* is pronounced *-dansu.*

temoto: small personal tansu for women to store hair ornaments, a mirror, cosmetics, etc.

Tōhoku: contemporary reference to the northeastern area of Honshu, including Fukushima, Miyagi, Yamagata, Iwate, Akita, and Aomori prefectures.

tonoko: powdered whetstone or baked earth used as a wood sealer.

tōshi: general term for any handle used to move a chest. Side, U-shaped handles through which a pole was passed for carrying a chest between two people may be called *bō-tōshi* or *sao-tōshi.* Elliptical side handles are called *mochiokuri.*

tsuzura: portable coffer with a detachable lid constructed of woven bamboo, reeds, or vines, often covered with traditional Japanese paper and then lacquered for clothing storage.

uchimono kanagu: forged hardware.

urushi: sap of the lacquer tree *Rhus verniciflua.*

uwaoki-tsuki chest: three-section stacking chest, the top section consisting of or including two sliding doors. Most always of twentieth-century provenance.

yarō: colloquial term used in northeastern Honshu to describe large, single-section, multiple-drawer personal tansu.

zushi: ancient term for free-standing, open-frame or partially enclosed cabinetry in which *kannon-biraki* doors were used in the structure. In the early Edo period, both *zushi* and *hitsu* were used to describe what later would be called tansu. In contemporary usage, a *zushi* is a small box with hinged double doors in which an image of the Buddha would be kept.

INDEX

The "weathermark" identifies this book as a production of John Weatherhill, Inc., publishers of fine books on Asia and the Pacific. Book design and typography: Nobu Miyazaki and Miriam F. Yamaguchi. Layout of illustrations: Nobu Miyazaki. Composition of the text: Samhwa Printing Co., Seoul. Printing of the text: Kenkyusha Printing Co., Tokyo. Engraving and printing of the plates, in four-color and monochrome offset: Nissha Printing Co., Kyoto. Binding: Makoto Binderies, Tokyo. The typeface used is Monotype Perpetua.